# the FIRST DAYS OF SCHOOL

## HOW TO BE AN EFFECTIVE TEACHER

### HARRY K. WONG

Some people go into teaching
because it is a job.
Some people go into teaching
to make a difference.

### ROSEMARY T. WONG

We are pleased to share with
the teaching profession
our contribution to making
a difference.

**HARRY K. WONG PUBLICATIONS, INC.**
**www.EffectiveTeaching.com**

This book has been printed on environmentally friendly paper. Join us in making a choice to save our planet.

**Dedicated to my father and mother,**
Who wanted me to be a brain surgeon.
I exceeded their expectations.
I became a scholar and a teacher.

_Harry K. Wong

**Dedicated to Mr. Frederick McKee,**
My first principal, whose evaluation of me said
I needed better "classroom management" skills.
Thank you for telling me I needed to improve my skills.
I did.  It worked!

_Rosemary T. Wong

Cover Images:  A tribute to real educators in real education settings.  You are making a difference in the lives of students and the world.
From right front cover to left back cover:  Edward Aguiles, Chelonnda Seroyer, Jeffrey W. Smith, Nile Mendoza Wilson, Elmo Sanchez, Jr.,
Sarah Jondahl, Theresa A. Borges, Cheryl Ralston, Hilton Jay, Kirk Gordon, Lena Nuccio-Lee, and Diana Greenhouse.

Copyright © 2009 by Harry K. Wong Publications, Inc.

ISBN:  978-0-9764233-1-7
Library of Congress Control Number:  2008903342

17

Printed in Singapore by Pristone Pte. Ltd.

Executive Producer:  Rosemary T. Wong

Graphic Design Team:  Heidi Heath Garwood, Nancy Roberts, Mark Van Slyke
Production Team:  Jean Bong, Tim Chen
Editorial Team:  Eric Gill, Megan Pincus Kajitani

Harry K. Wong Publications, Inc.
943 North Shoreline Boulevard
Mountain View, CA  94043-1932

Telephone:  650-965-7896
Facsimile:  650-965-7890
Internet:  www.EffectiveTeaching.com

# About the DVD, "Using THE FIRST DAYS OF SCHOOL"

## She Succeeded on Her First Day of School

**V**oted teacher-of-the-year, Chelonnda Seroyer never looked back after her first day of school.

But she could well have failed as a teacher because her student teaching experience was a disaster. Wisely, she took copious notes of that experience and reflected on what happened to prepare for her first teaching position in the English department at Bob Jones High School in Madison, Alabama.

Chelonnda spent two months poring through *The First Days of School* and using it as a guide for organizing for her first day of school. When the first day of school came, she had a script. She had a classroom management plan.

Standing at the classroom door, she greeted her students as they entered the room. She was nervous and uneasy. Then she had an eerie feeling. Turning around to look into her classroom, she saw that her students were seated at their desks—and at work!

And the **first second** of the **first minute** of the **first day of school** **had not even begun.** **She was already a success on her first day of school.**

From that moment on, she has never looked back on her career.

At the end of her first year as a teacher, she was awarded the school's Patriot Award, given to the first-year teacher who contributed the most to the school.

At the end of her second year as a teacher, she was given another Patriot Award for her contributions. This time she was selected from *all* the teachers in the school.

At the end of her fourth year, she was selected the school's teacher-of-the-year.

A veteran teacher said to her, "I have been here for 13 years and I have yet to receive a recognition. How do you do it?"

**Chelonnda said one word, "Procedures."**

**Chelonnda shares the procedures she uses in her first day of school script in the DVD, "Using THE FIRST DAYS OF SCHOOL," found inside the back cover of this book.**

# Contents

**A**  **Basic Understandings** _The Teacher

The successful teacher must know and practice the three characteristics of an effective teacher.

**B**  **First Characteristic** _Positive Expectations

The effective teacher has positive expectations for student success.

**C**  **Second Characteristic** _Classroom Management

The effective teacher is an extremely good classroom manager.

**D**   **Third Characteristic** **_Lesson Mastery**

The successful teacher knows how to design lessons to help students achieve.

**E**   **Future Understandings** **_The Professional**

The teacher who constantly learns and grows becomes a professional educator.

The DVD features Chelonnda Seroyer as she walks you through how she implements *The First Days of School* in her classroom.

## About the Authors

**Who are Harry and Rosemary Wong?**

They are teachers.

# Basic Understandings

## _The Teacher

The successful teacher must know and practice the three characteristics of an effective teacher.

# Unit  Basic Understandings _The Teacher

The successful teacher must know and practice the three characteristics of an effective teacher.

Unit A is correlated with Part 1: "The Effective Teacher" in the DVD series *The Effective Teacher*.

## Success on the First Day of School

> Successful teachers have a script or a plan ready for the first day of school.

THE KEY IDEA

**Your success during the school year will be determined by what you do on the first days of school.**

**W**hat you do on the first days of school will determine your success or failure for the rest of the school year. Knowing how to structure a successful first day of school will set the stage for an effective classroom and a successful school year.

College professor Douglas Brooks videotaped a series of teachers on their first day of school. Looking at the recording afterward, he made a startling discovery. The ineffective teachers began their first day of school by covering the subject matter or doing a fun activity. These teachers spent the rest of the school year chasing after the students.

Douglas M. Brooks,
Miami University of Ohio

**The effective teachers spent time organizing and structuring their classrooms so the students knew what to do to succeed.** He wrote his findings in an article, "The First Day of School."[1]

The most important thing to establish in the first week of school is **CONSISTENCY**. People want to know exactly what they are getting and what will be happening. Students do not want surprises or disorganization. Consistency prevents them from asking, "What are we doing today?"

Students want a safe, predictable, and nurturing environment—one that is consistent. Students like well-managed classes because no one yells at them, and learning takes place. Effective teachers spend the first two weeks teaching students to be in control of their own actions in a consistent classroom environment.

> " *The highest stake of all is our ability to help children realize their full potential.* "
>
> _Samuel J. Meisels

[1]Brooks, Douglas M. (May 1985). "The First Day of School." *Educational Leadership*, pp. 76–78.

### Hand in the Work

At a school in an at-risk community, (truly these students are "at-promise") a student said, "I like coming to this school because everyone knows what to **DO**. No one yells at us and we can get on with learning."

The student is not talking about behavior, which is addressed in Chapter 18. The student is talking about **DOING**, or getting things done as explained in Chapters 19 and 20. Summarizing the importance of *doing*, a seventh grade student said, "I have figured out how to succeed in school. Hand in the work!"

**Learning takes place when students get things done.**

**Effective teachers teach classroom management procedures that create consistency.** Their classrooms are caring, thought-provoking, challenging, and academically successful. A well-managed classroom is the foundation for learning in the classroom. Therefore, Unit C in this book may be the most important for you to read and implement as you start the first days of school.

**Effective teachers have lesson plans and procedures that produce student learning.** Unit D in this book will walk you through how to get your students to achieve.

## Effective Teachers Script Their First Day of School

A coach scripts the first 10 to 20 plays of a football game. A wedding coordinator has a plan or agenda for the sequence of events at a wedding. Likewise, an effective teacher is ready with a script or classroom management plan on the first day of school.

> **GoBe**
>
> Read below to find out how to access the **Go**ing **Be**yond folders at EffectiveTeaching.com.

### Going Beyond

The term "lagniappe" (pronounced "lan-yap," meaning "something extra") is used in Louisiana and Mississippi. It began as a little bonus that a shopkeeper might add to a purchase such as an extra donut (as in a baker's dozen), something for the road, or a complimentary dessert. Today it has become synonymous with the little extra things people do for each other.

When you see a **Go**ing **Be**yond or "**GoBe**" folder, go to EffectiveTeaching.com and select **Books** in the menu bar. Click on *The First Days of School* and look for the tab that says **Going Beyond**. Open the tab to access all of the GoBe folders found in the book. Every chapter has at least one GoBe that will take you to additional resources that go beyond the printed page.

Diana Greenhouse

Kazim Cicek

**Diana Greenhouse**, a teacher in Texas, says, "What an incredible first year of teaching this has been. When I look back at all I accomplished, it takes my breath away. My students learned and I loved every minute of teaching.

"And it all started with that very first minute of the first day. I started the school with a PowerPoint presentation of my classroom management plan."

**Kazim Cicek**, a teacher in Oklahoma, says he spent his first three years in the profession as a warrior. The students fought him and he fought them. Then, four days before the start of his fourth year—one that he did not want to start—he heard Harry Wong speak at a preschool meeting and had a "light bulb moment." Over a long weekend, he created a PowerPoint presentation of his classroom management plan.

At the end of his fourth year he said, "The wish I wished my students was also given to me. I, too, had a wonderful year."

Today, he is a very happy and successful teacher.

## teachers.net

The work of Diana Greenhouse and Kazim Cicek first appeared on the website teachers.net. Since June 2000, we have contributed to a monthly column featured on teachers.net.

We have highlighted examples from teachers who have shared with us their successful implementations of **The First Days of School**. The profiles encompass elementary, high school, and special ed teachers, and cover the range from English, science, technology, and fine arts instructors to librarians. College professors have been featured. There's even a teacher's first-day-of-school script in Spanish.

A cumulative, short summary of all past columns can be found in each June column. By all means, beg, borrow, and steal from these teachers—use their ideas to create your own successful classroom.

### GoBe

### Classroom Management Plans

Diana Greenhouse's and Kazim Cicek's PowerPoint presentations are in the **Go**ing **Be**yond folder for Chapter 1 at EffectiveTeaching.com.

### Don't Be a Pal

Our heart goes out to all the neophyte teachers who want to be their students' friend. Be friendly, caring, loving, and sensitive, but do not be their friend. They have enough on their hands with their own friends.

The students of today need you to be an adult role model they can look to with admiration and pride. If you become a student's friend, the student will start asking for favors, as people do of friends. And if a favor is not granted, the student becomes incensed, "I thought you were my friend. I hate you!"

**It is better to be a paragon than a pal.**

This teacher is ready on the first day of school.

---

> **Student achievement at the end of the year is directly related to the degree to which the teacher establishes good control of the classroom procedures in the very first week of the school year.**

**The effective teacher establishes good control of the class in the very first week of school.** Control does not involve threats or intimidation. Control means that you know (1) what you are doing, (2) your classroom procedures, and (3) your professional responsibilities. It is very reassuring to your students that you know what you are doing.

**There is overwhelming evidence that the first two to three weeks of school are critical in determining how well students will achieve for the remainder of the year.**

You must have everything ready and organized when school begins. **Your success during the school year will be determined by what you do on the first days of school.**

## Effective Teachers Produce Results

The subtitle of this book is "How to Be an Effective Teacher." Effective means "to effect," "to produce results."

When you interact with people, such as a plumber, salesperson, dentist, or lawyer, you expect that person to be effective—to produce results. Likewise, the effective teacher is someone who can produce learning.

To be effective, a person is firstly proficient. **Proficient** refers to someone who continually acquires knowledge and skills to, in turn, be able to teach effectively.

> **PROFICIENT:** possessing knowledge and skills
> **EFFECTIVE:** to produce results
>
> The **EFFECTIVE** teacher **IMPACTS** lives.

## The Four Stages of Teaching

**T**here are four stages to teaching,[2] yet many teachers never progress beyond the Survival stage. The purpose of *The First Days of School* is to get you out of stage two, Survival, and on to the third stage, Mastery, so you can be the difference in the lives of your students.

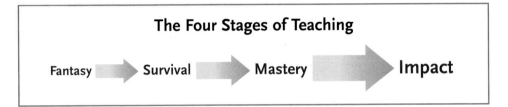

**Stage 1—Fantasy.** Many neophyte teachers have the naïve belief that to be a successful teacher, all they need to do is relate and be a friend to their students. They rarely talk about standards, assessment, or student achievement. Entertaining students with activities is their concept of teaching.

**Stage 2—Survival.** Teachers in the Survival stage have not developed instructional skills as explained in Unit D. They spend their time looking for busywork for the students to do, such as completing worksheets, watching videos, and doing seatwork—anything to keep the students quiet. Student learning and achievement are not their goals; they teach because it's a job and the paycheck is their Survival goal.

**Stage 3—Mastery.** Teachers who know how to achieve student success employ effective practices. These teachers know how to manage their classrooms. They teach for mastery, and have high expectations for their students. Effective teachers strive for Mastery by reading the literature and going to professional meetings. Student learning is their mission and student achievement is their Mastery goal.

**School**

**School is a powerful place.** People go to school to study, work, and produce—just like in an adult workplace. School is where people go to acquire knowledge, learn skills, and develop values that will make them productive citizens and help them grow to their fullest potential as human beings.

[2]Ryan, Kevin. (1986). *The Induction of New Teachers.* Bloomington, Ind.: Phi Delta Kappa.

## It's Never Too Late

*Teaching, unlike most professions, gives us the opportunity to start fresh each and every day, each and every year. You may stay in Survival mode your first few years, but that's highly unlikely if you read this book and implement the shared skills.*

*And if you're a veteran teacher, struggling to survive and reading this book for the first time, tomorrow is your new day, too.*

*I have been "surviving" for the last eight years. With the strategies I take away from this program, I finally can say, for the first time in nine years, I don't dread those first days.*

Becky Gibbs
Franklin Road Academy
Nashville, Tennessee

The effective teacher IS the difference.

**Stage 4—Impact.** Effective teachers make a difference in the lives of their students. These are the teachers to whom students come back years later and thank for affecting their lives. To make an impact on your students, you need to use effective teaching practices, which is the subject of this book. A student learns only when the teacher has an appreciable impact on the student's life. When you reach this stage, you have gone beyond Mastery; you have arrived as a teacher.

**When you reach the Impact stage**, you will return to the Fantasy stage—and fulfill your fantasy or dream of making a difference in the lives of your students. You'll also become a teacher-leader and live a happier life with a sense of pride and accomplishment knowing that you are contributing to the profession.

> Impact
>
> **Teachers universally say they go into teaching to make a difference.**
>
> **You more than make a difference.**
>
> **You ARE the difference.**

## Effective Teachers Impact Lives

T eachers who are proficient and effective are more capable of impacting the lives of students than teachers who are not proficient and effective.

The effective teacher knows how to bring the class to order quickly, explain rules and procedures, find out important information about the students, and let them know what to expect in the coming days. The next chapters will teach you these skills.

Relationships are created in an effectively run classroom. There is a trusting relationship between an effective teacher and the students. **Finding out about the students is important in an effectively run classroom.**

You were hired to impact lives. You were hired not so much to teach third grade, or history, or physical education, as to influence lives. Touch the life of a student, and you will have a student who will learn history, physical education, even science and math, close the windows, staple all the papers, and turn cartwheels to please you.

The beginning of school is critical. **What you do in the first days of school to affect the lives of your students will determine your success the rest of the year.**

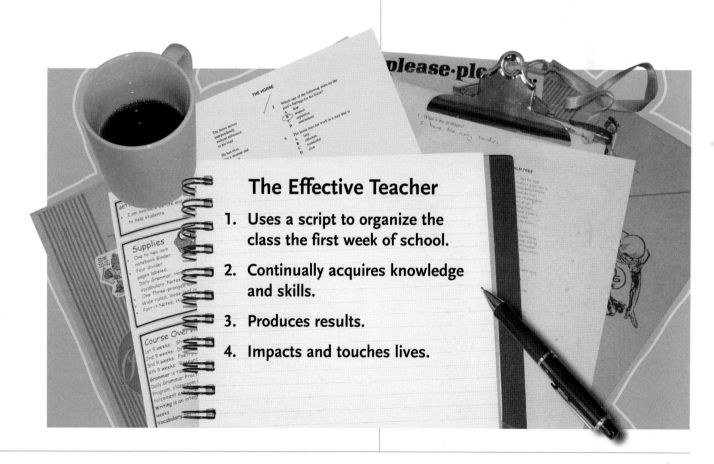

## The Effective Teacher

1. **Uses a script to organize the class the first week of school.**

2. **Continually acquires knowledge and skills.**

3. **Produces results.**

4. **Impacts and touches lives.**

## THE KEY IDEA

The beginning teacher must become proficient in the three characteristics of an effective teacher.

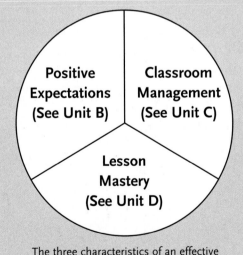

The three characteristics of an effective teacher and where to find them.

## The Effective Teacher

**The Three Characteristics of an Effective Teacher**

1. Has positive expectations for student success
2. Is an extremely good classroom manager
3. Knows how to design lessons for student mastery

**T**here are three characteristics of an effective teacher, and they apply to all teachers.[1] These characteristics are known, and you can easily learn how to be a very effective teacher.

**Teaching is a craft, a highly skilled craft that can be learned!**

**What works in a kindergarten classroom or a high school classroom also works with modification in any other classroom.**

The teacher with an ineffective classroom is constantly looking for activities to grab the students' attention. They are eager to present their lessons, do their exciting activities, and share their wonderful knowledge. But, none of these techniques will be successful until you become skilled in the characteristics of an effective teacher. Teaching is not covering chapters or doing activities.

**It's not what you put in; it's the outcome you get from the students.**

**Every one of us is both a student and a teacher.**

**We are at our best when we each teach ourselves what we need to learn.**

---

[1]Good, Thomas L., and Jere Brophy. (2007). *Looking in Classrooms.* Needham, Mass.: Allyn & Bacon, pp. 8, 9, 12, 47, 71, and 301.

Research consistently shows that of all the factors schools can control, the effective teacher has the greatest impact on student achievement.

Decade after decade of educational innovations and fads have not increased student achievement. **The only factor that increases student achievement is the significance of an effective teacher.**

## Positive Expectations

**P**ositive expectations, sometimes called high expectations, should not be confused with high standards. **Having positive expectations simply means that the teacher believes in the learner and that the learner can learn.**

The belief in positive expectations is based on research, which demonstrates that the learner will produce what the teacher expects the learner to produce. If you believe a student is a low-level, below-average, slow learner, the student will perform accordingly because these are the beliefs you transmit to the student. If you believe a student is a high-ability, above-average, capable learner, the student will perform at that level because these are the expectations you transmit to the student.

**It is essential that the teacher exhibit positive expectations toward all students.** Unit B discusses ways to convey positive expectations and explains the importance of positive expectations, an attitude that benefits the teacher and the student, as well as the overall classroom environment.

## Classroom Management

**C**lassroom management consists of the practices and procedures that a teacher uses to maintain an environment in which instruction and learning can occur.** For this to happen, the teacher must create a well-ordered environment.

An effective teacher has the greatest impact on student achievement.

**GoBe**

### Close to a Miracle

Stacy Hennessee's classroom was out of control. Then he experienced something close to a miracle. What he did is in the **Go**ing **Be**yond folder for Chapter 2 at EffectiveTeaching.com.

## Students Work Without the Teacher Present

*Dear Dr. Wong,*

*In my 23 years in the classroom, I have always felt that one of my greatest strengths is in the area of classroom management.*

*To illustrate, I called the administration one evening to inform them that I was ill and would not be present the next day. The following morning my students were standing in the hall outside my room when the first bell rang. The other teacher in the department opened my door to let the students in. As the day progressed, the classes came and went. In the afternoon a counselor came looking for me. My students said that they had not seen me all day and went back to business as usual.*

*My standing joke with the administration is that if I could get my students to keep quiet about my absence, I could stay home all week or maybe even take a trip to some South Seas island!*

*In closing, I have not had a serious discipline problem in over 15 years, and my day is free to spend however I wish at 3:15 P.M.*

*Procedures work!*

Richard L. Crewse
Concord High School
Elkhart, Indiana

Discipline has very little to do with classroom management. You don't discipline a store; you manage it. The same is true of a classroom. Unit C explains how to manage a classroom, applying the principle that a well-ordered environment leads to an effective classroom. **The effectiveness of such an environment is the result of how well the teacher learns the skill of managing the classroom.**

## Lesson Mastery

**M**astery refers to how well a student can demonstrate that a concept has been comprehended, or perform a skill at a level of proficiency, as determined by the teacher.** Unit D explains how to teach for mastery.

When a home is built, the contractor receives a set of blueprints from the architect. The blueprints specify the degree of competence that will be acceptable. The inspector who periodically checks on the construction always looks at the blueprint first and then checks the workmanship to see if the work has been performed to the degree of competence specified.

**Well-Ordered Environment + Positive Academic Expectations = Effective Classroom**

The classroom of Sarah Jondahl is structured for success.

Teaching is no different. To teach for mastery or competence, an effective teacher must do three things:

1. Know how to design lessons in which a student will be able to learn a concept or a skill to a goal or standard.

2. Know how to deliver the instruction to teach to the goal or standard.

3. Know how to assess and provide corrective action for learning so the student can master the concept or the skill.

**Student success in the subject matter of the class depends on how well the teacher designs lessons and checks for mastery.**

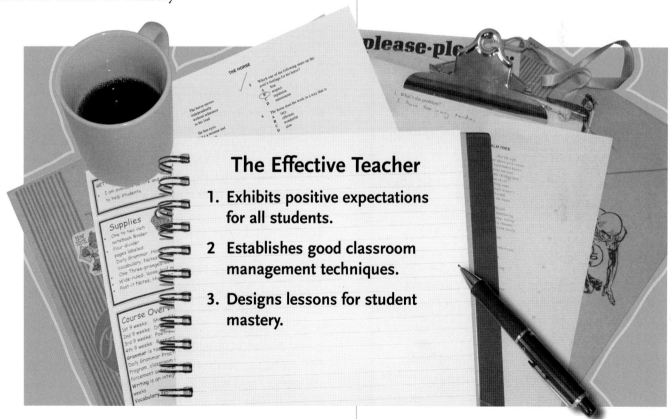

## The Effective Teacher

1. **Exhibits positive expectations for all students.**

2 **Establishes good classroom management techniques.**

3. **Designs lessons for student mastery.**

**3**

## THE KEY IDEA

**The beginning teacher must perform the full complement of skills while learning those skills.**

---

### The First Year of Teaching Is the Most Crucial

**New teachers feel**
Isolated,
Vulnerable, and
Deeply concerned with how
   they will be perceived, yet
Afraid to ask for help.

**They are hired,**
Given a key,
Told which room is theirs, and
Given no support.

**They are given the worst assignments.**
They feel frightened.
They feel humiliated.
They are given no help.
They want someone to give them hope,
   to tell them when their hardship will end.

---

## The First Year Can Be Successful

> Here's the biggest secret to teaching success:
> Beg, Borrow, and Steal!

I t's really not stealing. It's really research and learning. You walk into the classrooms of effective teachers, look around, and if you see something that you think might help you, say, "Gimme, gimme, gimme." There are many veteran teachers who will be happy to share with you and help you.

We are in a community of equals, not a community of experts. We are members of a common community. Don't be afraid to ask and learn. Through mutual support and sharing, we improve our profession.

Your first day of teaching will be an exciting, anticipated event but very frightening at the same time. **Yet you can succeed if you learn how to be effective on the first days of school.**

## Teacher Education Will Not Have Prepared You

T he schools of education are not to be blamed. No one ever said that education ends with a college degree. Some people enter teaching by way of an alternative certification route. Regardless, the best teachers are also the best students. Good teachers are continually improving themselves by going back to college; joining professional organizations; attending conventions, conferences, and workshops; participating in staff development meetings; and working cooperatively with others on the staff in collegial support networks and learning communities to improve student achievement.

## Student Teaching Will Not Have Prepared You

**Y**our master teacher is not to be blamed. No one ever trained your master teacher in what to teach you. Few student teachers enter teaching with any experience in what to do on the first day of school. Typically, the master teacher started the class and then turned the class over to the student teacher. **Thus, most student teachers enter the teaching profession with no training and no experience in what to do on the first day of school.**

Elmo Sanchez, Jr.,
first-year teacher

---

**The First Year of Teaching Can Be Frightening**

1. Teacher education will not have prepared you.
2. Student teaching will not have prepared you.
3. The district may not have prepared you.
4. Yet, you will be expected to perform immediately.

---

Beth A. Sommers,
first-year teacher

## Some Districts Have Induction Programs to Prepare You

**I**n teaching, entry into the profession can be sudden. In the business world, new employees receive comprehensive training from day one, allowing them to gradually gain knowledge, experience, and responsibility until retirement.

Have you ever wondered why your seemingly problem students do so well at a local store or fast-food restaurant? Restaurants such as McDonald's and Domino's Pizza have sophisticated training programs to prepare workers before they face the public. Go behind the scenes at any place of business and you will see workers in training reviewing videos, reading instruction manuals, and learning various aspects of their jobs. **Effective districts and schools, likewise, have a training or comprehensive induction program for all newly hired teachers.**

**Knowledge is weightless,
a treasure you can always carry easily.**

## Learning Is Ongoing

*Our induction program helped me have a very successful first year. Thanks to my administrator, the staff developer, and the book **The First Days of School**, my days have been very exciting and worthwhile. I have continued to use the tools provided in the district's induction program and the book to help me achieve success with my students each new year.*

Jaime A. Diaz
Tucson, Arizona

Jaime Diaz

**GoBe**

### 10 Questions to Ask

When you interview for a job, there are 10 questions you need to ask. These are in the **Go**ing **Be**yond folder for Chapter 3 at EffectiveTeaching.com.

Regretfully, in some schools, newly hired teachers are merely given a key to a room and told to go teach, leaving you to

**Figure it out yourself. Do it yourself. Keep it to yourself.**

> **The beginning teacher is expected to assume the same tasks and responsibilities as the most seasoned teacher on the staff.**

**What will really prepare you for teaching in your district is an organized new teacher induction program.** Induction is a structured multi-year program that will train and support you as you become an effective teacher. To learn more about induction, go to NewTeacher.com and read many of the articles on the website. Also, read *New Teacher Induction: How to Train, Support, and Retain New Teachers.*[1]

**Attention New Teachers: If you are a new teacher looking for a teaching job, you need to ask if the district has an induction program. Do not sign a contract until you ask.** Districts with induction programs care that you succeed. This entails more than simply giving you a mentor.

Effective districts want to help their newly hired teachers succeed. They offer induction programs that begin before the first day of school and may extend for several years thereafter. Induction is more than orientation, mentoring, or evaluation. It's the training a district gives to bring out the teacher you are meant to be. Please do not be so naïve to think that you can succeed on your own without help.

[1] Breaux, Annette, and Harry K. Wong. (2003). *New Teacher Induction: How to Train, Support, and Retain New Teachers.* Mountain View, Calif.: Harry K. Wong Publications, Inc.

## You Will Be Expected to Perform Immediately

**W**hen you become a first-year teacher, you will be an equal with all the other teachers. You will have the same students they teach, you will teach from the same curriculum, and you will have the same administrators. You will have the same duties and responsibilities as all the other teachers.

**Yet, you will be expected to be perfect on the first day of school and then get better each year.** You can do it, but you will be able to do it better if your district puts you through an induction program and you recognize that becoming an effective teacher is a never-ending learning process.

> You will be expected to perform
> your full complement of duties immediately
> while learning them at the same time.

**Education is not a product; it is a never-ending process.** The purpose of this book is to give you some insight, ideas, and choices about how to start your first days of school. Note the word, "choices." The quality of the choices you make today will dictate the quality of your opportunities tomorrow.

There are no pat answers in education, no simple answers, no quick-fixes, no sure model, no foolproof methods. There are teachers, who become effective because they make teaching a profession and not a job. **They continue to learn, and from their fund of knowledge they make choices about each appropriate strategy they should use.**

### Induction Can Help Beginning Teachers

Induction has three purposes:

1. To **reduce** the **intensity** of your transition into teaching

2. To help you **improve** your **teaching** effectiveness

3. To **increase** the **retention** of greater numbers of highly qualified teachers

The Lafourche Parish Public Schools induction program is so successful that Louisiana has adopted it as a statewide model for all school systems.

## Selected Professional Educational Organizations

American Alliance for Health, Physical Education, Recreation, and Dance
American Association of Family & Consumer Sciences
American Association of Physics Teachers
American Council on the Teaching of Foreign Languages
American Library Association
American School Counselor Association
American Speech-Language-Hearing Association
Association for Career and Technical Education
Association for Childhood Education International
Association for Children and Adults with Learning Disabilities
Association for Educational Communications and Technology
Association for Gifted and Talented Students
Association for Supervision and Curriculum Development
Comparative and International Education Society
Council for Exceptional Children
Council for Learning Disabilities
Educational Theatre Association
International Reading Association
International Society for Technology in Education
Kappa Delta Pi
Lutheran Education Association
National Alliance of Black School Educators
National Art Education Association
National Association for Bilingual Education
National Association for Gifted Children
National Association for Music Education
National Association for Sport and Physical Education
National Association for the Education of Young Children
National Association of Biology Teachers
National Association of Child Care Professionals
National Association of Elementary School Principals
National Association of School Nurses
National Association of Secondary School Principals
National Association of Special Education Teachers
National Business Education Association
National Catholic Education Association
National Council for the Social Studies
National Council of Teachers of English
National Council of Teachers of Mathematics
National Rural Education Association
National Science Teachers Association
National Society for the Gifted & Talented
Society for Music Teacher Education

Some school districts have model classrooms that are prepared before the first day of school. Induction program teachers visit these classrooms to see how a classroom can be set up for the start of school.

Your whole life is ahead of you, and it can be filled with happiness and success. If you want positive results from your professional career, know that your colleagues are your best resource.

**Work** in a collegial manner with your colleagues.

**Associate** with and learn from positive mentors and coaches.

**Join** a professional organization.

**Continue to learn** through classes, workshops, conferences, professional meetings, books, journals, CDs, DVDs, the Internet, and advanced degrees.

### GoBe

### Websites

Each of these organizations has a website, publishes a journal, and holds meetings. Many have state and local branches. See the **Go**ing **Be**yond folder for Chapter 3 at EffectiveTeaching.com for each group's website.

" *Hold fast to dreams for if dreams die*
*Life is a broken-winged bird that cannot fly.*
*Hold fast to dreams for when dreams go*
*Life is a barren field frozen with snow.*[2] "

_Langston Hughes

You now have the rest of the school year and your professional years ahead of you to truly enjoy. You can be a happy, successful, and exciting teacher.

**Inside Every Great Teacher**
**there is an even better one**
**waiting to come out.**

Some districts have learning communities where new teachers can seamlessly fit in immediately.

---

> **Life is fuller when you are chasing a challenge.**

### If Only Someone Would Start the Class

*I do not remember this teacher's name, but had it not been for her, I never would have made it this far. Bless her! Something happened to me before the first day of school when I began teaching 26 years ago in Los Angeles.*

*I was standing in the teachers' lounge when this experienced teacher came to me and said, "You don't know how to start, eh?"*

*I said, "How can you tell? If you can only start my classes for me and get them rolling, I'll be able to carry on."*

*No one had taught me how to start the first day of school.*

Gail Sutton
Portland, Oregon

---

[2]Hughes, Langston. (2004). "Dreams." *The Collected Poems of Langston Hughes.* Arnold Pampersad (ed.). New York: Alfred A. Knopf.

## You Can Have Any Job in Education in Three to Five Years With a Raise in Salary of 25 Percent or More

Because of the need for many more teachers in the future, there will be many opportunities for effective teachers.

Your future in education can be very rewarding, but only the teachers who strive for success will be rewarded. It's no different with students. Only those who work hard and have the most positive attitudes get the best grades. Here are some reasons why the future looks good for you.

- By 2013, U. S. schools will need to hire more than 2 million teachers and administrators to replace those retiring from the current teaching force and to meet the needs of a growing population of students.

- All kinds of job opportunities will be available—and not just in the classroom. Many teachers will become administrators or college professors, hold jobs in educational organizations, write software, become consultants, run educational programs for private businesses, open child-care centers, and embark on many other educationally related endeavors.

- Although teachers are in the learning profession, they are typically among the worst when it comes to wanting to learn how to improve their own competencies. Most teachers do not go to conferences, and they deride professional meetings.

- Because many teachers do not want to grow, those who do can have almost any position in education in three to five years at a salary 25 percent above what they are making right now.

There is a new sense of urgency about our schools, especially in closing the achievement gap. You can play an active role during this time of urgency—and be rewarded for your contribution.

Teaching is a profession, and like all professions, its members must continuously learn new knowledge and skills. The most effective way to continually acquire new knowledge and skills is to be part of a learning team where professionals share and learn from each other.

The teachers we hire today will become the teachers for the next generation. Their success will determine the success of an entire generation of students.

### The Greatest Threat

People seldom improve when they have no other model to copy but themselves. Build on the strengths of your colleagues, not the weaknesses of a few.

The greatest threat to a teacher who is not growing is a teacher who is growing. The stagnating teacher will do everything to discourage and prevent you from growing because your growth is perceived as a threat.

Do not listen to cynical, running-in-place teachers.

These are the people who make fun of administrators, schools of education, staff developers, conventions, conferences, and professional meetings (if they go, they sit in the back rows). They resist anything and anyone who wants to help you grow into the great teacher and person you are destined to be.

Avoid teachers who constantly complain and make excuses. Do not allow people who cannot control their own behavior to be in control of your behavior.

**Find yourself a coach, a colleague who will serve as your role model. Seek someone who will help you learn and give you inspiration. Find someone you can hold up as a symbol of the success you truly want to be. You are the only person on the face of the earth who can use your abilities. It is an awesome responsibility.**

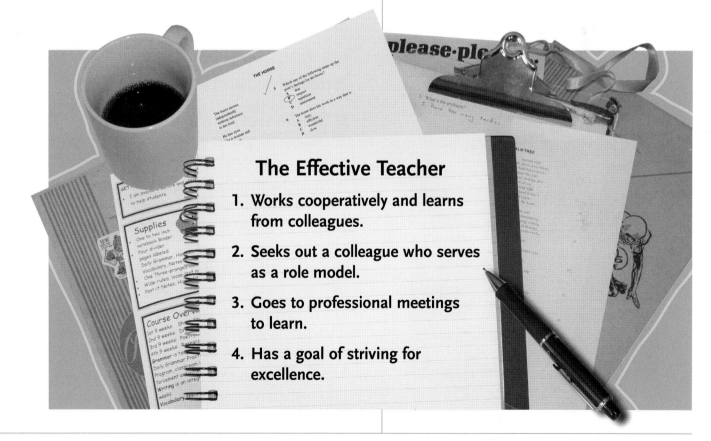

## The Effective Teacher

1. Works cooperatively and learns from colleagues.

2. Seeks out a colleague who serves as a role model.

3. Goes to professional meetings to learn.

4. Has a goal of striving for excellence.

**4**

## THE KEY IDEA

**The effectiveness of the teacher determines the level of student achievement.**

Alex Kajitani creates Math Raps to teach his middle school Algebra students.

## The Importance of Effective Teachers

**The greatest asset of a school is its people.**

**S**chool does not begin until the teacher walks into the classroom. It is the teacher—what the teacher knows and can do—that is the most significant factor in student achievement. **The more effective the teacher, the more successful the students.**

## The Difference Between an Effective Teacher and an Ineffective Teacher

**T**here's only one difference: The ineffective teacher is simply not doing what the effective teacher is doing. Do what the effective teacher is doing, and the ineffective teacher will be effective—instantly.

**Successful teachers are innovative planners, exceptional classroom managers, adept critical thinkers, and competent problem solvers.** Successful people MAKE themselves do the things unsuccessful people will not do.

**Ineffective teachers look for busywork** to kill class time. They are survivors. They whine that nothing useful ever applies to them, fully expecting others to tell them what to do.

The effective teacher is a creative teacher—one who can think, adapt, and implement. **Effective teachers steal from the best and learn from the rest.** They look at the resources available to them and reorganize those resources to work toward a goal.

Effective teachers are problem solvers. They analyze, synthesize, and create materials to help students learn.

> **A true professional and effective teacher is a learner who learns along with the students.**

Here are some observations on the importance of effective teachers:

- The most effective teachers can produce 9 months or more of learning, essentially a full year, than ineffective teachers.[1]

- Teacher expertise accounts for a greater difference in student performance—40 percent—than any other factor.[2]

- Students who have several effective teachers in a row make dramatic achievement gains, while those who have even two ineffective teachers in a row lose significant ground.[3]

- Teacher quality accounts for more than 90 percent of the variation in student achievement.[4]

- The single greatest effect on student achievement is not race, not poverty—it is the effectiveness of the teacher.[5]

- As teacher effectiveness increases, lower-achieving students are the first to benefit.[6]

## Teachers Want Success

It's the teachers and their instructional practices—not the curriculum programs or a change in the school structure—that improve student learning. **Teachers do not want programs; they want achievement for their students.**

### Quality Teaching

Research overwhelmingly supports the fact that teacher knowledge and skills are the most important factors influencing children's learning.[7] And for children from disadvantaged backgrounds or troubled home environments, quality teaching is even more important.

[1] Rowan B., R. Correnti, and R. Miller. (2002). "What Large-Scale Survey Research Tells Us About Teacher Effects on Student Achievement." *Teachers College Record*, 104, pp. 1525–1567.

[2] National Commission on Teaching and America's Future. (November 1997). *Doing What Matters Most: Investing in Quality Teaching.* NCTAF, 2100 M Street NW, Suite 660, Washington, D.C. 20037, p. 8.

[3] Sack, Joetta. "Class Size, Teacher Quality Take Center Stage at Hearing." *Education Week*, May 5, 1999, p. 22.

[4] National Commission on Teaching and America's Future, p. 9.

[5] Rivers, June C., and William L. Sanders. "Teacher Quality and Equity in Educational Opportunity: Findings and Policy Implications." Presented at the Hoover/PRI Teacher Quality Conference, Stanford University, May 12, 2000, p. 4.

[6] Sanders, William L. (1996). "Cumulative and Residual Effects of Teachers on Future Student Academic Achievement." University of Tennessee Value-Added Research and Assessment Center, p. 7.

[7] Hanushek, E. A., J. F. Kain, and S. G. Rivkin. (2001). *Why Public Schools Lose Teachers.* Cambridge, Mass.: National Bureau of Economic Research.

# Successful Teachers Come in All Subjects and Grade Levels

**Jeffrey W. Smith is a successful teacher.** There is nothing in *The First Days of School* about how to teach welding, yet Jeff Smith adapted what he read in this book and became America's foremost welding teacher.

He is a PROFESSIONAL educator. He practices professionalism, adhering to the codes of dress and conduct accepted by the welding industry.

He is a leader in welding education, integrating certification standards and requirements in his lessons. His students have the highest certification levels in Oklahoma, making his students the most accomplished junior welders in the state.

**Jeff Smith:** High School Vo-Tech Teacher. Every student Jeff has taught has passed and received the Oklahoma welding certification. All of his students have succeeded.

**Elizabeth Breaux:** Middle School Teacher. Liz teaches alternative education students in a high-poverty school who are typically one to three years behind their peers, yet she has no major problems, her students are successful, and she is basically stress free!

**Sarah Jondahl:** Elementary School Teacher. Sarah began teaching on her first day of school with a classroom management action plan binder. It has grown to two binders. She's organized for student success. The students love her and the parents do, too.

**Steve Geiman:** High School Physical Education Teacher. Steve adapts general classroom procedures to the gym. He says procedures used in the P.E. classroom are applicable to all classrooms.

**Chelonnda Seroyer:** High School English Teacher. Chelonnda was successful the moment her first student walked into her very first classroom. She had an assignment ready for her students and her students got to work.

**Julie Johnson:** Elementary School Teacher. Julie has been teaching for many years and she's never had problems getting her students to do their assignments. Her students beg to be tested.

**Robin Barlak:** Pre-school Special Education Teacher. Robin adapts procedures so her students can experience success. She makes learning enjoyable for teachers, classroom assistants, therapists, students, and parents.

**Norm Dannen:** High School English Teacher. Norm uses scoring guides so his students know up front what they are expected to learn and how they will be assessed.

**Karen Rogers:** High School Science Teacher. Karen shows her procedures with a PowerPoint presentation. She uses scoring guides so her students and their parents know what needs to be done.

**Susan Monfet:** College Instructor. Susan says, "The classroom management practices I teach my students also work in how I manage my college classroom."

**Effective teaching practices work in all classrooms: K–16.** Prepare yourself for an "Aha" or "light bulb" moment, and modify the technique for your classroom. Then, it's all yours to use with success.

## GoBe

### Stories of Successful Teachers

The complete story for each of these teachers can be found in the **Go**ing **Be**yond folder for Chapter 4 at EffectiveTeaching.com.

**Programs do not produce achievement; teachers produce student achievement.** Money is much better spent training and developing teachers than for buying one program after another. Educational leaders know that what matters most is whether schools can offer their neediest students good teachers who are trained in effective strategies to teach strong academic knowledge and skills.

## How to Improve Student Achievement

The ineffective teacher affects little, if any, growth in students. **The effective teacher, even in an ineffective school, produces improved student learning and increased student achievement.**

Imagine the student is achieving at the 50th percentile and the student is placed in one of the following situations. After two years, Robert Marzano's research concludes the following:

- If the student has an **ineffective teacher** in an **ineffective school**, **student achievement will drop** from the 50th percentile to the 3rd percentile.

- If the student has an **ineffective teacher** in an **effective school**, **student achievement will still drop** to the 37th percentile.

- However, if the student has an **effective teacher** in an **ineffective school**, **student achievement will rise** to the 63rd percentile.

**It's the teacher. It's the teacher.** Consider that we have average teachers in average schools. That's fine.

**But, if teachers and administrators can only slightly improve their effectiveness each year, there will be monumental gains in student achievement over the collective years.**

| School and Teacher Effectiveness Impact on Learning Entering School at 50th Percentile[8] | |
|---|---|
| Type of School and Type of Teacher | Percentile After Two Years |
| Ineffective school and Ineffective teacher | 3rd |
| Effective school and Ineffective teacher | 37th |
| Average school and Average teacher | 50th |
| Ineffective school and Effective teacher | 63rd |
| Effective school and Average teacher | 78th |
| Effective school and Effective teacher | 96th |

*" Perhaps the most valuable result of all education is the ability to make yourself do the thing you have to do, when it ought to be done, whether you like it or not. "*

_Thomas Huxley

[8]Marzano, Robert. (2003). *What Works in Schools: Translating Research into Action.* Arlington, Va.: Association for Supervision and Curriculum Development (ASCD), p. 74.

Some people can give thousands of reasons why they CANNOT succeed at something when all they need is one reason why they CAN succeed.

**GoBe**

### The Miracle of Teachers

Read what teachers have accomplished in elevating the success of students through the years in the Going Beyond folder for Chapter 4 at EffectiveTeaching.com.

These gaps in achievement exist when groups of students with relatively equal ability do not achieve in school at the same levels. Extensive research can be found on how to close the achievement gap. Schools that work on closing the achievement gap maintain these characteristics:[9]

- Keep a laser focus on learning for all students.
- Maintain a "no excuses" attitude.
- Use research and data to improve teacher practices.
- Involve everyone in improvement processes.
- Persist through difficulties and setbacks.
- Celebrate accomplishments.

**The achievement gap can be closed with a school of average to above-average teachers, but the school and the teachers must work together on improving student achievement.**

A student who has an outstanding teacher will remain ahead of her peers for at least the next few years. A student with an ineffective teacher will not be fully remediated for up to three years—even if that student has effective teachers.

The quality of the teacher, in any school setting, is the most critical component for IMPROVING STUDENT ACHIEVEMENT and closing achievement gaps.

Rita Zimmermann works with young minds in Fort Worth, Texas.

[9]National Education Association. (2006). *Closing Achievement Gaps: An Association Guide.* Washington, D.C.: National Education Association (NEA), p. 19.

## That Noble Title
# Teacher

As we begin each new school year, let us remember the fine nuances and the distinguishing essence of that proud word **Teacher**.

Let us be reminded of the tools you have at your command, because of your talents, your traits, and your training . . . and because you chose to become a **Teacher**.

**Teacher**—you are a poet, as you weave with your colorful magic language a passion for your subject. You create a vast and grand mosaic of curiosities to imagine, secrets to unfold, connections only to begin the cycle of learning.

**Teacher**—you are a physicist, as you bring magic, logic, reason, and wonder to the properties, changes, and interactions of our universe.

**Teacher**—you are a maestro, a master of composing, as you conduct and orchestrate individuals' thoughts and actions from discordant cacophony into harmonic resonance.

**Teacher**—you are an architect, as you provide each student a solid foundation, but always with a vision of the magnificent structure that is about to emerge.

**Teacher**—you are a gymnast, as you encourage the contortions and gyrations of thoughts and the flexing and strengthening of ideas.

**Teacher**—you are a diplomat and the ambassador of tact and sensitivity, as you facilitate productive, positive interactions among the multiplicity of personalities and cultures, beliefs, and ideals.

**Teacher**—you are a philosopher, as your actions and ethics convey meaning and hope to young people who look to you for guidance and example. As you prepare for your first day and each day, when your students enter and you encounter their attitudes, ranging from eager, enthusiastic anticipation to uncomfortable, uncertain apathy, recall the powers you have within . . . from poet to philosopher . . . and present yourself to those students as a person worthy of the noble title . . . Teacher.

Trish Marcuzzo
Omaha Public Schools, Nebraska

This essay is available as a color poster. See page 345.

## We Are Teachers

**W**hat teachers do is a miracle. Teachers accept all children from every imaginable situation and care for them, nurture them, and teach them. You are to be thanked for choosing such a noble profession.

The units in this book on positive expectations, classroom management, and lesson mastery will prepare you for your career as an effective teacher. It will be an exciting journey.

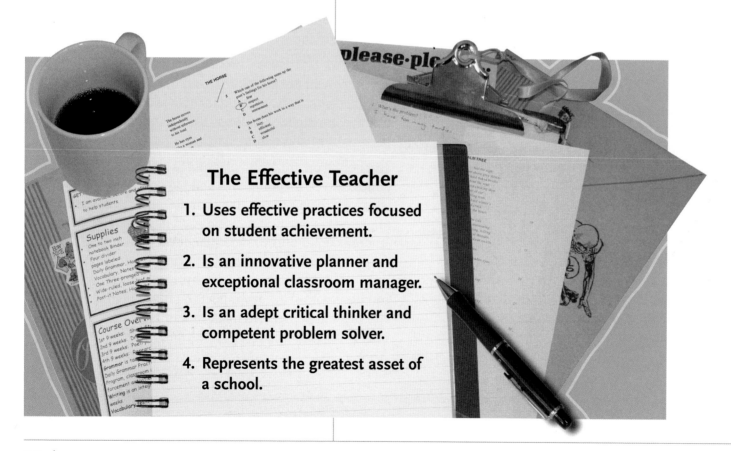

### The Effective Teacher

1. **Uses effective practices focused on student achievement.**

2. **Is an innovative planner and exceptional classroom manager.**

3. **Is an adept critical thinker and competent problem solver.**

4. **Represents the greatest asset of a school.**

## The Research Process

> People who know what to do and people who know how to do it will always be working for those who know why it is being done.

## THE KEY IDEA

**Effective teachers use proven, research-based practices that are employed by thousands of other teachers.**

esearch is the process of critical thinking and problem solving employed by thousands. It is this ability that sets humans apart from all other living things. Research is simply the use of the human mind to seek answers or, as some would say, to search for the "truth."

Research is not something only scientists do. Businesspeople do research; so do baseball players, chefs, plumbers, lawyers, dentists, artists, and actors. Students, when they write term papers, do research. To search and search and search, over and over again. That is why it is called re-search.

## It May Be Dangerous to Teach as You Were Taught

**U**nfortunately and erroneously, **many teachers teach as they were taught.** Many teachers teach as their academic college professors taught them, thinking that's the way to teach. No education professor, administrator, staff developer, or teacher at a workshop has ever said that the model of teaching presented in the box on the next page is the way to teach. Yet, many teachers think this is teaching.

### The Research Process

**Problem:** What do I want to know?
**Prediction:** What do I think is the right answer?
**Procedure:** How will I solve the problem?
**Data:** What will I look for?
**Conclusion:** What do the results tell me?

**Effective teachers use research to improve their effectiveness.**

When you change a recipe, you are doing research.

Regrettably, many teachers also succumb to teaching according to the latest fad, philosophy, or political agenda, never asking for the research evidence of its success. This is why Richard Elmore of Harvard University says, "Most decisions made in education, especially in urban schools, are made for the benefit of the adults—not the children."

Teachers who work in learning communities represent the greatest research asset in a school. What they learn is the greatest asset of the educational system, and it is to be shared.

Teaching is a profession, and like all professions, its members must learn new knowledge and skills continuously. Becoming a truly accomplished teacher is a journey, not a destination. A professional teacher will still be "learning to do it better" the day she or he retires.

- Ineffective teachers talk more about the gimmicks and games they are trying to find to "keep the kids quiet."

- Effective teachers talk more about the research they constantly look for to improve the achievement of their students.

**Always remember, student achievement and success are why teachers teach; our research successes are to be shared for the sake of the students.**

## Research Improves Student Achievement

Theme parks know when and where to send more food vendors. Airlines know how much to price each flight. Stores know your buying patterns. They use what is known as business intelligence or BI in industry terms. There is software that harvests data, trends, and information to help businesses make decisions.

**Schools do the same. They harvest student data to improve student achievement.** Led by Superintendent Joe Kitchens, the Western Heights School District in Oklahoma has seen math and reading scores increase up to 48 percent over a four-year period.

---

### This Model of Teaching Has NO Research to Support It

- Assign chapters to read.

- Answer the questions at the back of the chapter or on the worksheet.

- Deliver a lecture and have students take notes.

- Show a video or do an activity.

- Construct a test based on a number of points.

- Control the assignment of grades.

---

**Effective teachers do what the research tells us is most effective.**

**Effective teachers use proven, research-based practices.**

**Why would you do otherwise?**

---

Using software systems that mine student information, teachers have almost immediate access to their students' scores at any given time. Data drives teaching, learning, and continuous improvement in this diverse district, where 75 percent of the students qualify for free or reduced-price meals.

The research data allows teams of teachers to review and determine "how best" to prepare lessons for students who need differentiated instruction. Teachers know exactly where the child needs help, or has potential to excel.

The lesson-planning program software and benchmarking process both allow sharing among teachers. The staff uses data to improve student achievement.

Western Heights has taken the Oklahoma standards and aligned them with its own benchmarked tests, which the teachers and administrators created at higher levels than the state tests.

Using research data, they have broken down skills sets for each child by subject and level. The faculty shares this data to improve teaching and learning. **This sharing of research data is their formula for student achievement. That's success.**

Joe Kitchens, superintendant

### Western Heights School District's Keys to Success

- Grade level teams developed scope and sequence, objectives, and benchmark tests that exceed the Oklahoma standards for grade level subjects.

- Benchmark tests are given at the end of each nine-week period.

- Teachers consistently and annually review results of what's been taught and tested.

- Teachers have immediate access to each student's performance on each standard.

- Teachers have the technology to share lesson plans and tests to improve teaching and learning.

**Here's an "Aha."** Do you realize that if you come to Western Heights as a new teacher, you get the immediate impression that they know what they are doing, and you can be part of it and succeed?

### The Four Beliefs of an Effective Teacher

1. It is the teacher who makes the difference in the classroom.

2. By far the most important factor in school learning is the ability of the teacher.

3. There is an extensive body of research and knowledge about teaching that must be known by the teacher.

4. The teacher must be a decision maker, able to translate the research and body of knowledge about teaching into increased student learning.

_After Madeline Hunter

**GoBe**

**She Stopped the Video Frequently**

**Stacey Allred** taught a video-guided workshop on *The Effective Teacher*. She used "Aha" pages to reflect on the video. See her work in the **Go**ing **Be**yond folder for Chapter 5 at EffectiveTeaching.com.

## Educational Research That Applies to Every Teacher

John P. Rickards discovered two things:[1]

1. The most ineffective place to print questions is at the end of a textbook chapter.

2. It is ineffective to give a student all the questions for an assignment at one time, and then ask the student to answer all the questions and to turn them in all at one time.

**Rickards found that if you want a student to achieve high-level comprehension, you should intersperse the questions throughout the text or the assignment.** You do this to constantly assess the learning success of the students. Chapters 22 and 23 discuss this in greater detail.

You know that this is true from having taken reading comprehension tests. Reading comprehension tests are not written with pages of text, followed by a long list of questions. They constantly go back and forth, a paragraph or two of learning text followed by a few questions.

Put another way, no doctor asks questions when the patient is dead. A doctor intersperses questions during the treatment of a patient, constantly assessing the health of the patient.

Likewise, the effective teacher does not ask all the questions at the end of the discussion, class period, video, chapter, lecture, or meeting. **The effective teacher who wants high-level comprehension intersperses questions throughout all class activities. This is what the research tells us.**

## When Should You Ask Questions During a Video?

Educational research tells you, and Bob Wallace, a middle school teacher in New Jersey, shows you. He reported the following as a result of his research with his students.

He divided his students into three groups and did the following:

**Group 1:** Showed the students a video and gave them a test.

**Group 2:** Briefed the group on the video to be shown and then showed the same video shown to Group 1 and gave the same test.

**Group 3:** Briefed Group 3 exactly as he had Group 2 and then showed the same video.

However, during the video, he made frequent stops. During each stop, he asked questions and held class discussion. He then gave the same test he had given to Groups 1 and 2.

Guess which of the three groups scored the highest on the test? Group 3, of course.

[1]Rickards, John P. (November 1976). "Stimulating High-Level Comprehension by Interspersing Questions in Text Passages." *Educational Technology*, p. 13.

## Research on Improving Student Achievement

**Aligned Time on Task:  Students who are actively focused on educational goals do best in mastering the subject matter.**

> Research findings:  More than 130 studies support the obvious:  The more students study, the more they learn!  Time alone, however, does not suffice.  The lesson objectives, learning activities, and tests must be matched and emphasized.  (To see how this is implemented, refer to Chapters 22 and 23.)

**Learning Community:  People in small, research groups can support and increase one another's learning.**

> Research findings:  Academic achievement is greater when there is frequent exchange among teachers and students.  In addition, teachers and students learn teamwork skills that are essential in the workplace.  (To see how learning teams are implemented, consult Chapter 24.)

**Extensive Reading:  Extensive reading of material of many kinds, both in school and outside, results in substantial growth in the vocabulary, comprehension abilities, and information base of students.**

> Research findings:  Cognitive abilities, such as comprehension and vocabulary, are enhanced with increased time spent reading—inside and outside of school.  Studies show, however, that children spend no more than a few minutes a day on either assigned or independent reading.  School resources need to be provided for materials, and large blocks of time allocated for students to read.

**Wait Time:  Pausing after asking a question in the classroom results in an increase in achievement.**

> Research findings:  Students are usually given less than one second to respond to a question.  Increasing wait time from three to seven seconds, accompanied by a high-order question, results in students responding with more thoughtful answers and an increase in achievement.

**Improving achievement is no great mystery; nor is it an impossible task.**  The major principles of effective teaching are in the *Handbook of Research on Improving Student Achievement*.  The research for the handbook was sponsored by 29 leading education organizations serving 3 million members.  So if improving achievement is no great mystery, why can't we do it?  You'll learn how to apply this research in Units C and D.

Based on Gordon Cawelti (ed.).
*Handbook of Research on Improving Student Achievement.*  (2004).  Arlington, Va.:
Educational Research Service.

" *Research cannot and does not identify
the right or best way to teach,
nor does it suggest that certain instructional practices
should always or never be used.
But research can illuminate which instructional practices
are most likely to achieve desired results,
with which kinds of learners, and under what conditions.*[2] "

_Myriam Met

## The Effective Teacher

1. Understands the research process.

2. Uses proven, research-based teaching practices.

3. Uses research data to improve teaching and learning.

[2]Cawelti, Gordon (ed.). (2004). *Handbook of Research on Improving Student Achievement.* Arlington, Va.: Educational Research Service, p. 3.

# *First Characteristic*

## _Positive Expectations

The effective teacher has positive expectations for student success.

# Unit  First Characteristic _Positive Expectations

The effective teacher has positive expectations for student success.

Unit B is correlated with Part 2: "The First Days of School" and Part 8: "Positive Expectations" in the DVD series *The Effective Teacher*.

## Humans Have a Success Instinct

> There is absolutely no research correlation between success and family background, race, national origin, financial status, or even educational accomplishments. There is but one correlation with success, and that is ATTITUDE.

## THE KEY IDEA

**Your expectations of your students will greatly influence their achievement in your class and in their lives.**

ll living things live to survive. They spend their entire day instinctively seeking food and shelter and escaping predators.

**Humans have a success instinct.** This is what makes humans different from all other living things. They want success, and they strive for their success potential. You can accomplish anything with students if you set high expectations for behavior and performance by which you yourself abide.

### The Two Kinds of Expectations

- Positive or high expectations
- Negative or low expectations

## Positive and Negative Expectations

**K**nowing what you can or cannot achieve is called **EXPECTATION**. An expectation is what you believe will or will not happen.

Successful people have both the attitude and the determination to succeed.

> **Each child is living the only life he has—the only one he will ever have. The least we can do is not diminish it.**
>
> _Bill Page

### GoBe

**She Was the Turning Point in My Life**

Teaching is a journey of the heart. Read how a teacher turned a student's life around with positive expectations in the **Go**ing **Be**yond folder for Chapter 6 at EffectiveTeaching.com.

## Positive Expectations

An optimistic belief that whoever you teach or whatever you do will result in success or achievement. If you expect to be successful, you are constantly alert and aware of opportunities to help you be successful.

### Examples of Positive Expectations

- "What we achieve comes from how we work together."

- "I believe that every child can learn and will achieve to his or her fullest potential."

- "I am a good teacher, and I am proud that I am a professional educator."

- "I am always learning and that is why I enjoy going to conferences, workshops, and professional development meetings."

### Results of Positive Expectations

The odds are that what you want to happen will happen if you expend energy to make it happen. Therefore, predispose yourself to realize success personally and among the people you deal with, such as your students.

## Negative Expectations

A pessimistic belief that whoever you teach or whatever you do will not work out or will fail. Why bother to do anything or teach anyone at all? If you expect to fail, you are constantly looking for justification and proof of why you have failed.

### Examples of Negative Expectations

- "You don't understand the culture where I teach."

- "These kids just don't want to learn."

- "They can't read; they can't spell; they can't sit still; they can't behave."

- "Professional development meetings are boring; conferences have nothing to offer to me."

### Results of Negative Expectations

The odds are that what you expect not to happen won't happen if you expend energy to ensure that it doesn't happen. Therefore, do not predispose yourself to realize failure personally and among the people you deal with, such as your students.

It takes just as much energy to achieve positive results
as it does to achieve negative results.
So why waste your energy on failing
when that same energy can help
you and your students succeed?

| Expectations of | Negative or Low Expectations | Positive or High Expectations |
|---|---|---|
| Parents | I'll be happy if my children do not become involved with drugs. | I want each of my children to graduate in the top ten of their class. |
| Students | This class is boring. Why do we have to study this junk? | My dream and intention is to be a teacher. |
| Teachers | Professional meetings are so boring. Why do we have to listen to this garbage? | I learn so much and meet so many interesting people at conferences. |

## Expectations Are Different from Standards

**E**xpectations should not be confused with standards. Standards are levels of achievement. Teachers who practice positive expectations will help their students reach high standards.

Example: "This will be an exciting class, and you are
going to have the most memorable year you have ever had;
as a result, you will do very well."

### FLOWING WELLS HIGH SCHOOL KEYS TO SUCCESS

*Whether you think you can or think you can't—you are right.*
Henry Ford

*All our dreams can come true—if we have the courage to pursue them.*
Walt Disney

*No legacy is so rich as honesty.*
William Shakespeare

*I do the very best I know how, the very best I can, and I mean to keep on doing so until the end.*
Abraham Lincoln

*In the middle of difficulty lies opportunity.*
Albert Einstein

*Success is the maximum utilization of the ability that you have.*
Zig Ziglar

The most successful schools have
expectations that everyone will succeed.

" *The greatest discovery of my generation is
that a human being can alter his life
by altering his attitude of mind.* "
_William James

Teachers who practice negative expectations will prevent students from reaching high standards.

> **Example: "No one in this class will earn an A. I will make the work too hard for you to do."**

People are molded more by the depth of their convictions or expectations than by the height of their intelligence. Success involves converting people, not to your way of knowing, but to your way of feeling. People can refuse words, but they cannot refuse an attitude or an expectation.

## The Classic Research on Expectations

The classic research on expectations was done in the 1960s by Robert Rosenthal of Harvard University and Lenore Jacobson of the South San Francisco schools.[1] They fed erroneous information to a group of South San Francisco elementary school teachers and watched the teachers make the results come true.

In the spring of the preceding school year, the students at Oak School were pretested. When school began that fall, the researchers and the administrators told the teachers they were special teachers who were to be part of a special experiment.

They were told, "Based on a pretest, we have identified 20 percent of your students who are special. They will be 'spurters' or 'bloomers' and are a designated group of students of whom greater intellectual growth is expected."

The names were really selected at random, but the teachers were led to believe that the status of being special children was based on scores on the pretest, the Harvard Test of Inflected Acquisition, a fictitious test.

---

**Expectations**

**Give your students more than they expect, and you will get back more than you ever expected.**

**Student success is limited only by adult expectations.**

---

[1]Rosenthal, Robert, and Lenore Jacobson. (1968). *Pygmalion in the Classroom.* New York: Holt, Rinehart and Winston.

"As a special reward for your teaching excellence," they were told, "we are going to give you this information, but on two conditions:

1. You must not tell the students that you know that they are special.

2. You must not tell the parents that their children are special.

**"Thus we expect and know that you will do extremely well with these special students."**

Eight months later, all the students were tested again, and a comparison was made of the designated special students and the undesignated students, as measured by IQ scores. The results showed a significant gain in intellectual growth for the 20 percent who were designated special in the primary grades but no significant gains to the undesignated students.

The administrators brought the teachers in, showed them the growth results of their students, and congratulated them on their spectacular success with their students.

The teachers said, "Of course, we had special students to work with. It was easy, and they learned so fast."

The administrators and researcher said, "We'd like to tell you the truth. The so-called special children were picked at random. We made no selections based on IQ or aptitude."

"Then it must have been us," said the teachers, "because you said we were special teachers selected to be part of a special experiment."

## Teachers Get What They Expect

Teacher expectations and student achievement research has been known for more than 50 years. **It states that teacher expectations play a significant role in determining how well and how much students learn.**[2]

Some teachers unknowingly could be stifling the learning of students who are not achieving. We know about the inconsistent expectations teachers have for high-, average-, and low-achieving students. For instance, on latency or wait-time, teachers often give high-achieving students more time to respond or perform than the time given to low-achieving students.

Now, take this sentence: "Teachers often give high-achieving students more _____ than low-achieving students" and complete the sentence by inserting the following teacher expectations:

| | | |
|---|---|---|
| Opportunity | Affirmation | Proximity |
| Individual help | Praise | Questions |
| Rephrasing | Feelings | Desisting |

Information on a teacher expectation and student achievement (or TESA) program can be found at http://streamer.lacoe.edu/tesa/. TESA has isolated 15 teacher-student interactions and constructed a course on how best to bring out the fullest potential of those students waiting to be fulfilled.

The program is based on expectation theory, which conveys that teachers make inferences about students that can have a damaging effect on certain students. **This "self-fulfilling prophecy" suggests that what you expect from a student is what the student gives back to you.**

[2] Bamburg, Jerry. (1994). "Raising Expectations to Improve Student Learning." North Central Regional Educational Laboratory. ED 378 290.

## Development

From conception to age 4, the individual develops 50 percent of his mature intelligence; from ages 4 to 8 he develops another 30 percent; and from ages 8 to 17 the remaining 20 percent.

Research indicates that a child's first four years are the most important growing period for academic achievement. **And all subsequent learning in school is affected, and in large part determined, by what a child has learned by the age of 9 or at least by the end of grade 3.**

When school and home environments are mutually reinforcing, learning is likely to be greatest. **The nature of the learning environment is most critical during the periods of most rapid change in learning—the early years of school.**[3]

*Children are like wet cement. Whatever falls on them makes an impression.*

_Haim Ginott

[3] Bloom, Benjamin S. (1964). *Stability and Change in Human Characteristics.* New York: Wiley, pp. 68, 88, 110, and 128.

"We need to tell you something else, too," replied the researcher. "All the teachers were involved in this experiment. None of you were designated special over any other teacher."

This was a perfectly designed experiment. There was only one experimental variable—**EXPECTATIONS**.

1.  The expectations of the administrators toward the teachers were stated explicitly. "You are special teachers, and these 20 percent of your students are special students who show potential for intellectual growth. Thus we expect and know that you will do extremely well with these special students."

2.  The expectations of the teachers toward the students were conveyed implicitly and were unspoken. Because the teachers believed they had some very special students in the school, their body language, personalities, and attitudes influenced their teaching and expectations of their students.

As the researchers stated, "The results suggest rather strongly that children who are expected by their teachers to gain intellectually in fact do show greater intellectual gains after one year than do children of whom such gains are not expected."

Following the original study, many additional studies have been undertaken. Some have been able to replicate the findings, while others have not. Regardless, educators and parents are very keen in the power of expectations to affect student outcomes.

> **Students tend to learn as little or as much as their teachers expect. Teachers who set and communicate high expectations to all their students obtain greater academic performance from these students than teachers who set low expectations.**[4]

[4] U.S. Department of Education. (1986). *What Works: Research About Teaching and Learning.* Washington, D.C.: U.S. Government Printing Office, p. 7.

# The Two Most Important Groups of People for Young People

### A Tribute to My Parents

*Before I was five years old, my parents said something to me over and over again. They even got my relatives to say it to me, as well as my neighbors and the local merchants.*

*Several times a day, I would hear, "Little Harry Wong, when you grow up, what kind of a doctor are you going to be?" This was accompanied by their pointing out to me, as positive role models, that my uncles were all doctors and that my cousins were studying to be doctors.*

*They told me that it was a foregone conclusion that I would be admitted to medical school, even though the competition was tough in those days. What they wanted to know was what I planned to specialize in.*

*Not being in kindergarten yet, I said, "I don't know."*

*And then came their reply, "You're going to be a brain surgeon, aren't you?" In other words, they believed that I had the intelligence to be the ultimate of all doctors, so brilliant that I could even operate on other people's brains.*

*My parents conveyed a message of high or positive expectations to me. For this I will be forever grateful to them, and I send them my love.*

*_Harry K. Wong*

> ## Things My Parents and Teachers Never Said to Me
>
> You are dumb.
> You are stupid.
> You are no good.
> You will never amount to anything.
> You don't belong in this class; you were placed here against my wishes.
> Look at it this way, summer vacation is only 10 months away.

### A Tribute to My Teachers

*The other reason I achieved success in school and life was my teachers. In elementary school, I remember distinctly that my teachers had a saying that they would repeat often, year after year. This saying became a driving force or expectation in my life.*

*They would say, "You can be anything you want to be. You can even be president of the United States." The message of expectation I received was that I could be a world leader or a leader in whatever field I chose.*

*Young people get very little urging to become leaders or heroes. Rather, they receive messages from the media and from friends that it's not cool to succeed in school. Luckily, I was born and raised in San Francisco's Chinatown, where crowded conditions and poverty did not matter. I had a family, good schools, and a culture. A favorite "put-down" when I was growing up was "rice bucket," which was applied to someone who was so lazy and useless that all he did was sit around all day and eat until he looked like a bucket of rice. We were expected to make more of ourselves than that. We were all expected to work hard and do well in school, and this expectation was reinforced by wonderful teachers who embraced a culture that assured us success would result from hard work.*

*My teachers conveyed to me a message of highly positive expectations, a powerful message that told me I was smart and good enough to be anything I wanted to be, even to hold the highest office in the nation.*

*I thank my teachers for having that expectation of me.*

*_Harry K. Wong*

> ❝ **My teacher thought I was smarter than I was—so I was.** ❞
>
> _Six-year-old

What parents and teachers convey to young people in their formative years as expectations will influence young people to achieve accordingly.

**Your expectations of your students will greatly influence their achievement in your class, in their lives, and ultimately in the world.**

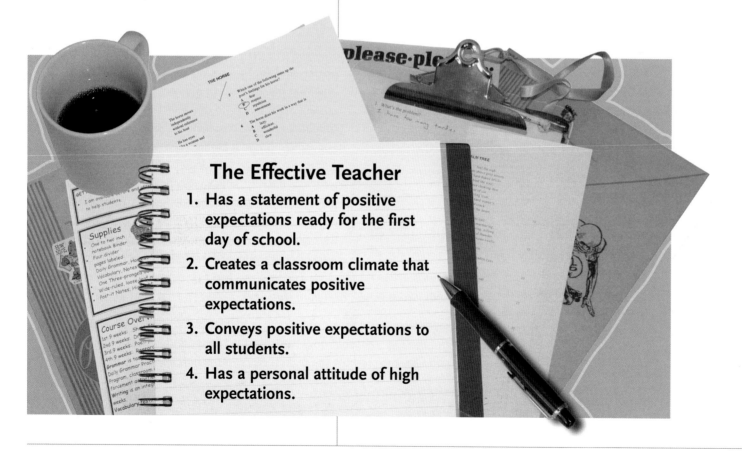

### The Effective Teacher

1. Has a statement of positive expectations ready for the first day of school.

2. Creates a classroom climate that communicates positive expectations.

3. Conveys positive expectations to all students.

4. Has a personal attitude of high expectations.

## Celebrate the First Day of School

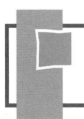

> The most important day of a person's education is the First Day of School, not Graduation Day.

## THE KEY IDEA

**The more the school and the family are joined as partners in educating young people, the greater the children's chances for success.**

If school does not begin with the proper, positive expectations, there may not be a Graduation Day. The Class of 2009 failed to graduate 1.3 million students, or one student dropping out of school every 27 seconds.[1]

For some students, graduation is not a day to celebrate a joyful sense of accomplishment. Rather it is a day to mock respect, act stupid, make fun of the educational system, show disrespect to parents and teachers, and engage in wild parties that make you wonder if any educating ever took place.

> The proper day to celebrate in all the schools of a country is the First Day of School.

Celebrating the **First Day of School** must become a tradition of all educational systems. This day of celebration must include everyone associated with and interested in the education of the future citizens of the world.

In addition to everyone at the school site, the celebration should include parents, the business community, and the neighborhood. It is important that students see that everyone is interested in helping them all succeed.

Effective schools celebrate the First Day of School.

[1]"Analysis Finds Graduation Rates Moving Up." (May 31, 2011). *Education Week.*

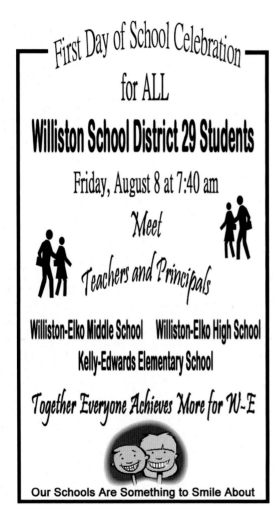

This announcement appears each year in the local Williston, South Carolina, newspaper.

**The more the school, the family, and the community are joined as partners in the cause of educating young people, the greater each child's chance for success.**

## Welcome Them to School

Just as you go on a vacation with high expectations, students come to school with high expectations, also. They come to get an education, meet friends, participate, have fun, study, and learn. Their entire day revolves around school and their friends. It is an exciting time in their lives.

Therefore, the personnel of the school should extend greetings to the students before they come to school and upon their arrival. Everyone should be involved in planning the students' welcome to the school. "Everyone" means administrators, teachers, classified staff, district personnel, parents, and the business community. **The successful education of young people is an interrelated, community team effort.**

### How to Welcome Them to School

- Organize a **First Day of School** celebration.

- Stand at the bus stop and welcome them on the First Day of School. Wave and smile like it's Aunt Mabel whom you have not seen in 14 years and her airplane has just pulled up to the jet bridge.

- Stand at the front entrances of the school. Have at least one greeter at every entrance so no one will fail to receive a warm, friendly welcome.

- Bring out the school band to play at the curb or near the entrance.

- If you don't have a band, have a group of students and teachers assembled to bring a welcome smile on the First Day of School.

- Hang up a banner welcoming students to school.

- Distribute a school newspaper extolling the virtues of the school and the wonderful school spirit of the teachers and the students.

- Have guides in the hall. Hang up directional signs to help students get to their classrooms.

- Have your name and room number clearly visible on the classroom door along with your personal greeting of welcome.

- Let the first message spoken over the public address system be one of welcome and positive expectations for the school year.

> **We must TEACH and SHOW our students—**
>
> 1. **That we can be responsible for one another.**
> 2. **That school is a place to gain knowledge.**
> 3. **That school is a place to give and receive love.**
> 4. **That school is a place to become successful.**

**School is not a place** where students come to listen to lectures, fill in worksheets, and endure boredom. Nor is it a place reserved for those who can tolerate the drab and dirty look of many schools.

**School is a concept** wherein students are welcome to learn and enhance the quality of their lives without fear of intimidation or harm, guided by hospitable and caring people in a clean and orderly environment.

> **School is not a place; school is a concept.**

Everyone needs to be welcomed on the first day of school.

> **Schools should be built better and kept up better than banks because there's more wealth in them.**
>
> _Martin Haberman

## You Will All Succeed

You will think that I'm in love with Japanese education. I'm not, but here is an anecdote that illustrates my point.

When our daughter took our granddaughter to her first day of kindergarten in Japan, she walked in casually dressed, as we might do in the United States, thinking she would drop the child off and go home. Well, not at all.

First, she discovered that all of the other parents were dressed up in their finest for a full day of ceremonies in celebration of the first day of school. They were in the room with the children, and there were speakers on the platform with a big banner that said, "Welcome to Kindergarten. You Will All Succeed."

Ernest L. Boyer
"On Parents, School and the Workplace."
(Fall 1988). Kappa Delta Pi *Record*, p. 8.

### GoBe

**First Day of School Celebrations**

Resources for creating a First Day of School Celebration at your school can be found in the **Go**ing **Be**yond folder for Chapter 7 at EffectiveTeaching.com.

## Haughton High School Welcomes You

**A week before school begins, Haughton High School in Louisiana, welcomes incoming freshmen.**

Busses are provided for those who need a ride for the half-day program. The incoming freshmen gather in the auditorium. They are taught the school song and the Buccaneer Spirit Cheer. Teachers, nurses, bus drivers, and cafeteria workers are all introduced. Messages of welcome and high expectation flow.

They are given their schedules, shown their lockers, the cafeteria, the gym, the media center, and their classrooms. No one needs to worry or be mocked on the first day of school because they now know the school.

The students rotate through success groups where they are taught how to get off to a good start and given tips on staying out of trouble.

They meet their counselor and can plan for their success! **This is how they are welcomed to a school that cares that they succeed.**

There is no greater gift one human being can give another than the opportunity to learn and grow in a loving and nurturing learning environment.

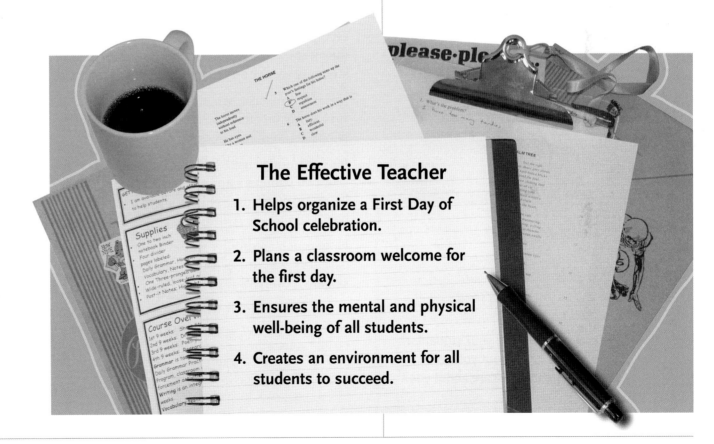

## The Effective Teacher

1. Helps organize a First Day of School celebration.

2. Plans a classroom welcome for the first day.

3. Ensures the mental and physical well-being of all students.

4. Creates an environment for all students to succeed.

**8**

## THE KEY IDEA

The effective teacher dresses appropriately as a professional educator to model success.

### Dress Perception

*As you are dressed,
so shall you be perceived;
and as you are perceived,
so shall you be treated.*

**Always dress better than your students.
If you do not care about yourself,
why should the students care about you?**

## You Are Treated as You Are Dressed

> You do not get a second chance to make a first impression.

Interviewers tell us they make an initial judgment on an interviewee in 20 seconds. Salespeople know they have seven seconds to make an impression. **Effective teachers know that the clothes they wear and the smile that dresses their face are the first things students see when they are greeted at the door.**

Make no mistake, we judge others by their dress, and they judge us, too. It may not be fair. It may not be right. But people tend to treat other people as they are dressed.

**It's common sense. You will be treated as you are dressed.** A salesperson sees two shoppers approaching, one appropriately dressed and the other inappropriately dressed. You know very well who will get immediate and better service.

How much credibility would a bank have if the teller who processes your paycheck was dressed in jeans and wore a T-shirt emblazoned with the slogan "Poverty Sucks"?

In an ideal world, it would be wonderful to be accepted for ourselves alone, not for our appearance. In the real world, however, our all-too-visible selves are under constant scrutiny.

The fact is, most people think that the cover is the book, the box front is the cereal, and the leather jacket is the person. We all make judgments. We look at someone and judge status, income, even occupation.

> **It is not what is
> but what is perceived that counts.**

## You Are a Walking, Talking Advertisement

This may be a superficial world, but it is the way the world works, so saying that something is superficial will not make it go away. You are much better off making your dress work for you than allowing it to work against you.

> " *Give an elementary student three days,
> and the student will mirror you.
> Give a high school student ten days,
> and the student will mirror you.* "
> _Charles Galloway

### Teachers Are Happier and Better Equipped to Deal with Challenges Today

- The proportion of teachers who are "very satisfied" with their careers increased from 40% in 1984 to 62% in 2008.
- More teachers today (66%) feel respected by society than in 1984 (47%).
- 66% of teachers believe they earn a decent salary—almost double the number of teachers who believed that in 1984.
- Far more teachers today (75%) report that they would advise a young person to pursue a career in teaching (45%).
- Two-thirds (67%) of teachers agree that the training teachers receive today does a good job of preparing them for the classroom, compared to 46% of teachers in 1984.
- 44% rate the availability of teaching materials and supplies as excellent, compared to 22% of teachers in 1984.
- Teachers feel better equipped to address important challenges to student learning (poverty, problems speaking and understanding English, lack of parental support, and poor health).

Statistics compiled from
*The MetLife Survey of the American Teacher:
Past, Present, and Future.*
"A Survey of Teachers, Principals, and Students."
Reported October 2008.

Successful teachers dress for success.

Yes, ties take time to tie and sometimes get uncomfortable.

However, a tie tells everyone you meet, "I respect you, my job, and myself, and I'm willing to take the time to show it."

The key is looking professional, not just looking good. **The advantage of looking professional is that it keeps you from self-destructing in the first few seconds, before your students make any hasty judgments about you.**

**The effective teacher dresses appropriately as a professional educator to model success.** The important word is *appropriately*. We often see signs like this one:

One of the reasons we have schools is for students to learn what is appropriate. Young people learn what is appropriate in society by looking at their adult role models. Your dress, your actions, and your words are what young people will take to be appropriate.

By the end of the first or second week, the entire class will have taken signals from you as to how they should behave for the rest of the school year.

We are walking, talking advertisements for who we are. We are walking, talking advertisements for who we believe we are as professional educators.

When you walk into class late, you have just made a statement. When you walk into class late with a can of soda or a cup of coffee in your hand and a scowl on your face, you are making a statement.

When you walk into class early—when you're standing at the door with a smile and an extended hand of welcome, the assignments are on the chalkboard, the room and materials are ready, and there is a positive classroom climate—you are making a statement.

When you allow teasing in class, you are making a statement. When you refuse to tolerate teasing in class, you are making a statement. **The statement that you make influences how the students will behave and achieve in class. And how students behave and achieve in class will determine your success as a teacher.**

> **Every time you act,
> you validate who you are.**

The experts tell us that teenagers get their values from their friends. That's true to the extent that there is a values vacuum to be filled. It is imperative that the parents get there first. New teachers get their values from other teachers. It is imperative that there exists a school or district induction program coupled with a coaching program staffed by dedicated, professional, role-model teachers to influence new teachers.

## Dress for Respect

Clothing may not make a person, but it can be a contributing factor in unmaking a person. Whether we want to admit it or not, our appearance affects how we are perceived and received in definite ways. Clothing has nothing to do with students liking a teacher. But clothing definitely has an effect on students' respect for a teacher, and respect is what a teacher must have if learning is to take place.

**Even as a Substitute Teacher**

*My daughter, who just started a school counselor's job in a Phoenix school, agrees with me that we can win the kids over with our appearance.*

*She said: "I dressed very nicely as a substitute teacher. The kids held the door for me. One on each side! That's pretty scary and wonderful that they are influenced so easily by appearance."*

_As shared with Harry Wong

Research reveals that the clothing worn by teachers affects the work, attitude, and discipline of students. You dress for four main effects:

1. Respect
2. Credibility
3. Acceptance
4. Authority

The effective teacher uses these four traits as assets in relating to students, peers, administrators, parents, and the community. If you have these four traits, you have a much greater chance of influencing young people to learn than someone who lacks these four traits.

You can be sure that students notice how their teachers are dressed, in the same way they notice the appropriateness of their own and each other's dress.

Kids see their parents go to work each day, dressed in business attire or institutional uniforms. Then they come to school and observe the attire of teachers—professionals who are considered middle-class intellectuals with college degrees, competent people with teaching credentials. You can see why the teaching profession has a difficult time gaining respect and credibility.

You can also see why some teachers have great difficulty reaching and influencing students—and if teachers cannot reach students, no teaching or learning will take place. Not only are these teachers unable to reach students, but they also leave school at the end of the day frustrated over their own inadequacies. These inadequacies are evident in how they dress. **For when you select your clothes each day, you are making a statement about yourself to the world.**

Make no mistake about reality. Teachers have a responsibility to encourage learning, and learning begins by gaining and keeping the respect of students. **Your respect begins with your appearance.**

---

### Could Not Believe What I Saw

*After Christmas vacation, one of my students left some pictures of the class holiday party on my desk. I took a look at myself and I could not believe how I looked. I looked like I didn't care about myself.*

*The next day I came to school more appropriately dressed, and they all noticed and commented on how nice I looked. I was so happy, and they made me feel so good.*

*I now spend more time caring about who I am. The students care about me. I am proud of who I am. And they are also so much better behaved now as a result of who I represent.*

Fifth-grade teacher,
Iowa

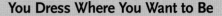

## What's Out

- Tennis shoes are for sports and exercise.
- Sweatshirts and sweat suits are best left for the gym.
- T-shirts and see-through shirts lessen being taken seriously.
- Mini-skirts, low-rise pants, and low-cut shirts aren't for the classroom.
- Flip-flops are for vacations and lounging.
- Trendy clothes do not establish authority and should be left to students.
- Save blue jeans for after school or weekends.
- Excessive jewelry or excessive fragrance is distracting.

## What's In

- Bright colors are enjoyed by elementary students.
- Soft, muted tones are recommended for secondary school.
- Men can't miss with a tie on a collared shirt.
- A career dress or skirt, pants, and blouse are appropriate for women.
- Clean clothes convey good hygiene.
- Pressed clothes tell people you care.
- Neat, cleanly tailored clothes establish confidence.
- Career clothes prepare students for a future in the competitive, global world economy.

**GoBe**

### Dress for Success

The research on appropriate dress for professionals is found in the **Go**ing **Be**yond folder for Chapter 8 at EffectiveTeaching.com.

### You Dress Where You Want to Be

DeRutha Richardson, a Business Education teacher at Muskogee High School in Oklahoma, was about to embark on a class project about perceptions and professional image.

On the first day of the project, she came to class dressed in the most negative manner she could conjure up. She wore an old ill-fitting jacket over a long, fishtail dress and wore tennis shoes with flannel socks over her stockings. She slicked her hair back, wore no makeup, and even faked a missing-tooth effect.

She was amazed at what happened in the classroom.

She lost all control of the class, could not get the students' attention and endured 15 minutes of pure classroom chaos. She had to leave the classroom and return dressed in a professional manner before she could restore order in the classroom.

Her students, who soon will be entering the job force, experienced firsthand the importance of appropriate dress for any occasion. Dress is the silent language that will make or break her students in their professional careers.

"Projecting Professional Images." (March 2007). www.kodak.com/global/en/consumer/education/lessonPlans/lessonPlan018.shtml.

Every profession has its appropriate attire.

If you are appropriately dressed, students will comment when you look nice, and if something is out of place, they will tell you because they know that you are a person who cares about yourself. But if you consistently come to school inappropriately dressed, they will not say a word because they surmise that if you do not care about yourself, they need not care about you. **Dress appropriately because it is very important to know that people care about you.**

When people care about you, they will respect you, learn from you, and buy from you. And as a professional educator, you are selling your students knowledge and success for the future.

## Preparing Students for the World

**W**hat does it mean to dress appropriately? You expect your students to use appropriate English, write papers using an appropriate form, and display appropriate behavior and manners. Right? Then you understand about appropriate dress.

It is universally agreed that one major function of schools is to prepare young people for tomorrow's world. Yes, the world, not a particular city, state, or country. **We live in a competitive, global world economy where people work for companies that are international in scope.** It is likely that many of your students will work for a company that will have offices all over the world.

> **If you want to succeed in the world, you must think globally.**

If we are to prepare students for tomorrow's world, we need to know the world. If you do not know the world, take some time to do some research. Stand at a major airport and watch passengers disembark from American Airlines, Lufthansa, and Singapore Air Lines.

Then go to the business district of a large city and observe the dress of the people—the executives, store owners, salespeople, and support service people. And speaking of support people, have you ever noticed that the school secretary almost always comes to school more appropriately dressed than a lot of the teachers?

Having observed the world, after you have dressed in the morning, look at yourself in the mirror before you go to school to face your students, all of whom will see you as a model of success in tomorrow's thriving world. Ask yourself these three questions:

1. Would a real estate agency hire you dressed as you are?

2. Would McDonald's allow you to hand food to a customer dressed as you are?

3. Would you have confidence sending your loving child, grandchild, godchild, niece, or nephew to school to be taught by a teacher dressed as you are?

The school secretary conveys her competence by dressing appropriately.

Even criminals have a clear sense of the nonverbal messages people give out. In an eye-opening experiment, groups of convicted muggers were shown videos of people walking along the street. Overwhelmingly, the muggers picked people who walked slowly, with stooped shoulders, who looked helpless, disheveled, and downtrodden. They rejected people who walked erect, purposefully, and confidently. These latter people conveyed the message that they were in control of their lives.

**Your dress announces to the world whether you care or do not care about yourself.** The entire public can read this message. As a teacher, which of the two statements do you make?

1. I am one of a group of poor, underpaid, slovenly, dour, and unappreciated people.

2. I am one of a group of professional, proud, devoted, dedicated, responsible, and appreciated people.

> " *That she call in sick someday,*
> *we all live in fear.*
> *We would have to cancel school*
> *if the secretary wasn't here.* "
>
> Dave Arnold, Head Custodian
> Brownstown Elem. School, Illinois

**Dress Your Mind!**

This message is also conveyed to your students at your school, as well as to the administration and your colleagues, many of who find the very casual dress of many educators totally unacceptable.

People in sales, management, and leadership training will all tell you the same thing. **By how you behave, you convey to the world a message of who you are and what you expect of life.**

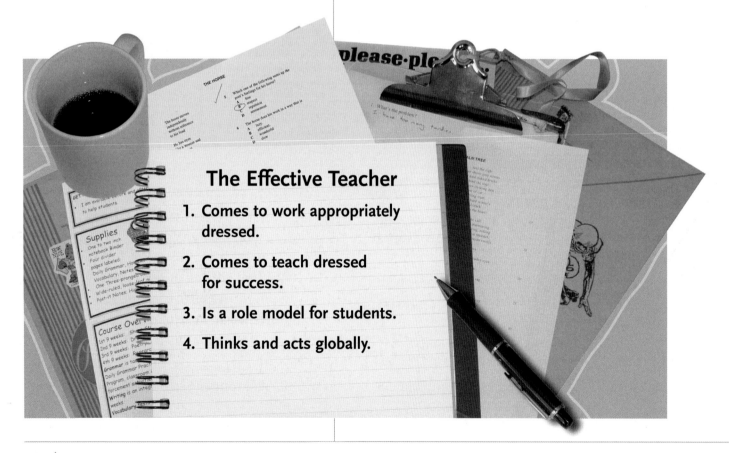

### The Effective Teacher

1. **Comes to work appropriately dressed.**

2. **Comes to teach dressed for success.**

3. **Is a role model for students.**

4. **Thinks and acts globally.**

## Invitational Education

**Effective teachers have the power and the ability to invite students and colleagues to learn together each day in every class.**

**There must be people, places, policies, procedures, and programs working together to invite people to realize their fullest potential.**

**T**he parents of 25 out of 30 students came to Back-to-School Night! Cindy Wong, a teacher in San Jose, California, sent an invitation home with each of her students. She also had her students copy a letter and leave it on their desks, along with a paper crane and a personal letter for their parents. They were so excited to tell their parents about a "special" surprise awaiting them. Some parents explained that their children said they just had to come to get their presents! This resulted in 25 out of 30 students being represented at Back-to-School Night.

Dear Parents,

Welcome to your child's classroom! What happens in this classroom will affect your child's future. Your child's time here will be well spent. He or she may even come home exhausted from all the thinking done during the day. But I will make every minute count. We have a fantastic group of children in this class. I am looking forward to a terrific year ahead. With your help, we can make it happen.

Sincerely,

*Mrs. Wong*

Dear Mom,

Thank you for caring about me and taking the time to come and learn about my class. We have been learning about a young girl named Sadako who bravely fought leukemia. She believed in good-luck signs. The crane was one sign, a symbol of peace and dreams come true. Here is a crane I made especially for you. With it, I wish you love, peace, and everlasting happiness. I love you!

Love, Emilio

Cindy Wong then asked each parent to write a note to his or her child and leave it on the desk. The students couldn't wait to come to school the next day to find their surprises on their desks. What an invitation!

**Why Was I Not Invited?**

*It upsets me to this day. When I was in junior high school, I had straight A's and was in the honors class. One day, the teacher went around the class and gave invitations to several students, but not me. They were asked to join the National Honor Society. To this day, I am still puzzled and disappointed that I was not invited.*

*—Rosemary Tripi Wong*

" *No one has yet fully realized the wealth of sympathy, kindness, and generosity hidden in the soul of a child. The effort of every true educator should be to unlock that treasure.* "

*—Emma Goldman*

## The Basis of Being Inviting

> **The basis of being inviting is building relationships.**

**T**he effective teacher builds relationships with the parents. Invite parents to be partners in unleashing the potential of their children. Refer back to Chapter 7 to see how schools invite parents and children to school before the first day of school.

The effective teacher is deliberately inviting. We all like to be invited to go shopping, to attend a party, to join a group. Most of us have the common courtesy to greet people at the door, exchange pleasantries when introduced to others, and offer food or drink to a visitor. These are all obvious, expected, and practiced. These same concepts should be practiced in the classroom at all grade levels.

Walk around and see if your classroom is inviting. What's a student's or visitor's first impression?

- Is the door clearly marked?
- Are welcome and information signs posted?
- Are signs written in jargon?
- Is the first assignment clear and understandable?
- Are there clues that show you care for young people?

**The effective teacher is committed to seeing all people as able, valuable, responsible, and possessing untapped potential in all worthwhile areas of human endeavor.**

The person who is asked or complimented is INVITED. The person who is not asked or complimented is DISINVITED. This concept was formulated by William W. Purkey and is known as invitational education.[1]

[1] Purkey, William W., and John Novak. (1996). *Inviting School Success.* Belmont, Calif.: Wadsworth; Purkey, William W., and Betty L. Siegel. (2003). *Becoming an Invitational Leader.* Atlanta: Humanics Trade Group.

## Success Is Easy

Theresa A. Borges of American High School in Miami says, "Success is easy. Pay attention to the students. Like a detective, listen to what they have to say.

- I notice and compliment a new haircut and new shirt and especially a right answer.
- I analyze handwriting for original work; I offer lunchtime tutoring.
- I call back every parent by the end of the same day.
- I never get a second request from a parent for a contact or phone call.
- I visit students in the hospital, go to funerals (unfortunately), and make awards for students who achieve perfect scores on tests.
- I put stickers on perfect papers, even in Algebra 2.
- I read about our athletes in the paper and go to games that I can attend.
- I know what video games they like and the things you can learn on MySpace.

"Of course knowing your curriculum is vital; but knowing your students takes time and leads to success."

Theresa Borges knows how to invite her students to learn.

> **" Until I was 13,
> I thought my name was SHUT UP. "**
>
> _Joe Namath

*I have come to a frightening conclusion.
I am the decisive element in the classroom.
It is my personal approach that creates the climate.
It is my daily mood that makes the weather.
As a teacher I possess tremendous power to make a child's life miserable or joyous.
I can be a tool of torture or an instrument of inspiration.
I can humiliate or humor, hurt or heal.
In all situations it is my response that decides whether a crisis will be escalated or de-escalated, and a child humanized or dehumanized.*

Haim Ginott,
*Teacher and Child.* (1976).
Avon Books.

Even the outside of the classroom door contributes to creating a welcoming, invitational atmosphere.

## Are You Invitational or Disinvitational?

### Inviting Verbal Comments

"Good morning."
"Congratulations."
"I appreciate your help."
"Tell me about it."

### Disinviting Verbal Comments

"It won't work."
"I don't care what you do."
"You can't do that."
"Because I said so, that's why."

### Inviting Personal Behaviors

Smiling
Listening
Thumbs up or high five
Holding a door open

### Disinviting Personal Behaviors

Sneering
Looking at your watch
Shoving
Letting a door close on a person behind you

### Inviting Physical Environment

Fresh paint
Living plants
Clean walls
Comfortable furniture

### Disinviting Physical Environment

Dark corridors
No plants
Bad odor
Beat-up or uncomfortable furniture

### Inviting Thoughts (Self-Talk)

"Making mistakes is all right."
"I've misplaced my keys."
"I could learn to do that."
"Sometimes I have to think what to say."

### Disinviting Thoughts (Self-Talk)

"Why am I so stupid?"
"I've lost my keys again."
"I never could do that."
"I never know what to say; I'm so slow to catch on."

## You Are a Significant Person

**I**nvitational education states that all individuals have significant people in their lives. These include teachers, leaders, mentors, colleagues, bosses, parents, relatives, coaches, administrators, spouses, and close friends. Everyone is special.

Students are influenced more by the depth of your conviction than the height of your intelligence. The goal is changing students, not to your way of thinking, but to your way of feeling.

**Students can refuse words,
but they cannot refuse an invitational attitude.**

> **The invitational messages that are extended exist in the minds of the significant people who influence the lives of other people.**

Effective teachers have the power and the ability to invite students and colleagues **to learn together each day in every class**. Attentiveness, expectancy, attitude, enthusiasm, and evaluation are the primary forces behind a teacher's being inviting or disinviting. These are the characteristics that significantly influence a student's self-concept and increase or decrease the probability of student learning.

Wayne Hill of Mesa, Arizona, has a way of telling his students that they are significant people.

*On the first day of class, before introduction of the class, I greet the students by holding up a $20 bill and asking who would like the $20. Obviously, many hands go up. I crumble the bill and again ask the same questions, and hands go up. I throw the bill onto the floor, stomp, and smash the bill into the floor. I hold it up and again ask the same question. All hands go up.*

*I ask the students why they still want the $20 after I have crushed, stomped, and smashed it. Their response is always, "Because it is still worth $20; it has not lost its value."*

*I explain to the students that sometimes in life we feel like we have been stepped on and made to feel dirty. But never forget that someone at home or someone here at school cares about you. I tell them, "You are special to me. Don't ever forget."*

*When I discuss the dismissal procedure for the class, I explain that I dismiss the class, not the bell. I dismiss the class only after all students are seated and quiet. I simply say, "Don't ever forget." The class responds, "We are special."*

*They leave the class and often I hear the kids repeating as they walk out the door, "We are special." When they see me on the campus, they shout out to me, "Hello, Mr. Hill. We are special."*

## If Only the Finest Birds in the Forest Dared Sing, How Quiet the Forest Would Be

*If only the best readers dared read,*
*how ignorant our country would be.*
*If only the best singers dared sing,*
*how sad our country would be.*
*If only the best athletes engaged in sports,*
*how weak our country would be.*
*If only the best lovers made love,*
*where would you and I be?*

*I would be tired!*

_William W. Purkey

---

**"You are important to me as a person."**
**This is the message that we all need to convey**
**to our students and our colleagues every day.**

Every teacher, every professor, every educator ought to spend time in a kindergarten or first-grade class each year just to look at and feel the excitement there. Children get excited about everything in the world. All the world is their stage, and there is nothing they cannot do, even though they cannot read, write, or spell. Yet they are ready to do anything you want them to do.

Then look at their teachers. They know their charges cannot read, write, spell, or even speak correctly. Some of these students do not even know how to eat, use the bathroom, or hang up their jackets without help. Yet these teachers do not complain that they have a bunch of low achievers. Instead, their classrooms and their demeanors sparkle with invitational attitudes toward learning, treating everyone as high achievers.

---

### Everyone Is a VIP

Oklahoma City principal Sharon Creager keeps a "VIP book" in her office with this inscription on the inside cover:

**Congratulations to these**
**Very Important Pupils,**
**who have distinguished**
**themselves in various ways.**
**These are the stars**
**of our future.**

Teachers send students to the office to have their names entered in the VIP book. The book is on permanent display in the hall and has never been vandalized. Each morning, the new VIP names are read on the morning announcements.

All children have the capacity to achieve.

## The Four Levels of Invitational Education

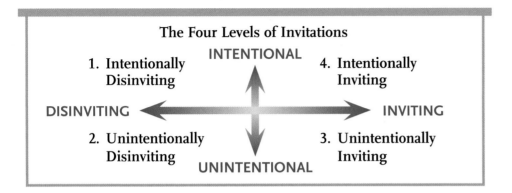

**The Four Levels of Invitations**

INTENTIONAL

1. Intentionally Disinviting

4. Intentionally Inviting

DISINVITING ← → INVITING

2. Unintentionally Disinviting

3. Unintentionally Inviting

UNINTENTIONAL

**T**here are four levels of invitations that are issued to students. These levels can determine your effectiveness as a teacher.

**1. Intentionally Disinviting.** This is the bottom level at which a few curmudgeonly teachers operate. They deliberately demean, discourage, defeat, and dissuade students. They use expressions like these:

> "Why do you bother coming to school?"
> "I've only given one A in the 16 years that I've been teaching."
> "You will never amount to anything."

And they never smile.

**2. Unintentionally Disinviting.** Some teachers are oblivious to the fact that they are negative people. They feel that they are well-meaning but are seen by others as chauvinistic, condescending, racist, sexist, patronizing, or thoughtless. They make comments like these:

> "I teach only students who want to learn."
> "If you don't want to learn, that's your problem."
> "These people just don't have the capacity to do any better."
> "I was hired to teach history, not to do these other things."

And they keep their arms folded when interacting with students.

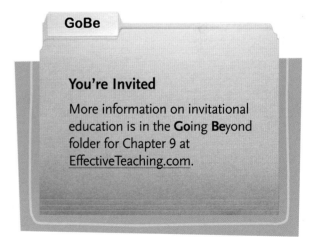

**GoBe**

**You're Invited**

More information on invitational education is in the **Go**ing **Be**yond folder for Chapter 9 at EffectiveTeaching.com.

**3. Unintentionally Inviting.** These are the "natural-born teachers." Such teachers are generally well-liked and effective but are unaware of why they are effective. They are usually affable, and this characteristic often hides the fact that their students may not be learning to their fullest potential. These teachers are sincere, they try very hard, and we generally like to have them as friends. They offer remarks like these:

> "Aren't you sweet!"
> "Charge! Let's go, team!"
> "That's neat."
> "Just try harder."

And they bubble with excitement.

**4. Intentionally Inviting.** Intentionally inviting teachers have a professional attitude, work diligently and consistently, and strive to be more effective teachers. They have a sound philosophy of education and can analyze the process of student learning. Most important, they are purposively and explicitly invitational. They know what it means to be invitational, and they work at it. They say things like this:

> "Good morning. Have a great day."
> "If you try this, you'll be sensational."
> "I know that someday you will be the best at . . ."
> "Would you like to help me?"

They also use the proper emotion at the appropriate time.

> **Effective teachers know how to open the door**
> **and invite their students to learn.**

When you apply the power of POSITIVE EXPECTATIONS and INVITATIONAL EDUCATION, you become a very powerful and effective teacher.

Eric Abrams, a former principal at Douglas Elementary School in Tucson, Arizona, intentionally invited his students to communicate with him.

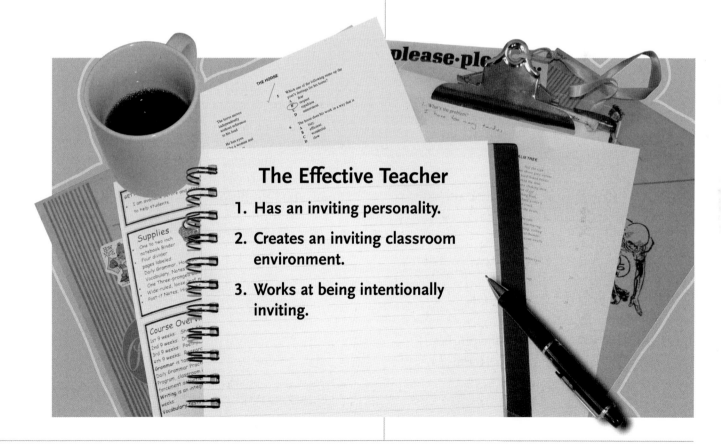

**The Effective Teacher**

1. Has an inviting personality.

2. Creates an inviting classroom environment.

3. Works at being intentionally inviting.

**10**

## THE KEY IDEA

The heart of education is the education of the heart.

## Five Significant Concepts

> When you look at truly effective teachers, you will also find caring, warm, lovable people.

**E**ffective teaching is all about teacher-student relationships. The easiest way to build relationships with students is to use a well-managed classroom where students are on task, allowing you to spend one-to-one time with them. Students, parents, teachers, everyone thrives on connections.

Students need role models. Students need heroes they can look up to—someone to connect with—and that someone can be a teacher. The success of a person's journey through life can be influenced by the significant people with whom we make connections. Significant people understand and use five significant concepts that help people achieve whatever they want in life. These concepts are addressing a person by name, saying "please" and "thank you," smiling, and showing care and warmth.

---

**The Five Significant Concepts
That Enhance Positive Expectations**

1. Name
2. Please
3. Thank You
4. Smile
5. Love

---

## Address Each Student by Name

**E**ffective salespeople employ a very simple but valuable technique. They find out your name, introduce themselves to you, and then use your proper name every 7 to 10 sentences when they talk with you. Why? **When you address someone by name, you are treating that person with dignity and respect.**

Your name is very important. It identifies and dignifies you. Other people in the world may have the same name as yours, but as far as you are concerned, you are the only person in the world with your name. It is a name that you can easily hear called above the din of a crowd. And when you hear your name, you pay attention. Salespeople know this when they use your name. You pay attention. You pay attention because you are important!

Effective teachers use names, especially when they want a student to do something or behave in a certain way.

**When you address a student, use the student's name.**

Use a student's name in a friendly, respectful manner. Never address a student in an angry or condescending tone. This is a put-down of a person's identity and dignity.

**Pronounce the student's name correctly.** A person's name is precious and personal. It is that person's property. It is imperative that students hear the correct pronunciation of names. Failure to do so will tell the students they do not have to respect each other's names and as a result can tease, mock, and make fun of each other's names.

When you use a person's name, you are saying to that person, "You are important. You are important enough for me to identify you by name."

When you use a person's name, you are saying, "I care enough to know who you are."

Important people have business cards—and who is more important than a teacher?

**The depth of your heart determines the height of your dreams.**

### Repetition Is the Key

For a child to learn something new, you need to repeat it an average of eight times.

For a child to unlearn an old behavior and replace it with a new behavior, you need to repeat the new behavior an average of 28 times.

Twenty of those times are used to eliminate the old behavior, and eight of the times are used to learn the new behavior.

_After Madeline Hunter

People in our culture are starved for attention.

- The average child receives an estimated 12 minutes of attention each day from his or her parents.
- By age 18, most Americans have spent more time in front of the television than they have with friends or parents.
- The average adolescent spends more than three hours alone every day.
- Loneliness is the number one problem of the elderly, many of whom are afraid to venture out of their homes or apartments.

The Carnegie Foundation surveyed 22,000 teachers.

- 90 percent said that a lack of parental support was a problem at their schools.
- 89 percent said that there were abused or neglected children at their schools.
- 69 percent stated that poor health was a problem for their students.
- 68 percent reported that some children were undernourished.
- 100 percent described their students as "emotionally needy and starved for attention and affection."

## Say "Please," Please

Cultured, polite people can be identified by their manners. The heart of courtesy is respect for persons. **Courtesy and respect convey a message that says, "I am paying attention to you."** The neglect of courtesy leads to the collapse of community and this can be seen in ineffective schools and classrooms where people demean one another.

People who neglect to say "please," even when speaking to children, are teaching impressionable youngsters that it is all right to bark orders and to run roughshod over the dignity of others. The youngsters may not react or respond, but they resent the lack of courtesy implicit in such treatment.

When you fail to say "please" and couch your request as an order, you are slowly chipping away at that person's freedom and dignity, and many of our children come to school, having been yelled at all day and night, with none of their freedom and dignity intact.

When you say, "Would you please get me a bottle of glue?" it is in fact shorthand for saying, "If you please—if it gives you pleasure—get me a bottle of glue." You are asking the person not only to help but also to feel kindly toward you. "Please" is an acknowledgment of that kindness. When you say "please," you are in effect saying, "I respect you and your kindness and your worth as a human being."

- Kindness begins with the word *please*.

- Cultured, polite, and well-mannered people automatically use the word *please*. They have learned appropriate behavior.

- Repetitive use of the word *please* is important if a child is to learn to use the word *please* in his or her life.

- *Please* is usually used when you ask someone to do something for you. Thus the most effective way to use *please* is to precede the word with the person's name, as in "Trevor, *please* . . ."

- Consider adding the word *please* to instructions on your worksheets, assignments, and other papers that you distribute in class.

## I Really Appreciate What You Did, "Thank You"

**Y**ou really cannot use *please* without using *thank you*. The two just go together. Not using the two together would be like having a knife without a fork, a belt without a buckle, a letter without an envelope. When you say "thank you," you are acknowledging that someone did something kindly for **YOU** and not because you ordered **THEM** to do it.

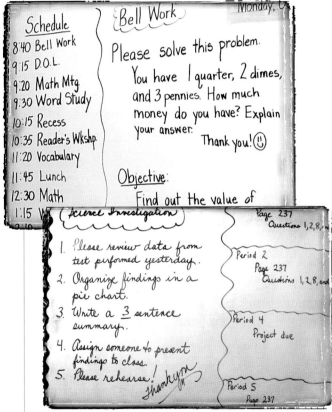

*Please* and *thank you* are used in these teachers' classrooms.

**"Thank you" says to others that you appreciate their effort and kindness.** If you have expectations that students will work hard and will learn to be kind, then saying "thank you" is your way of acknowledging they have been kind and diligent and that you appreciate what they have done for you.

- *Thank you* is the perfect transition; it paves the way to the next request, lesson, activity, or task in class. It makes whatever you want done next much easier.

- The most effective way to use *thank you* is to use it with the person's name: "I truly appreciate what you did. *Thank you*, George" or "George, I truly appreciate what you did. *Thank you*."

- Consider adding the words *thank you* to instructions on your worksheets, assignments, and other papers that you distribute in class.

## A Smile, the Frosting on the Cake

If you truly want to achieve maximum effectiveness when you use a person's name and say "please" and "thank you," SMILE. It requires no effort and is even easier than frowning. Smiling uses far fewer muscles than frowning and hence is less tiring to do. But like using please and thank you, smiling is a behavioral trait that is learned.

A smile is like that sprig of parsley on the dinner plate, the extra pat on the back when a job has been done well, or the extra hug that says, "I really love you." It's the frosting on the cake, the little lagniappe that sets you apart. It communicates three things:

1. You are a person who knows the ultimate of hospitality and graciousness.

2. You have that little extra bit of polish or panache that marks you as a cultured person.

3. You feel good about yourself and want others to feel good about themselves, too.

**A smile is the universal language of understanding, peace, and harmony.** If, indeed, we want the next generation to have a world of peace and understanding, we need to teach its sign—a smile.

A smile is the most effective way to create a positive climate, to disarm an angry person, and to convey the message, "Do not be afraid of me; I am here to help you."

- There is no need for a great big smile; a controlled, slight, disarming smile is all you need.

- Accompany the smile with the name of the person.

- As you smile and speak, use momentary pauses. This is called timing. Every performer knows that the key to delivering a speech, telling a joke, or giving a performance is timing. This is the pregnant pause before speaking an important or emotional line or the punch line.

> **" A smile is a light to tell people that your heart is connected with theirs. "**
>
> Lynn Birdsong
> Howard County Public Schools, Maryland

### Notes in a Lunch Box

Every day, along with a frosted cupcake, Kimberley jotted down a few words of loving encouragement on a note that she placed in her son Kenny's lunch bag. And every afternoon, Kenny returned his lunch bag with her note inside.

Kimberley often wondered if he even read the notes. One day, Kenny returned his lunch bag without the note. Out of curiosity, his mother asked, "Honey, where's your note?"

Kenny looked at her, not sure if he had done something wrong. "I gave it to Tim," he said. "His mother doesn't give him notes and I, well . . . I thought he could use mine."

"You did?" Kimberley questioned.

"Yeah. His mother is really sick and he's so sad right now," Kenny explained. "Maybe you can write a note for him tomorrow or maybe I can give him the one you wrote last Thursday. That was a good one."

**There Will Never Be a Shortage of Love**

Love is the reason for teaching.
It costs nothing, yet it is the most precious
    thing one can possess.
The more we give, the more it is returned.
It heals and protects,
    soothes and strengthens.
Love has other names, such as
    forgiveness . . .
    tolerance . . .
    mercy . . .
    encouragement . . .
    aid . . .
    sympathy . . .
    affection . . .
    friendliness . . .
    and cheer.
No matter how much love we give to others,
    more rushes in to take its place.
It is, really, "the gift that keeps on giving."
Give love in abundance—
    every day.

**Technique for Smiling, Speaking, and Pausing**

**Step 1. SMILE.** Smile as you approach the student, even if your first impulse is to behave harshly toward the student.

**Step 2. FEEDBACK.** Observe the reaction to your smile. Are you receiving a smile in return, or at least a signal that the student is relaxing and receptive to your approach?

**Step 3. PAUSE.** (Timing, timing.)

**Step 4. NAME.** Say "Nathan" with a slight smile.

**Step 5. PAUSE.**

**Step 6. PLEASE.** Add "please," followed by your request. Do this in a calm, firm voice, accompanied by a slight, nonthreatening smile.

**Step 7. PAUSE.**

**Step 8. THANK YOU.** End with "Thank you, Nathan" and a slight smile.

### Example

*Nathan, please stop talking to Joey and get to work on your assignment. Thank you, Nathan.* (Slight smile.)

**Practice this in a mirror, over and over again.**

## It All Adds Up to Love

**O**nly two things are necessary for a happy and successful life: being lovable and being capable. The effective teacher never stops looking for ways of being more and more capable.

**When you look at the truly effective teachers, you will also find caring, warm, lovable people.** Years later, when students remember their most significant teachers, the ones they will remember most are the ones who really cared about them. Effective teachers know they cannot get a student to learn unless that student knows the teacher cares.

Ineffective teachers think all they have to do is offer a product, as in "I was hired to teach history" or "I was hired to teach third grade."

**Effective teachers offer more than a product; they offer a service, too. Effective teachers can help students learn as well as enhance the quality of their lives.** They offer this service consistently because they are practicing this same belief on themselves as they increase their own effectiveness in life.

The sincerest form of service requires no money, no training, no special clothes, and no college degrees. **The sincerest form of service comes from listening, caring, and loving.**

> Love is the reason for teaching.
> It costs nothing,
> yet it is the most precious thing one can possess.

**You don't need to tell all the members of a class that you love them, but you certainly can show it.** If you choose to be a significant and effective person in a student's life, you must demonstrate your care and love both implicitly through your body language and explicitly through what you say.

**When significant people use significant words and actions, they increase the likelihood of eliciting positive behaviors from other people. Thank you for being a positive role model for your students.**

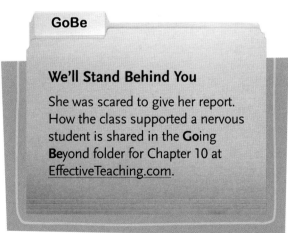

**GoBe**

**We'll Stand Behind You**

She was scared to give her report. How the class supported a nervous student is shared in the **Go**ing **Be**yond folder for Chapter 10 at EffectiveTeaching.com.

## Teachers Do It All

There are no commercial programs, no websites, and no books on teaching love as a unit. We are our best source—each of us. What we are, our attitudes and behaviors, reflect on to others and teach them about love. **The best teachers teach from both the head and the heart.**

Effective teaching has very little to do with programs and structural changes. Programs do not teach kids. Changing class size does not teach kids. Teachers teach kids.

- Programs do not make mean teachers nice.
- Programs do not turn ineffective teachers into effective teachers.
- Programs do not understand that half the class does not speak English.
- Programs do not give a student a caring smile or a kind touch.
- Programs do not say "please" or "thank you."
- Programs do not believe in kids.

Teachers do all this and more.

> *Love is life . . . And if you miss love, you miss life.*
>
> _Leo Buscaglia

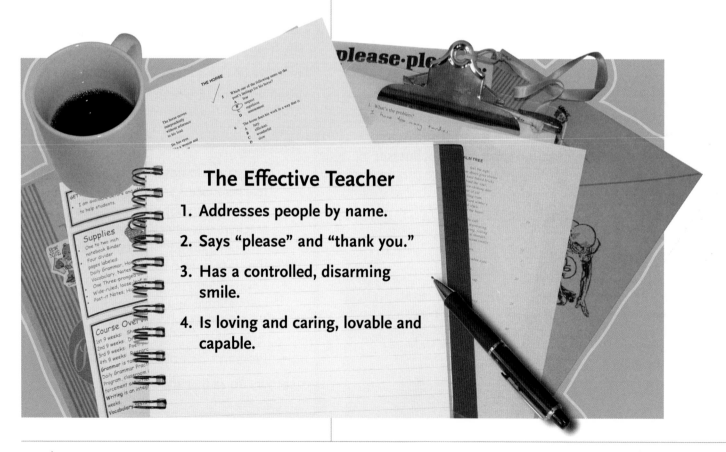

### The Effective Teacher

1. Addresses people by name.

2. Says "please" and "thank you."

3. Has a controlled, disarming smile.

4. Is loving and caring, lovable and capable.

# Unit C

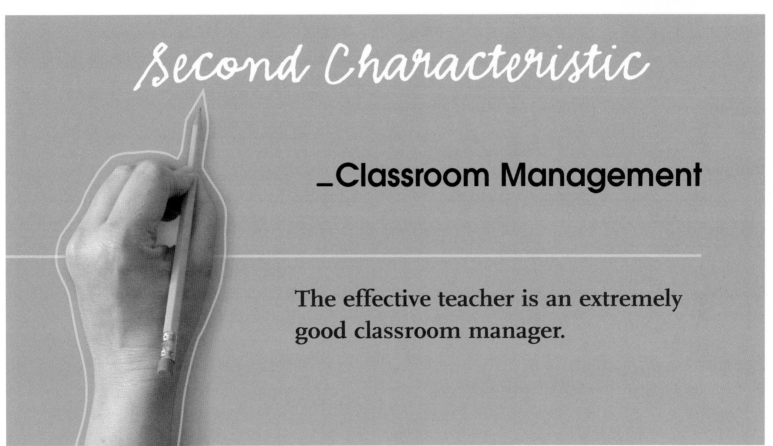

## Second Characteristic

### _Classroom Management

The effective teacher is an extremely good classroom manager.

# Unit  Second Characteristic _Classrooom Management

The effective teacher is an extremely good classroom manager.

Unit C is correlated with Part 3: "Discipline and Procedures" and Part 4: "Procedures and Routines" in the DVD series *The Effective Teacher*.

11

## THE KEY IDEA

The effective teacher is able to organize a well-managed classroom where students can learn in a task-oriented environment.

### 28 Factors

Here are some of the 28 factors governing student learning listed in rank order:

1. Classroom Management
2. Instructional/learning process
3. Parental and home support

28. District demographics

**Classroom Management is the most important factor governing student learning.**

## The First Thing You Need to Know

Classroom management overarches everything in the curriculum.

## Possibly the Most Important Unit in This Book

**W**e have identified the single most important factor that governs student learning. In a study reviewing 11,000 pieces of research that spanned 50 years, three researchers determined that there are 28 factors that influence student learning and placed them in rank order. (See the chart to the left.) **The most important factor governing student learning is Classroom Management.**[1] Thus, Unit C may be the most important unit for you.

**The least important factor is the demographics of the student body.** That is, race, skin color, gender, national and religious background, and the financial status of the family are the least important factors that determine student achievement.

So, once and for all,
let's stop using the demographics or culture
of the students as an excuse for
the lack of achievement.

[1]Wang, Margaret, Geneva Haertel, and Herbert Walberg. (December 1993/January 1994). "What Helps Students Learn?" *Educational Leadership*, pp. 74–79.

**How you manage the classroom is the primary determinant of how well your students will learn.** *The First Days of School* is based on the following research findings:

- Effective teachers have three characteristics:[2]
    1. They have classroom management skills.
    2. They teach for lesson mastery.
    3. They practice positive expectations.

- Classroom management skills are of primary importance in determining teaching success.[3]

- The number one factor governing student learning is classroom management.[4]

- The first day of school is the most important of the school year. Effective classroom management practices must begin on the first day of school.[5]

Based on these findings, this is a statement of dignity for the teaching profession:

**It is the teacher—**
**what the teacher knows and can do—**
**that makes the difference in the classroom.**

It is the principal who makes the difference in the school.

It is the teacher who makes the difference in the classroom.

[2]Good, Thomas, and Jere Brophy. (2007). *Looking in Classrooms.* Needham, Mass.: Allyn & Bacon, pp. 8, 9, 12, 47, 71, and 301.

[3]Emmer, Edmund T., Carolyn M. Evertson, and Murray E. Worsham. (2003). *Classroom Management for Secondary Teachers.* Boston: Allyn & Bacon; Evertson, Carolyn M., Edmund T. Emmer, and Murray E. Worsham. (2006). *Classroom Management for Elementary Teachers.* Boston: Allyn & Bacon.

[4]Wang, Haertel, and Walberg.

[5]Brooks, Douglas. (May 1986). "The First Day of School." *Educational Leadership*, pp. 76–79.

## Effective Teachers Manage Their Classrooms

**T**he fact that you know how to cook a steak does not make you a successful restaurateur. For that, you need to know about accounting procedures; federal, state, and local regulations; sanitation laws; union agreements; and worker and customer relationships. How to cook a steak is the last thing you need to know. The first thing you need to know is how to manage the restaurant.

The fact that you have a college degree in English does not make you an English teacher. The first thing you need to know is how to have a well-managed classroom and then in Unit D, how to deliver the instruction and assess for student learning.

> **Effective teachers MANAGE their classrooms.**
> **Ineffective teachers DISCIPLINE their classrooms.**

Students want a well-managed classroom more than the teachers do because it provides them with security in the classroom that is CONSISTENT. There are no surprises and no yelling in a classroom where everyone—teacher and students—knows what is happening. Consistency comes from implementing procedures and routines.

**Nothing will send kids into orbit faster than letting them suspect that their teacher is disorganized.** Disorganized teachers think only about presenting lessons, lectures, worksheets, videos, activities—never management. And when classrooms aren't managed, they become chaotic and less productive.

Alice Waters, who introduced California cuisine to the world, is noted not only for her skill in the kitchen but also for her skill in running her restaurant, Chez Panisse, in Berkeley, California.

Therefore, the most important thing a teacher can provide in the classroom during the first week of school is CONSISTENCY. **Classroom practices and procedures must be predictable and consistent.** The students must know from day to day how the classroom is structured and organized. If they break a pencil point, they know what to do. If they are tardy, or they need help from the teacher, or they must walk down the hall, or they need to move from one activity to another, they know what to do. There is no yelling of instructions.

Think back to Chapter 1 and the student from the high-poverty school in an at-risk community who said,

> "I like coming to this school because **everyone knows what to do.** As a result, no one is yelling and screaming at us, and we can get on with learning."

The key word in the student's statement is "do." In an effective classroom, the students are responsible for doing the procedures organized for their learning. In an ineffective classroom, the teacher is constantly concerned with student behavior.

## What Is Classroom Management?

**C**lassroom management refers to all of the things a teacher does to organize students, space, time, and materials so student learning can take place.

Brophy and Evertson say, "Almost all surveys of teacher effectiveness report that classroom management skills are of primary importance in determining teaching success, whether it is measured by student learning or by ratings. Thus, management skills are crucial and fundamental. **A teacher who is grossly inadequate in classroom management skills is probably not going to accomplish much.**"[6]

> **"** *The aim of education is to provide children with a sense of purpose and a sense of possibility and with skills and habits of thinking that will help them live in the world.* **"**
>
> _Alice Waters

**GoBe**

**The Edible Schoolyard**

Read how Alice Waters put her "aim of education" quote into action in the Going Beyond folder for Chapter 11 at EffectiveTeaching.com.

---

[6]Brophy, Jere, and Carolyn M. Evertson. (1976). *Learning from Teaching: A Developmental Perspective.* Needham Heights, Mass.: Allyn & Bacon.

> **Too many teachers do not teach.**
>
> They do activities.
> And when problems arise, they discipline.
>
> Many classrooms are unmanaged.
>
> And when classrooms are not organized, little is accomplished in them.

Classroom management skill includes the things a teacher must do toward two ends:

1. Foster student involvement and cooperation in all classroom activities

2. Establish a productive working environment

**A well-managed classroom has a set of procedures and routines that structure the classroom.** (See Chapters 19 and 20.) The procedures and routines organize the classroom so that the myriad of activities that take place there function smoothly and stress free. These activities may include reading, taking notes, participating in group work, taking part in class discussions, participating in games, and producing materials. An effective teacher has every student involved and cooperating in all of these activities and more.

Unit C will help you accomplish the dual goals of fostering student involvement and creating a productive working atmosphere so you can be a very effective teacher. In an effective classroom, there is structure that provides for an environment conducive to learning. The students are working; they are paying attention; they are cooperative and respectful of each other; they exhibit self-discipline; and they remain on task. All materials are ready and organized; the furniture is arranged for productive work; and a calm and positive climate prevails.

## Characteristics of a Well-Managed Classroom

You expect a department store to be well managed. When asked what that means, you would probably list some of these characteristics:

- **The store:** Its layout, organization, and cleanliness
- **The merchandise:** Its display, accessibility, and availability
- **The staff:** Their management, efficiency, knowledge, and friendliness

You could probably do the same for a restaurant, an airline, or a doctor's office. In fact, you have probably said more than once, "If I ran this place, I would do things differently."

Well, since you run a classroom, what is it that you do? It is called classroom management, and the characteristics of a well-managed classroom are well known. Unit C is devoted to getting you up to speed as quickly as possible with everything you need to know about how to get your classroom running and organized for student success.

> ### The Characteristics of a Well-Managed Classroom[7]
>
> 1. Students are deeply involved with their work, especially with academic, teacher-led instruction.
>
> 2. Students know what is expected of them and are generally successful.
>
> 3. There is relatively little wasted time, confusion, or disruption.
>
> 4. The climate of the classroom is work-oriented but relaxed and pleasant.

(1) This room is arranged for productive work.
(2) This room has a positive climate.
(3) The students are on task.
(4) The students are cooperative and respectful of one another.

---

[7]Emmer, Evertson, and Worsham; Evertson, Emmer, and Worsham.

**Techniques to Help You Implement the Four Characteristics of a Well-Managed Classroom**

| Characteristics | Effective Teacher | Ineffective Teacher |
|---|---|---|
| 1. High level of student involvement with work | Students are working. (See page 123.) | Teacher is working. |
| 2. Clear student expectations | Students know that assignments are based on objectives. (See page 238.) | Teacher says, "Read Chapter 3 and know the material." |
| | Students know that tests are based on objectives. (See page 246.) | "I'll give you a test covering everything in Chapter 3." |
| 3. Relatively little wasted time, confusion, or disruption | Teacher has procedures and routines. (See page 165.) | Teacher makes up rules and punishes according to his or her mood. |
| | Teacher starts class immediately. (See page 123.) | Teacher takes roll and dallies. |
| | Teacher has assignments posted. (See page 124.) | Students ask for assignments repeatedly. |
| 4. Work-oriented but relaxed and pleasant climate | Teacher has invested time in practicing procedures until they become routines. (See page 176.) | Teacher tells but does not rehearse procedures. |
| | Teacher knows how to bring class to attention. (See page 182.) | Teacher yells and flicks light switch. |
| | Teacher knows how to praise the deed and encourage the student. (See page 184.) | Teacher uses generalized praise or none at all. |

Arthur Kavanaugh,
Wissahickon Middle School

### It Works So Well, It's Scary

*I start each class with a "Constitution minute" (CM). The CMs are actual transcripts from NBC Radio that were broadcast during the bicentennial of the U.S. Constitution.*

*Several weeks before—*

- *Each student is given a copy of the actual transcript.*
- *Each student is assigned a date of delivery in front of the class.*
- *Transcripts are to be memorized.*
- *Ideas for effective presentation are discussed.*
- *Procedures for the presenters' expectations are discussed.*
- *Procedures for the listeners' expectations are discussed.*

*On the day of the delivery—*

- *The student presenter proceeds to the front of the room ready to present his or her CM before the class begins.*
- *The rest of the class is seated and ready to listen and take a few brief notes.*
- *One minute after the bell rings, the presenter begins the CM.*
- *Approximately one minute later, the CM is over and the presenter sits down.*
- *The class checks the front board for the schedule, procedure, or assignment for the day.*

*During this time, I sit quietly in the back of the room and listen, grading the presentation, taking the roll, and so on.*

*The class automatically starts itself.*

- *They're quiet.*
- *They're organized.*
- *They're ready to learn.*
- *They know what is expected.*

*It works so well, it's scary.*

*Within two minutes, the class is ready and I haven't said a word and yet we have accomplished one learning activity—all managed by procedures.*

Arthur H. Kavanaugh
Ambler, Pennsylvania

## A Task-Oriented and Predictable Environment

**A** well-managed classroom has a task-oriented environment where students know what is expected of them and how to succeed. According to research, most students will make better achievement gains in a well-managed classroom.

**A well-managed classroom has a predictable environment.** Both teacher and students know what to do and what is supposed to happen in the classroom. Because you have chosen to manage the classroom environment, you should be able to close your eyes and not only envision learning taking place but also know why it is taking place.

It is the responsibility of the teacher to manage a classroom and to ensure that a task-oriented and predictable environment has been established.

## The Effective Teacher

1. Works on having a well-managed classroom.

2. Establishes consistency in the classroom.

3. Has students working on task.

4. Has a classroom with little confusion or wasted time.

# Why Effective Teachers Have a Minimum of Problems

> The effective teacher has a minimum of student misbehavior problems to handle.
>
> The ineffective teacher is constantly fighting student misbehavior problems.
>
> Yet the situation is easy to remedy.

**D**on't be ineffective—you and your students will pay for it. Ineffective teachers have classrooms that are not ready. Confusion leads to problems, problems lead to misbehavior, and misbehavior leads to constant struggling between teacher and students. The ineffective teachers, each day, become more stressed, burned out, frazzled, negative, cynical, and angry. They quickly learn to blame everyone and everything else for their problems.

---

### Effective Teachers Are Ready

**Effective Teachers Have the Room Ready.**
Unit C: Classroom Management

**Effective Teachers Have the Work Ready.**
Unit D: Lesson Mastery

**Effective Teachers Have Themselves Ready.**
Unit A: Basic Understandings
Unit B: Positive Expectations

---

## THE KEY IDEA

**Teachers who are ready maximize student learning and minimize student misbehavior.**

### Half of Your Effectiveness Is Determined Before You Leave Home

- **The amount of work you will accomplish will be determined before you even leave for work.**

- **Half of what you will accomplish in a day will be determined before you even leave home.**

- **Three-quarters of what you will accomplish in a day will be determined before you enter the school door.**

You need to prepare yourself, both academically and attitudinally, before you leave home and as you travel to school. You increase the chance of student successes and decrease the chance of student disruptions if the materials, classroom climate, and teacher are ready before the students arrive.

**Evertson and Anderson were the first to show the importance of effective classroom management at the beginning of the school year.**[1] They showed that teacher training was essential to achieve better classroom management practices. Through training to become effective teachers, they had classrooms ready.[2]

Effective teachers prevented problems by implementing a plan at the beginning of the school year. This plan had the following components:

- Used time as effectively as possible.

- Implemented group strategies with high levels of involvement and low levels of misbehavior.

- Selected lesson formats and academic tasks conducive to high student involvement.

- Communicated clear procedures of participation.

Because effective teachers had the classroom ready, they were able to prevent many behavioral problems from occurring. Effective teachers are effective because they have far fewer student problems and are therefore able to get their students to work and to achieve.

Consequently, effective teachers incur far less stress in having to deal with behavior problems and are able to leave each day feeling happy, accomplished, and proud.

Instead of waiting for crises to arise, the effective teacher plans and is ready.

---

[1]Evertson, Carolyn M., and L. Anderson. (1979). "Beginning School." *Educational Horizons*, 57(4), pp. 164–168; Emmer, Edmund T., Carolyn M. Evertson, and L. Anderson. (1980). "Effective Classroom Management at the Beginning of the School Year." *Elementary School Journal*, 80(5), pp. 219–231.

[2]Evertson, Carolyn M. (1985). "Training Teachers in Classroom Management: An Experiment in Secondary Classrooms." *Journal of Educational Research*, 79, pp. 51–58; Evertson, Carolyn M. (1989). "Improving Elementary Classroom Management: A School-Based Training Program for Beginning the Year." *Journal of Educational Research*, 83(2), pp. 82–90.

### A Successful Restaurant Is Ready

**The Table Is Ready.** The table is set and waiting when you arrive at your reservation time.

**The Dining Room Is Ready.** The ambiance is conducive to a pleasant dining experience.

**The Staff Is Ready.** You can expect good service because the staff is rehearsed and trained and has high expectations that you will enjoy your dinner.

### A Successful Teacher Is Ready

**The Work Is Ready.** The desks, books, papers, assignments, and materials are ready when the bell rings.

**The Room Is Ready.** The classroom has a positive environment that is work-oriented.

**The Teacher Is Ready.** The teacher has a warm, positive attitude and has positive expectations that all students will succeed.

**Have your classroom ready, every single day, especially the first days of school.** This is obvious. When you walk into a restaurant, an office, or a store, you expect it to be ready—for YOU. You become upset if things aren't ready.

When people come to your home for a dinner party, you increase the possibility of having a successful dinner if your table is ready. When your team or group goes out to compete or perform, you increase the chances of winning if your team or group is ready. When the students come to a club meeting, they will probably have a successful meeting if the agenda has been well-thought out.

**Most Important Words**

The three most important words to a painter, pilot, or chef are **preparation, preparation, preparation**.

The three most important words to a teacher are **preparation, preparation, preparation**.

A cluttered or barren room sends a negative message to your pupils that you don't care for them. A well-organized, attractive room sends a positive message that you respect them enough to provide a pleasant environment, and they will return the respect to you. A pleasant room feels good and calms people down. Invite your students to enter a room where you are prepared.

" *All battles are won before they are fought.* "

_Sun Tzu

## Before You Do Anything Else

**Organization is the key to effectiveness.**
Dust. Clean. Polish. Arrange. Decorate. Imagine royalty is coming. Who's more important than your students?

Get a collection of cleaning supplies—liquids, sponges, mops, and rags. Spray and dust. Spray and clean. Spray and rub. Spray and polish.

Get a bunch of folders and those plastic containers used for storage. Arrange your units of study in each and label. Discard, sort, and consolidate. Everything has its place. You will have learning organized for the year and will not hobble from day to day wondering what to do next.

**Research proves that a school's and classroom's cleanliness, orderliness, and character influences the students' behavior and the ability of a teacher to teach.**[3]

You know very well that if a client calls and you are not ready, you will lose the sale. If you are not prepared for your interview, you may not have another one. If you are not ready when the teacher calls on you, you may receive a poor grade or low score.

In the real world, you would be fired if you were not ready. For this real world, our students must be ready. We teach readiness by modeling readiness: in our work, in our class environment, in ourselves. People who are not organized send a loud message that they are not ready to teach.

> **Readiness is the primary determinant of teacher effectiveness.**

Prepare the classroom for learning.

[3] Lackney, J. A. (1996). *Teachers as Placemakers: Investigating Teachers' Use of the Physical Environment in Instructional Design.* Madison: University of Wisconsin, College of Engineering, School Design Research Studio. http://www.engr.wisc.edu/.

## Before You Move a Single Desk . . .

**B**efore you move any furniture or put anything on the classroom walls, here are some truisms:

1. A climate of work is what you want to establish during the first week of school.

2. The first week of school should stress large-group organization and student procedures.

3. Spend your time on classroom management of student procedures rather than making your classroom look like a showcase. A few bare but clean bulletin boards, shelves, and plant containers won't disturb anyone.

4. Do not overarrange or overdecorate your room for the opening of school.

5. Your room should be neat and pleasant, but don't spend time making it the ultimate room you want by Back-to-School Night.

6. Don't bother having the learning center, classroom library, or resource center complete. (You don't need a learning center on the first day of school. Wait a week or so after the students have the classroom rules and procedures and routines down pat before you allow them to work at the learning center.)

The following examples, like most examples in this book, are generalized and conceptual. Apply and adapt the examples to your grade level and situation.

## Prepare the Floor Space

- Count the number of desks and chairs needed. Arrange to have damaged furniture replaced and sufficient furniture brought in to the room. Ask for needed items well ahead of time. Do not be hostile if things are not as you want them, especially if your requests are made at the last minute.

The classroom should be arranged so that students and furniture don't get in the way of learning.

**Four Basic Rules of Organization**

1. **Separate school from personal work.** The students are your priority. Don't get sidetracked by a personal matter.

2. **Clear your desktop.** Have labeled vertical files where you can see categories of papers rather than a catchall pile of papers and materials on your desk.

3. **Create a place for incoming and outgoing papers.** Know where to put papers incoming for you and where to put papers to be returned to the students.

4. **Consolidate, consolidate, consolidate.** Get small boxes, clear plastic containers, magazine files, and desk organizers. The few minutes you spend to consolidate will save you hours of searching for items.

> Left-brain people have files.
> Right-brain people have piles.
> Scatter-brain people have piles of files!

- Administrators and custodians are truly helpful people and want quality education for the children as much as you do. Get to know them, and you'll discover that they are competent, cooperative, compassionate, and helpful. They are not the ogres the negative teachers want you to believe they are. They will assist you with your needs.

- Even if you plan to change your room arrangement during the school year, it is wise to begin the year with the desks in rows facing the teacher. This minimizes distractions, allows you to monitor behavior more readily, and helps you to recognize and become familiar with the students in your class.

- Desks do not have to be in traditional rows, but all chairs should face forward so that all eyes are focused on you.

- Place students' desks where students can easily see you during whole-class or small-group instruction.

- Keep high-traffic areas clear. Don't put desks, chairs, or tables in front of doors, water fountains, sinks, pencil sharpeners, or your desk.

- Have a strategic location ready for students who need to be isolated from the rest of the class.

**GoBe**

**Students Who Face the Board Learn More**

Seating arrangement impacts student learning and, amazingly, student health! Read more about this in the **Going Beyond** folder for Chapter 12 at EffectiveTeaching.com.

## Prepare the Work Area

- Arrange work areas and desks so that you can easily see and monitor all the students and areas no matter where you are in the room.

- Students should be able to see you, as well as frequently used whiteboards, bulletin boards, screens, demonstration areas, and displays.

- Keep traffic areas clear. Allow enough clearance to move up and down and around the last seat in the row.

- Keep clear access to storage areas, bookcases, cabinets, and doors.

- Learn the regulations regarding fires, earthquakes, tornadoes, hurricanes, and other natural disasters, and have the classroom ready for such emergencies.

- Make sure that you have enough chairs for the work areas.

- Be sure that you have all necessary materials for your work areas, such as books, lab supplies, media, activity cards, tools, and instruments.

- Test any electrical or mechanical equipment to make sure it works before you intend to use it.

- Use tote trays, boxes, coffee cans, plastic containers, or whatever to store the materials students will need. Arrange your room for these to be readily accessible to the students. (See page 208 for this procedure.)

## Prepare the Student Area

- Save yourself from having a throbbing head. Plan areas for students' belongings now. Provide space for their binders, backpacks, books, lunch bags, umbrellas, shoes, show-and-tell items, lost-and-found items, skateboards, and projects.

- Provide a space for students to hang their jackets.

---

### When to Prepare

You don't build your football team on game day.

You don't drill a water well when you get thirsty.

And you don't discuss procedures once an emergency has begun. That's not the time to discuss what should be done.

**Preparation is the key for teacher success.**

---

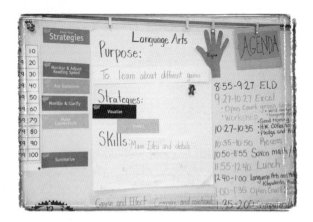

## Prepare the Wall Space

**T**he most effective classes are those where students are self-disciplined, self-motivated, and self-responsible learners. Teach your students to consult the bulletin boards for assignments and information on what to do and how to do it. (See Chapters 15, 19, and 20.)

- Cover one or more bulletin boards with colored paper and trim, and leave it bare. The purpose of this bulletin board is to display student work, not to be decorated by a teacher to look like a department store show window.

- Display your classroom rules in a prominent place. You can relocate it after the first week. (See Chapter 18.)

- Post procedures, duties, calendar, clock, emergency information, maps, schedules, menus, charts, decorations, birthdays, and student work.

- Have a consistent place for listing the day's or week's assignments.

- Post a large example of the proper heading or style for papers to be done in class.

- Post examples of tests students will take, assignments they will turn in, and papers they will write.

- Display the feature topic, theme, chapter, or skill for the day or the current unit.

## Prepare the Bookcases

- Do not place the bookcases or display walls where they obstruct any lines of vision.

- Rotate materials on the shelves and leave out only those items you are willing to allow students to handle.

- Do not place books or other loose materials near an exit where they can easily disappear or where they may hide emergency information.

## Prepare the Teacher Area

**M**aximize your proximity to students and frequently used materials and equipment. Time is lost when teachers and students waste steps to reach each other, gather materials, or use classroom equipment.

The closer you are to your students, the more you will minimize your classroom behavior problems. When the teacher is physically close to the students and can get to them quickly, their on-task behavior increases. When the teacher is far from a student and cannot get to the student quickly, the student is more likely to stop working and disrupt others. **Maximize your proximity to minimize your problems.**

> A teacher's discipline problems
> are directly proportional to
> the teacher's distance from the students.

The closer the teacher is to the students, the less likely behavior problems will occur in the classroom.

- Place the teacher's desk, file, and other equipment so they do not interfere with the flow of traffic. Do not create a barrier between yourself and your students. Place your desk so that you can move quickly to a student to assist, reinforce, or discipline.

- Place the teacher's desk so that you can easily monitor the classroom while at your desk or working with individual students.

- Place the teacher's desk away from the door so that no one can take things from your desk and quickly walk out.

- If you choose to have everything on and in your desk treated as personal property, make this clear during your teaching of classroom procedures and routines.

## Prepare the Teaching Materials

- Have a letter ready with the materials you want your students to bring from home. Have a place and a procedure ready to store these materials when they bring the items to the classroom.

- Have a method ready for matching students to a desk. Have name cards ready and on the students' desks. Or use an overhead transparency or PowerPoint slide correlating desk arrangement with students' names.

- Have your basic materials ready for the first week of school. These include books, papers, pencils, rulers, glue, chalk, felt pens, stapler, tape, clipboard, crayons, felt-tip markers, construction paper, instruments, calculators, supplies, manipulatives, playground equipment, and computer software. Buy a bell or a timer if you wish to use either as a signal.

- Find and organize containers for your materials. Use copy paper boxes, crates, coffee cans, milk cartons, and shoeboxes to store materials. Label your containers, and place in each an inventory card listing everything that should be in the container.

- Store seldom-used materials out of the way, but be sure they are inventoried and ready for immediate use.

- Place electronic media near outlets and where the students will not trip over the wires. Have an extension cord and an adapter plug handy.

- Organize and file your masters, lesson plans, and computer disks. Do likewise with your extra worksheets so they are immediately ready for any students who were absent or who need extra help.

Use labeled containers with an inventory card to hold materials for each activity or unit of study.

## Finally, Prepare Yourself

- Keep your briefcase, handbag, keys, and other valuables in a safe and secure location.

- Have emergency materials handy, such as tissue, bacterial wipes or gel, rags, paper towels, soap, first-aid kit, and extra lunch money. Store these for your use, not the students'.

- Obtain a teacher's manual for each textbook you will use in your class.

- Obtain a supply of the forms that are used for daily school routines, such as attendance, tardy slips, hall passes, and referral forms. You will use these forms each day, so place them where you can find them immediately.

To be an effective teacher, be prepared. **Teachers who are ready maximize student learning and minimize student misbehavior.**

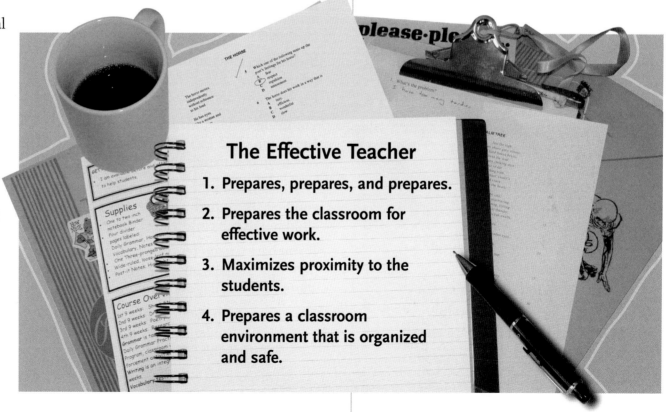

## The Effective Teacher

1. **Prepares, prepares, and prepares.**

2. **Prepares the classroom for effective work.**

3. **Maximizes proximity to the students.**

4. **Prepares a classroom environment that is organized and safe.**

**13**

## THE KEY IDEA

Right or wrong, accurate or not, your reputation will precede you.

### Your Image Enhances Sales

**HALLMARK:** "When you care enough to send the very best"

**LEXUS:** "Relentless pursuit of perfection"

**TIMEX:** "It takes a licking and keeps on ticking"

**De BEERS:** "A diamond is forever."

**L'ORÉAL:** "Because you're worth it."

## Your Reputation Precedes You

The way you introduce yourself on the first day can determine how much respect and success you will have for the rest of the school year.

**P**eople have reputations. You know of people who are sweet, kind, honest, industrious, and dependable, and others who are sleazy, curmudgeonly, arrogant, lazy, and undependable.

**Businesses have reputations.** Some have terrible service, sell shoddy merchandise, and do not guarantee their products. Other businesses can be trusted consistently.

Companies with good images, such as IBM, Coca-Cola, Lexus, Hallmark, Nordstrom, and Hewlett-Packard, enhance their sales. They know that people buy from companies they trust. Their image precedes a sale.

**Whether you want it to or not, your reputation will precede you.** Even before you first see your students, your success at winning their respect and attention may have already been predetermined by your reputation.

If you have a good reputation, the students will enter your classroom with high expectations, and this will work to your benefit. Building a reputation starts your first day and continues from there.

- A good reputation opens doors for you. If you have a good reputation, people (students) will flock to you. Exhibit integrity and honesty, and be approachable. The buzz of the students will reflect these positive traits.

- If you have a poor reputation, the students will enter with low expectations, and this will be to your detriment. The buzz of the students will be the buzz saw of your demise in the classroom.

Whether you like it or not, students will talk about you, parents will talk about you, the administration will talk about you, and colleagues will talk about you.

Everyone likes and supports a winner. Parents want their children in the classes of teachers with outstanding reputations. Teachers with poor reputations often get what's left after all the sifting and shuffling of students and teachers has been done.

You will attract better students, have a minimum of problems on the first day of school, and generally be much happier with your job if you have students who want to be in your class. It makes no sense to be a teacher that no one wants to have as a teacher.

**Protect your reputation by maintaining a positive image. You have nothing to lose and everything to gain.**

## Preschool Invitation or Visit

Here are some welcoming techniques used by effective teachers. Apply and adapt the examples to your situation.

1. **Send a letter home to parents BEFORE school begins.**

   - Tell the parents that you are looking forward to having their child in your class.

   - Ask them to put the date of the school's open house on their calendars, and explain why it is important to attend. You will be explaining homework, grading, discipline, and classroom procedures.

   - Include information on what materials you want the students to have ready for school.

### A Reputation of Love

Jone M. Couzins teaches in Ohio. On the last day of the school year she asks her seventh grade classes to write letters of advice to the next year's seventh graders. Because her seventh graders are among the most anxious in the building on the first day, she distributes the letters to the incoming seventh graders.

She tells them the letters are meant to help them adjust to life at the school. After reading the letters, their assignment is to answer a letter and compare their own experiences during the first week of school to the experiences and advice from the present eighth grade student whose letter they received.

Of all the comments made by the new students, the one that surfaced most often was. "I know that I'm going to like Mrs. Couzins' class because she said she loves kids."

2. **Send a letter home to each student BEFORE school begins.**

- Connect before school starts. Send a postcard of welcome. Email the family.

- Tell the students who you are.

- Invite them to call or email you if they have questions.

- Help them prepare by listing the materials they will need. They will be ready if you are ready. Do not surprise your students.

- Tell them *your* expectations, not theirs.

3. **Visit the home of each student BEFORE school begins (check to be sure that this is an appropriate thing to do).**

- Introduce yourself.

- Bring with you the letters just described.

- Share with the parents how they can help.

## Am I in the Right Room?

Douglas Brooks discovered that the very first thing a student wants to know on the first day of school is, "Am I in the right room?"[1] **Finding the correct room on the first day of school can be one of the most frightening experiences for a student.** There is nothing more embarrassing than to discover that you are in the wrong room—15 minutes after class has begun.

*Dear Dr. Wong,*

*When I came home from your in-service meeting, I asked my 13-year-old son the following question: "What's the most frightening thing about the first day of school?"*

*After thinking for a moment, he said, "Two things—having the teacher mispronounce your name and walking into the wrong classroom."*

Classroom teacher
Garland, Texas

[1]Brooks, Douglas. (May 1985). "The First Day of School." *Educational Leadership*, pp. 76–78.

## How to Communicate Quickly with Parents

Communicating with parents and students has never been easier. Use the Internet to your advantage to convey words of welcome before students arrive in your classroom. Let everyone know you're wired for learning.

**Bring your classroom to the parents and let them be an observer to all that goes on.** You don't have to be a technology expert to make it happen. Involve the students in the planning and dissemination of information. **Parents will appreciate the immediacy of the contact and you will appreciate the time-saving benefits of using the Internet as a tool of engagement.**

Here are some ways to get started:

1. **Before school begins, send an email introducing yourself to the parents.** These are items to include in the email:
   - A picture of you
   - An audio or video welcome
   - A picture of the classroom
   - Beginning and ending time of school
   - General curriculum for the first month
   - Best ways to get in touch with you
   - Ways you'll communicate with them
   - Expectations of students
   - Homework policy
   - Special supplies needed
   - Dates to save on their calendars
   - Eagerness you have for the school year
   - An attachment letter of welcome to the student
     - This letter includes the first homework assignment to be brought to class on the first day of school. Make it fun and easy.

2. Many school districts host **teacher-made websites**. Use the site to share homework, projects, and what the students are learning. If your school doesn't host a site, most teenagers know how to make one—if you don't. Ask for help. Start small—just post homework and expand as you get comfortable with the technology.

3. **Host a webcam session.** Create a link for parents to login "live" to watch a lesson being presented, the culmination of a class project, or a special celebration. Keep the camera off except for times you want to broadcast.

4. Use your **interactive white board** to accumulate and store work and messages. At the end of the day, download, save, and email to parents. For those without email, print it for students to take home to share.

5. **Blog.** In simple terms, a blog is a website where you write your thoughts on an ongoing basis. The latest information shows up at the top, so your visitors can read what's new. You can choose whether you want to accept comments at your blog site or use it as a one-way street of communication.

In 2003 an estimated 93 percent of public school classrooms had Internet access.[2] The technology is there for you to use not only in the classroom as a teaching tool, but also as a means of keeping the lines of communication open with parents and guardians wherever they may be in the world.

---

[2]National Center for Education Statistics. U.S. Department of Education.

Bond with your students. Jackie Routhenstein of New Jersey has a welcome sign on her classroom door.

Effective teachers, when possible, place student's names on their desks. This is highly cherished by those students who do not have a place to call "home" at home.

## How to Greet Students on Day 1

**S** tand at the classroom door with a big smile and a ready handshake—every day. You do this when company comes or when meeting people. Airline, restaurant, and auto dealership personnel do it. Effective teachers do what is obvious—not what everyone else is doing at school. If you're the only one standing at the door with a smile, does that make you wrong and the others right? Of course not! It makes you more effective at what you do.

Here is a successful technique used by many effective teachers for greeting students on the first day of school.

**Step 1.** Post the following information next to the classroom door:

- Your name
- Room number
- Section or period, if appropriate
- Grade level or subject
- An appropriate welcome or greeting

The students can see the information on the wall and can compare it to the correct information on their registration forms. This is no different from finding flight information displayed on a screen at an airport, a doctor's name on the office door, or movie information, times, and prices at a theater box office.

**Step 2.** Stand at the door on the first day of school. Have a smile on your face, hand ready to shake the students' hands, and a look that says you can't wait to meet them.

Chris Bennett, a theater-arts teacher in Tennessee, gives his students a theater ticket when he greets them at the door of the auditorium, which is their classroom.

**Step 3.** As they stand there, wondering if you are the right teacher and this is the correct room, welcome them to a new school year and tell them the following information:

- Your name
- Room number
- Section or period, if appropriate
- Anything else appropriate, such as seating assignment

**Step 4.** Check each student's registration card, and if the student is in the wrong place or is lost, help the student or find a guide who will.

**Step 5.** After you greet a student, the student should be able to enter the classroom and see the same information displayed in the room:

- Your name
- Room number
- Section or period, if appropriate
- Grade level or subject
- An appropriate welcome or greeting

Because the students are exposed to the same information three times, it is highly unlikely that any students will be in the wrong place on the first day of school. Their anxiety level and their tendency to be confrontational are reduced, and they will feel welcome and at ease.

What has just been suggested as an effective and cordial way to start a new year should be obvious. Have you ever gone somewhere on an errand or for an appointment and been unable to find the right address, building, or office? You know how frustrating that can be.

**Everything possible should be done to welcome the students and to make sure they know where to go and how to get there on time.**

Steven C. Zickafoose of Florida has a trifold ready for distribution.

*I love to stand at the door on the first day with a giant smile on my face, hand stuck out in an invitational pose, waiting for those "little bundles of joy" to come down the hall.*

### How NOT to Start the First Day of School

The ineffective teacher suddenly appears through the door just as the bell rings. The teacher's name and the room number are nowhere to be found. The teacher regards the class with an icy stare. The first day of school goes like this:

1. The teacher stands behind the desk, glaring, inspecting everyone walking in with a look that says, "You're infringing on my space."

2. The teacher never mentions his or her name, the room number, the class, the grade level, or the period.

3. The teacher announces that he or she will call the roll.

4. The teacher also announces that as the roll is called, the seating assignments will be changed so that everyone is seated in alphabetical order. A collective groan arises. (See "Succeeding With Your First Request," page 114.)

5. The teacher calls the first student and points to the student sitting in the first chair and demands, "Up." That student rolls his eyes, shuffles forward, and leans against the wall.

6. The teacher then points to the first student and says, "You, sit there."

7. As each student is dislodged from his or her chair, students lounge along the wall.

8. The students are all looking at each other, shaking their heads, "Who is this disorganized person? Our teacher? It's going to be a long year!"

## Seating Chart and First Assignment

If you choose to have assigned seats, tell each student this fact upon entering the door. Do not rearrange the seating after the class is all seated. The students will question why they have to move and why they can't sit near a friend.

---

### How to Help Students Find Their Assigned Seats

- Have names on place cards on the desks.

- Have names written on a seating chart transparency or a PowerPoint slide that is projected onto a screen.

- As you greet students at the door, give them an index card with a letter and a number on it, such as B5, A8, C3, and ask them to find their seats based on the seating chart that is projected. Do not use this method if you think it will be too difficult for your students to figure out two coordinates. You want them in their seats when the bell rings, not running around confused.

---

As the students go to their assigned seats, inform them they will find their first assignment at their seat or posted. Tell them to start to work on it immediately!

The first assignment should be short, interesting, and easy to complete. It should lead to success for all students. It may simply be an information form that will not be scored.

**You greatly increase the probability that school will start successfully for you and your students when these four points are true:**

1. You have your room ready.
2. You are at the door.
3. You have assigned seats.
4. You have the first assignment ready.

The important thing is to make a statement to your students about your efficiency and competence as a classroom manager and teacher. **What you do on the first day may well determine how much respect and success you will have for the rest of the school year.**

## How Students Are to Enter the Room

**I**t may be possible to meet and line up your students in an area outside your classroom. This is an ideal strategy to use for teaching students how-to-enter-the-classroom procedures while welcoming them to class.

You need to begin teaching procedures and routines the moment you meet students at the door on the first day of school. (More on this in Chapter 19.)

Ask any student who enters the room inappropriately to return to the door and enter appropriately. You do not send the student out of the room but rather to the door. You do not want to send anyone "out of the room" in the very first minute; "out of the room" has a negative, humiliating connotation. Do not make dubious remarks like this:

"Try coming in again correctly."
"We walk into this room like ladies and gentlemen."
"You walk in properly, understand?"

### Sharing Who You Are

Display some information about yourself. Post your diploma. Graphically describe your personality and expectations with interesting

All About Me!

world maps or photos of places you've visited, movie posters, etc. Limit the display of personal items such as family photos or your own children's artwork. The more your students know about your personality, the more likely they are to respect you; however, the more they know about your personal life, the less likely they are to view you as their teacher.

Let your students know who you are.

As soon as possible, put something on a bulletin board from each student with the student's name on it. Displaying something from every student makes each one feel like a part of the class. The more they know about one another, the more likely they are to identify with and respect one another as equals.

Jeanne Bayless of Nevada says, "I see nice straight lines. I see quiet fingers. And I see some great smiles. You are ready. You are invited in."

## How to Speak to the Class

**Stand up when you address the class,** and speak in short, clear sentences or phrases. Students have a way of turning off long, complex sentences. Your purpose is to establish sureness and understanding, not to impress with your intelligence. Most importantly, students will gauge their confidence in you by how you say what you want to say.

**You do not need to speak loudly.** The most effective teachers have a firm but gentle voice. Learn to "speak loudly" with your tone, not your volume. When you speak softly, the class listens carefully. You modulate the noise level of the class by the loudness of your voice. And on those rare occasions when you may need to raise your voice, you will have twice as much impact.

**Learn to use nonverbal language.** A nod, a smile, a stare, a frown, a raised eyebrow, or a gesture is often all that is needed, and it does not even disturb the class at work. Body language can speak volumes. Use it to manage the classroom and minimize disruptions.

**Rather, calmly but firmly, do the following:**

1. Ask the student to return to the door.
2. Tell the student why.
3. Give directions for correctly entering the room.
4. Check for understanding.
5. Acknowledge the understanding.

### Example

*Todd, please come back to the door. I am sorry, but that is not the way you enter our classroom. You were noisy, you did not go to your seat, and you pushed Ann.*

*When you enter this classroom, you walk in quietly, go directly to your seat, and get to work immediately on the assignment that is posted. Are there any questions?*

*Thank you, Todd. Now show me that you can go to your seat properly.*

Don't forget the importance of using the student's name, of saying please, and saying thank you. (See Chapter 10.)

Your manner and voice should be gentle and calm. Smile generously, but be firm. Your voice should communicate that you are not the least bit flustered or angry. You are simply in control and know what you expect from your students, and you are communicating this expectation.

**It is a mistake to let any misbehavior, such as entering a room inappropriately, go unchallenged under the rationale that you will have time to deal with this later.** Effective teachers know that it will be much more difficult to correct misbehavior at a later date.

Ineffective teachers bark and yell, have no guidelines or expectations, and assume that misbehavior will correct itself. Asking students to enter the classroom according to a set of procedures indicates there are definite boundaries to what they can and cannot do in your classroom.

It is important that you state the correct procedure for entering the room at any time of the day. Rehearse this procedure until it becomes automatic. Praise the students when it is done properly, and encourage them to make it a routine every day. It is best to save what has been explained in this paragraph until after you have introduced yourself, as suggested below.

## Your Important First Words

**T**here are two major things you want to state at the outset on the first day of school: your name and your expectations. It's in your best interest not only to tell the class your name but to pronounce it so they will call you by the name you want.

Students want to know who you are as a person and if you will treat them as people. It is important that you dispel any fears they may have about being in your class. The best way to do this is to smile, exude caring, and communicate positive expectations.

### One Teacher's Welcome

*Welcome. Welcome to another school year.*

*My name is Mr. Wong. There it is on the chalkboard. It is spelled W-O-N-G and is pronounced "Wong." I would like to be addressed as Mr. Wong, please. Thank you. I am looking forward to being your teacher this year. Relax.*

*I am a veteran teacher with over 30 years' experience. Outside of class, I go to workshops, conferences, professional meetings, college classes, and seminars. I also read the professional journals and work together with my fellow teachers in professional organizations. I keep up-to-date in my teaching skills. Most important, I love to teach! I enjoy teaching, and I am proud to be a teacher. So you can relax. You are in good hands this year with me.*

### You Will . . .

On the first days of school, learn to begin many of your sentences with "You will . . ." An alternative would be, "The class procedure is . . ." The first few days are critical. This cannot be stressed enough.

Your mission is to establish student habits, called procedures in this book, or routines. If not, **students will develop their own habit patterns in classes where teachers do not teach procedures and communicate expectations**. These habit patterns spread, and soon the entire class develops its own agenda, its own curriculum, and its own set of procedures. It's the third day of school, perhaps, and you have already lost your class.

The effective teacher has a classroom management plan right from the start to prevent the classroom from becoming a breeding ground for confusion and discontent.

*You are going to have one of the greatest educational experiences of your life. This classroom will be well-organized, and you will feel well-cared for while you are in it. We will not only study [subject], but I will also share with you some life skills and secrets that will help you succeed in the years ahead. I can assure you that if you should run into me at the mall 25 years from now, you will say, "You were right, Mr. Wong. That was the most memorable, exciting, and fascinating class I ever had."*

*So welcome!*

## Script for the First Day of School

**Y**ou are probably as anxious as your students on the first day of school. Effective teachers have a script ready for the first day of school. As you prepare your room and yourself for this all-important day, prepare for the students who will spend their first day with you. They will come with equal amounts of anticipation and anxiety. You can heighten their anticipation (and ease your nerves!) with a well-organized and welcoming room. You can allay their anxieties with a well-organized lesson. **With a first day of school script, they will see that you know what you are doing.**

Melissa Boone-Hand

Melissa Boone-Hand of Texas began her first year of teaching in an elementary school with a script. She detailed what she would wear, where she would stand, what she would say, how the room would be arranged, and what the students would do. She was ready. The students became ready. Today, she is a successful teacher-leader.

---

**GoBe**

### First Day of School Scripts

The scripts of these successful teachers, Melissa, Sacha, and John, are in the Going Beyond folder for Chapter 13 at EffectiveTeaching.com.

---

Sacha Mike

John Schmidt

Sacha Mike, a middle school teacher in Washington, had an assistant principal who did not think she would last a week—what terrible expectations. Today, her colleagues think she is awesome.

John T. Schmidt of Illinois is so successful that the Homewood-Flossmoor High School District in Illinois uses him as a demonstration teacher in the district's new teacher induction program—after teaching for just two years!

**Students will perform better when they know what the teacher expects of them.** Being prepared is the best strategy to use to prevent problems, because

> **If you do not structure your classroom,
> the students will structure the classroom for you.**

## Your Room Is an Introduction to You

- Have a place ready with a schedule, rules and procedures, a calendar, and a big welcome.

- Have an assignment posted before the students walk in. For consistency, post the assignment in the same location every day.

- Have your script ready for the first day of school.

The students now know what the classroom expectations are. They have an immediate assurance that you are organized and ready for what matters most: **Their Success!**

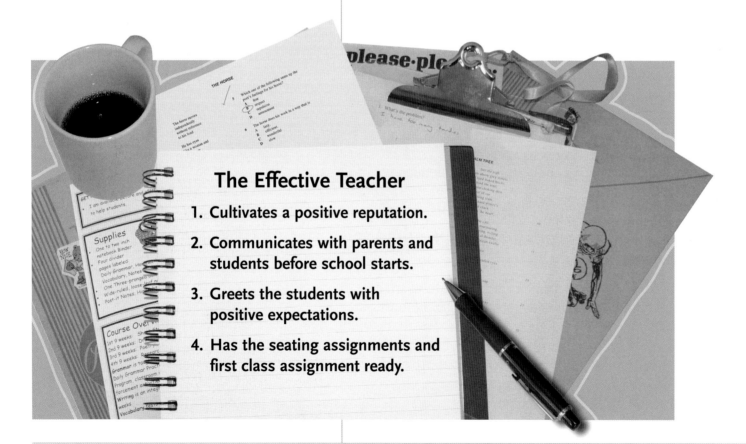

### The Effective Teacher

1. Cultivates a positive reputation.

2. Communicates with parents and students before school starts.

3. Greets the students with positive expectations.

4. Has the seating assignments and first class assignment ready.

# Your Very First Set of Directions to Your Class

> How the class reacts to your first directions will be an indication of how students will react to your directions for the remainder of the year.

## THE KEY IDEA

**Arrange seats for the students to accomplish what you want them to accomplish.**

**Y**ou can tell right away how successful you will be in giving directions by the success of your first request. Your very first instructions to your students will probably be to tell each one of them where to sit.

They will react in one of two ways:

1. They will follow your orders promptly and courteously.

2. They will grumble and argue over everything you want them to do for the rest of the year.

Yes, the rest of the year! Here's why.

Greeting students sets a positive tone for the school day.

> **Greet your students as they enter the classroom.**

One of the most successful techniques is to meet and greet your students at the door as they enter the classroom or line them up in an area for your greeting and instructions before entering the classroom.

"Good morning. Here's your seating assignment."

# Succeeding With Your First Request

## The Effective Teacher

- Is present in the room or at the door when the students arrive.
- Assigns seating to everyone upon entering the room.
- Has an assignment on each desk ready for the students.

What you do the instant a student enters the school, the library, the office, or the classroom communicates immediately if the student is welcome there.

The teacher is standing at the door with a smile and an extended hand to shake. The teacher bids everyone to enter, and each student receives a nonthreatening smile that conveys a message of safety. The welcome mat or red carpet is at the door for the class. This conveys a positive message to the students.

**People welcome people.** Textbooks, chalkboards, lectures, worksheets, and examinations do not welcome students to school. Teachers, bus drivers, food service workers, administrators, secretaries, aides, custodians, and counselors invite students to have a successful experience at school.

Upon entering the classroom, the students find a pleasant environment. Your name, the room number, the period, and the class name are on the chalkboard. Directions for seating (whether assigned or open) are reiterated. Information about the first assignment, which is on the desks or posted for all to see, is clearly stated and tells the students to get to work even before the bell rings. The message you are relating to these students is that the classroom is a safe, positive, work-oriented environment where every second will be devoted to success and learning.

If students are invited to have successful experiences in the classroom, they will know they are welcome, appreciated, cared for, and wanted. **And if the students feel wanted, they will be more likely to accede to your directions and requests.**

### How to Make Your First Request Effective

**Step 1.** Check each registration card at the door.

**Step 2.** Put a friendly smile on your face.

**Step 3.** Look each student in the eyes and verbally welcome and acknowledge each one. "Hello, come on in;" or "Glad to see you" are inviting comments.

**Step 4.** Lower your voice to a firm but soft tone. Speak slowly and tell the student if seating is open or assigned. (See page 116.)

**Step 5.** Follow this with, "When you sit down, you will find an activity on your desk (or posted). I think you will enjoy doing it. Please begin working on it right away. Thank you." (See page 127.)

# Failing With Your First Request

### The Ineffective Teacher

- Is nowhere in sight when students arrive.
- Reshuffles the whole class after everyone has found a seat.
- Grumbles about all the administrative details that must be done before class can begin.

Imagine the students walking into the classroom with no teacher in sight. Some students find a chair; others wander around. But they all ask, "Who's the teacher? Is this the right room? Is this history?" And they all respond, "I don't know."

The bell rings, and suddenly a teacher appears from an office or from around a corner, like a monster from a dungeon. It is Cold Start Charlie, the perennial ineffective teacher. He can always be found in the faculty lounge, gulping coffee, and puffing away on his cigarettes. Before the first day of school, he's already griping about the same thing he's been griping about for years.

Hurrying down to his classroom, he arrives just as the bell rings. The students immediately read the menacing look that dares anyone to breathe out of unison. He never introduces himself and may or may not identify the class or period. Standing in front of the class with the posture of a drill sergeant, he says, "When I call your name, come up and bring your registration card for me to sign."

When seemingly everyone has been registered, he looks up and asks if everyone has been called. One hand goes up. Discovering that the student is in the wrong classroom, Cold Start Charlie tells him where he should be. As the student leaves the room, all eyes are focused on him, with two

messages behind the stares, "Dummy. How can you be so stupid as to be in the wrong room?" and "Isn't he lucky not having to put up with this jerk of a teacher for the rest of the year!"

A student has just been humiliated because a teacher was not prepared and acted in a noninvitational manner. And the students' first impression of Cold Start will be reflected in their work for the rest of the year.

### Your First Request Will Be Ineffective . . .

1. If you are not in the room when the students enter.

2. If you do not check any of the registration cards before the students enter the room.

3. If you do not tell the students your name, the room number, the period or grade level, and the class.

4. If you do not welcome the students.

5. If you reshuffle the class after everyone has taken a seat.

6. If you grumble that you have to do administrative work.

7. If you have provided no assignment and the students have nothing to do while you register the class.

Group activity

Story time

Test, video, or lecture

## Seating Arrangements or Seating Assignments?

S hould I assign seats or allow students to sit wherever they choose? That question is appropriate only after you decide what you want the students to do. Seating assignment is not the issue. Seating assignments come after seating arrangements are determined. **Seating arrangements take priority.**

> **The purpose of arranging seats is to accomplish classroom tasks.**

**The teacher must know what the students are to accomplish before arranging the seating.** Then the desks are arranged to maximize the accomplishment of the tasks and to minimize behavior problems. After the seats are arranged, students may be assigned seating in whatever order is desired.

## Arrange Seats for Communication

S eating arrangements may not be the most exciting topic, but the placement of chairs can profoundly affect the outcome of a lesson. **The main purpose of a seating arrangement is communication.**

- The effective teacher uses a variety of activities to engage the students during the school year.
- A variety of seating arrangements will be used.
- The best seating arrangement is conducive to communicating.

> **How people communicate will determine the success of what you want to accomplish.**

Is the teacher communicating with the students? Are the students communicating with each other? Are the students communicating with an audience? Are the students communicating with a computer? Are the students communicating with a distance-learning teacher?

Chris Bennett teaches theater arts. His class is in the auditorium and the seats are bolted to the floor in rows. He communicates with the students; they communicate with each other; and they communicate with the other students on the stage in this manner. What better way to have a sense of the audience than to sit in rows of seats.

LaMoine Motz is a high school science teacher. His classrooms feature inquiry-based science activities. The students are in "lab groups," meaning they are in small groups engaged in activities. This same arrangement is used whenever small groups are engaged in work, regardless of grade level or subject.

Tony Tringale teaches fifth grade. During social studies, he finds that a horseshoe-shape arrangement is best because of his lecture-discussion style. He talks, and he leads lots of discussions. In this seating arrangement, the students see him and they see each other.

Performing arts

Discussion or demonstration

**Diana Greenhouse sets up a double circle of chairs for her "Inner-Outer Discussion."** The inner circle of chairs faces in, and the outer circle of chairs faces out. The chairs are back-to-back, making an inner and an outer circle of seats. (See page 274 for information on this technique.)

Students sit in a circle with their backs to each other.

Robin Barlak's classroom.

Angelica Garcia teaches performing arts. During music, her younger students sit on the floor facing her. An "x" on the floor indicates where they are to sit. Her older students stand in rows of risers facing her.

Robin Barlak teaches preschool special education. For her students, several of whom are severely disabled, the students sit in a half circle on the rug, in the same place each day, facing her during large-group time.

Steve Geiman teaches physical education. There are no seats, unless you consider the bleacher seats in fixed rows. Sometimes the students stand in columns and rows, sometimes huddled around the coach, and sometimes in lines facing different directions for drills.

### Seating Arrangements

Seats are arranged to coincide with the specific task you have designed.

#### Examples

- First-day registration and procedures
- Cooperative learning
- Listening to a lecture
- Sitting to hear a story
- Class discussion and interaction
- Small-group activity
- Taking a test
- Individual research or deskwork

### Seating Assignments

Seats are assigned to maximize learning and classroom management and minimize behavioral problems.

#### Examples

- By age
- By height
- In alphabetical order
- For peer-group tutoring
- For paired problem solving
- Placing lower-performing and more challenging students at the front of the room

## Seating Arrangements

To determine seating arrangements for the accomplishment of classroom tasks, you need to ask the following three questions, in order:

1. **What do I want to do?**
   Do I want to read a story; do small-group activities; teach discipline, procedures, and routines; lecture; show a video; conduct a chorus; lead exercises; have individual study?

2. **What kind of seating arrangements are possible?**
   You may be limited by the size or shape of the room or the available tables and chairs in the room.

Whatever the classroom arrangement, do not seat students with their backs to you or to the front of the classroom on the first day of school. If you are their focus of attention, as you should be at the start of school, the students will acknowledge your importance and listen to what you are communicating to them.

### What If the Chairs Cannot Be Moved?

If the chairs are bolted in place, you are restricted to that arrangement and must adapt your activities to that seating plan.

You may be sharing a room that is used primarily for a different grade level or subject. Or, more importantly, you may be sharing a room that is the primary room of another teacher.

For your own sense of sanity, adjust your classroom instructions and teaching techniques. You have no doubt been in situations where circumstances and budgets dictated the terms—for example, you could invite only 75 guests to a wedding reception and it had to be held in your home instead of at the ballroom of The Palace Hotel.

*Accept that all things are not the way you want them, and don't obsess about it.*

*Learn to nourish your body and go on improving the quality of your life.*

### 3. Which seating arrangement will I use?

Different seating arrangements need to be used to accomplish various tasks efficiently. The students must sit in a way that helps facilitate what you want them to accomplish.

There is no one form of seating that should be permanently used the entire school year. Change the seating in your room as frequently as you deem necessary for your purposes.

The only way for students to learn how your classroom is organized and structured is to have the seats arranged so that every pair of eyes will be looking at you. If you want to teach your rules, procedures, and routines, do not arrange the room in a series of centers or circles in which half the students have their backs to you. Discipline rules, procedures, and routines are explained in Chapters 18 to 20. These are best taught with the chairs arranged in columns and rows.

**GoBe**

**Assorted Seating Configurations**

Different activities have different seating arrangements. Various seating configurations are in the **Go**ing **Be**yond folder for Chapter 14 at EffectiveTeaching.com.

### Problems When Students Have Their Backs to You

1. You explain a rule of discipline, and the students sitting in a small group look at each other and roll their eyes toward the sky. They have just invalidated the rule by their defiant actions.

2. You explain a procedure, and half the students must turn around and write it down and then turn around again. You have just invalidated the procedure for teaching procedures.

3. You explain another procedure, and you cannot tell if half the students, with their backs to you, understand because you cannot see them practicing the procedure. You have just invalidated a routine of making sure students are learning.

## Seating Assignments

**T**he effective teacher assigns students to their seats on the first day of school. Don't make finding one's seat on the first day of school a frustrating treasure hunt. The task should be over in a matter of seconds. It is not a topic for class discussion. It should then be a closed issue because you are the teacher in charge of the instructional program. When you wish to rearrange the room furniture and equipment, or the seating, deal with the changes in the same expedient way.

**You will have a much more effective class, most of the time, if you assign students to their seats.** For group work, you should assign students to their groups and then assign the groups to their workstations or seating arrangements. If you are hosting a dinner party with guests at three separate tables, for instance, you don't ask your guests to get their own utensils out of the drawer and then sit wherever they please. If you are a good host, you tell your guests where you'd like them to sit.

Airlines, theaters, and restaurants—the good ones—will designate a seat or seat you in a chair of mutual choice. Do likewise in the classroom. You are the teacher, the conductor, the facilitator.

---

**Reasons for a Seating Chart**

1. **Facilitates roll taking**
2. **Aids name memorization**
3. **Separates problem students**

---

Seating assignments are sometimes made for social and behavioral reasons. When you do not want certain students to sit together, separate them. Before going to an assembly, say, "Please wait for me to place you before you take your seat."

Seating assignments will help expedite roll taking, which should be done without interrupting students during the "bellwork" assignment. (See page 135.)

Seating assignments are not permanent. Use small sticky notes with students' names on them. This will allow you to easily move a student.

Seating assignments and seating arrangements should not become issues in the classroom. **Student success and the instructional program are your major focus.**

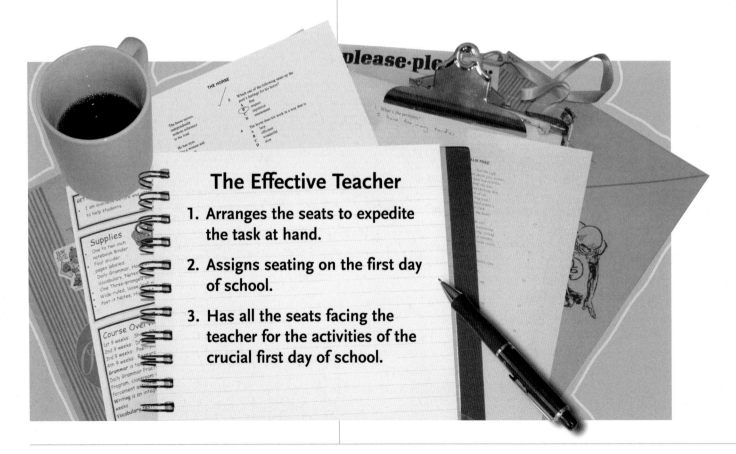

### The Effective Teacher

1. **Arranges the seats to expedite the task at hand.**

2. **Assigns seating on the first day of school.**

3. **Has all the seats facing the teacher for the activities of the crucial first day of school.**

## Your First Priority When Class Starts

> Your very first priority when the class starts is to get the students to work.

**Have an assignment ready and posted when the students enter the classroom.**

**M**any large department stores have a greeter as you enter the building. They welcome you with a nice smile and say, "Would you like a basket?" and all but push one into your hands. You take it because they want you to have this basket, and it's big, because they want you to fill the big basket and spend and spend even more. And you feel so good because your presence as a potential customer has been acknowledged.

Effective teachers do the same. They greet students at the door with a smile and say, "Here's your assignment."

**The students take it and get to work, right away. That's why these teachers and their students are so successful.**

This is no fantasy. It happens every day in thousands of classrooms. The students walk in, sit down, and get to work. No one even tells them to do this. In some countries it is the teacher who goes from class to class. Regardless, the students are in the room and they all know what to do.

## Daily and In the Same Place

**Y**our first priority is not to take roll; it is to get the students to work immediately. It is no different in the private sector, even for the students who work part time. Workers do not stand around waiting for directions or asking questions like, "What do you want me to do?" They are expected to begin working at the appointed hour.

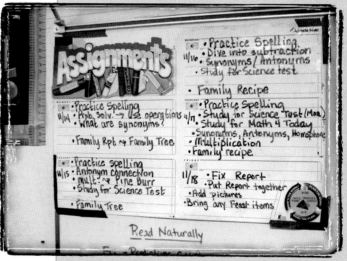

Assignments should be posted daily, always in the same place.

> ### Sample Assignments
>
> **For the students to get to work immediately, an assignment must be posted.**
>
> #### Sample Elementary Assignment
>
> SPELLING:
>
> 1. Number your paper from 1 to 15.
> 2. Take a practice spelling test.
> 3. Exchange papers with your spelling partner.
> 4. Correct tests.
> 5. Write words missed five times each.
>
> #### Sample Secondary Assignment
>
> 1. Review criteria for haiku. Use chart on board, or see page 76 in text.
> 2. Compose a haiku about winter.
> 3. Give it a one-word title. The title cannot be used in the body of the haiku.

When class begins, you can easily get students to work if three criteria have been met:

1. They have an assignment.
2. They know where to find the assignment.
3. They know why they are to do the assignment.

**Common sense and research on the effective classroom emphatically tells you to POST YOUR ASSIGNMENTS EVERY DAY!**

**Post the assignments in the same place every day.** Even if it is the same assignment, post it. Once they know the assignment is in the same place every day, there is no need to waste class time for students to ask, "What is the assignment?" or "What am I supposed to do?"

> ### Assignments Are to Be Posted Daily and Consistently
>
> 1. Post an assignment before the students enter the room.
> 2. Post the assignment in the same location every day.

## Are We Doing Anything Today?

The ineffective teacher keeps the assignment a mystery until it is announced. **It may be announced in different ways and posted in different places each day.**

Sometimes there may be no assignment, even though the students ask for one. This may be because the teacher does not know what should be done, what students are to learn, or how to teach it.

You can always identify classes where no assignments are posted. Ineffective teachers say things like this:

"Where did we leave off yesterday?"
(Translation: I have no control.)
"Open your books so that we can take turns reading."
(For what reason?)
"Sit quietly and do the worksheet."
(To master what?)
"Let's watch this movie."
(To learn what?)
"You can have a free study period."
(Translation: I do not have an assignment for you. I am unprepared.)

**The textbook is not the curriculum.** Having students fill in worksheets to keep them busy and quiet is not the curriculum. Teachers who have no curriculum follow the textbook, page by page, cover to cover, and look for busywork for the students. When this happens, you have students who walk into the classroom and say things like this:

"Are you going to show us a video?"
"Are you going to read to us?"
"Are you going to lecture to us?"
"Are you going to let us have a study period?"

Or worse yet,

"Are we going to do anything today?"
"Are we going to do anything important today?"
"Did I miss anything important while I was absent?"

In classes where students make comments like these, they take no responsibility for their work. The teacher is the only responsible person in the classroom. That's why they ask the teacher what is going to happen. They look to the teacher for direction, for entertainment, and for work.

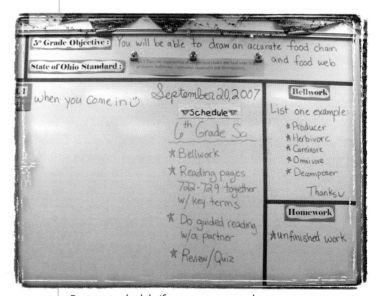

Post your schedule if you want your students ready to learn.

## One Month of Instruction Lost

**Shirley Hord, of the Southwest Educational Development Laboratory, discovered that 3 to 17 minutes are wasted at the beginning of each class period each school year.** That is, from the time the first student enters the classroom until instruction actually begins, wasted time can range from 9 percent to 32 percent of total class time.

Assuming ten minutes are wasted per classroom period, that translates into one hour for a six-period school day. Multiplying that by a 180-day school year equals 180 hours wasted during a school year. **Given a six-hour school day schedule, this equates to one month of school wasted each year.**

Policymakers talk about extending the school year. There is no need to extend the school year, because

**Effective teachers know how to guard instructional time as their most precious resource, packing as much as they can into class time.**

## It's All In How You Start

In tennis you are allowed two serves for each point. How you play the first serve will allow you to dictate the point.

In knitting, how you begin the first row will determine your success with the rest of the stitches. In fact, you can expect to start all over again if you find out later that you began incorrectly.

In dating, know that the first sentence out of your mouth will determine if you will be allowed a second sentence!

**To prepare the students for the day's instruction, they should be told to enter the classroom and begin with a morning or class routine.**

The effective teacher

- Has a bellwork assignment already posted before the students enter the classroom.
- Posts it in the same location every day.

### A Sample Typical Morning Routine

- Quietly walk into the classroom.
- Remove coat or jacket. Hang it up.
- Empty backpack or book bag.
- Have two sharpened pencils, books, and materials ready.
- Hand in all completed homework.
- Read the agenda for the day.
- **Begin BELLWORK assignment on your own.**

**Opening assignments can be posted on the chalkboard, a bulletin board, or a transparency, or can be distributed when the students enter the classroom.** If you are a floating, migrant, or resource teacher who has to move from room to room, have the assignment on a transparency, on a flip chart, or on your laptop ready to display the second you enter the classroom.

In classes such as physical education and K–1, the assignment does not have to be posted. If it is not, the procedure is rehearsed and is repeated daily so that when students come to class they just know what to do.

The P.E. teachers of Wilson Memorial High School, Virginia.

Effective teachers have different names for these opening assignments. These are some common terms for this activity:

| | |
|---|---|
| Assignment | Energizer |
| Bell Ringer | Opening Activity |
| Bellwork | Prime Time |
| Do Now | Sponge Activity |
| DOL (Daily Oral Language) | WOD (Word of the Day) |

## Opening Assignments

For a DOL, one teacher wrote the following on the board:

*Wendy she said me and josh was lying but he wasn't*

The students are to reorder the words to form a sentence.

**A teacher in Arizona has a set of bellwork assignments prepared for the entire school year.** These are on transparencies, one for each day, and are stored in a binder on the cart under the transparency projector. Each night before she leaves, she places the next day's assignment on the projector ready for the next morning. She also has a student trained to turn the projector on if she is late coming into the classroom.

As you develop your own set of assignments, (or purchase them commercially[1]) keep them so you will have them ready for the following year. The best bellwork assignments are those related to that day's work, with a transition or a motivation to what is to follow. A common bellwork in elementary schools, especially K–4, is silent reading until the lesson begins.

Make this a productive time for your students. If you blow this prime time with nonproductive tasks such as roll taking or paper shuffling, you will jeopardize the success of the entire class period.

[1] www.dailybite.com

### Daily Geography Practice

Debra S. Lindsey of Alabama teaches fifth grade science and social studies in 90-minute blocks. She uses a bellwork activity, "Daily Geography Practice." It is consistent, so the students do not have to ask questions and will know what to do everyday.

*Daily Geography Practice* is commercially produced by Evan-Moor Educational Publishers and can be found at a teacher supply store or on the Internet. Each week the students have a map of the week and two questions to answer daily. The students know that the procedure is to answer in complete sentences and use correct grammar.

Debra says that at the end of the year, not only do the students have excellent map skills, they also are writing great sentences in her subject areas on daily work and tests.

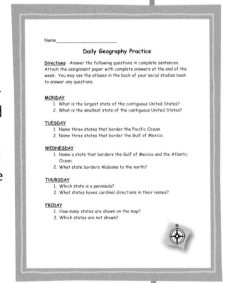

**Bellwork assignments are not graded.** Do not begin a class by threatening the students. A bellwork assignment is a procedure and procedures are not rules. Thus, they have no consequences or punishments.

## Effective Schools Have Schoolwide Procedures

Wanda Bradford is the principal at Harris Elementary School in Bakersfield, California. She showed various parts from the video series, *The Effective Teacher*, to her staff. She did not mandate anything; rather, her teachers chose to start each day with a bellwork assignment. Thus, this became a consistent school wide procedure.

She reports, "We start each day with a structured opening. Each teacher has a daily opening and the students start the day on task." She describes the success of her school in a poem:

*Each day begins with learning
when students come to class.
And without a lot of chatting,
they start the day on task.*

*With assignments clearly posted
students need not be told,
to quiet down and get to work
while the teacher takes the roll.*

*If daily routines are followed
less wasted time is spent.
Classes will run smoothly
with great class management.*

*Research has been proven
achievement gains will rise,
when effective teachers start the day
with time that's maximized.*

Wanda Bradford and her students from Harris Elementary.

The goal of her poem is student achievement; the teachers achieved this by using routines to manage their classrooms.

Think about Harris School in Bakersfield. Better yet, think about your own school. Imagine . . .

- The students walk into a class, sit down, and immediately get to work. No one tells them what to do; they know where to find the assignment.

- They go to their next class, sit down, and get to work.

- And on to the next class

- The next class

- And the next

And this becomes the prevailing culture of the school. The next year the students go from 3rd to 4th grade, 6th to 7th grade, and 11th to 12th grade, and this is the prevailing culture in the school district.

### Just Think . . .

- Just think how much easier life would be if the teachers supported each other with routines that were consistent from classroom to classroom.

- Just think what the achievement of these students would be if this were the prevailing culture of the school.

- Just think how effective the schools would be if this were the prevailing culture of the entire district.

To accomplish all of this, no money is spent. No costly, faddish programs are installed. Nothing is controversial and the concept works regardless of what grade is taught, what subject is taught, and what educational philosophy is espoused by the district.

---

### Ready to Show Up and Work

Daniel Furman,[2] of the Fund for Colorado's Future, reports that employers complained that high school graduates "would not come into an interview dressed appropriately. They would not come prepared to talk about the job they were interviewing for.

"If they were lucky enough to land a job, they didn't realize they had to show up to work on time Monday through Friday."

---

[2] Olson, L. (June 12, 2007). "What Does 'Ready' Mean?" *Education Week.*

---

**GoBe**

### The Workers Start the Day

In a fifth grade class and a high school business class, students start the class, rather than the teacher. To see how this is done, go to the **Go**ing **Be**yond folder for Chapter 15 at EffectiveTeaching.com.

The key is that the staff works together as a family. This creates a sense of consistency, making life so much easier for everyone. And, most importantly, student achievement is increased because there is more time for instruction and learning.

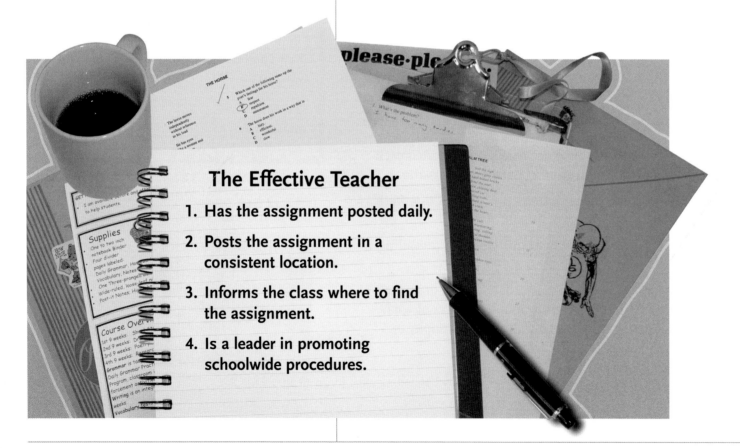

### The Effective Teacher

1. Has the assignment posted daily.

2. Posts the assignment in a consistent location.

3. Informs the class where to find the assignment.

4. Is a leader in promoting schoolwide procedures.

## The Results of Effective Roll Taking

The effective teacher starts the class immediately with an assignment, not roll taking.

Simplify the roll-taking process so it does not take away from instructional time.

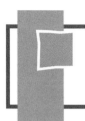ecky Hughes, a Kansas band teacher, doesn't even take roll. Each of her students' names is on a musical note, Velcroed to a chart. When students enter the classroom, they know the procedure. They take their names and put them into the envelope next to the chart.

A designated student is already hitting "C" on the piano and everyone tunes up in their seats. When the bell rings, Becky raises her baton; when the bell stops ringing, she brings the baton down. They play. No yelling at the students to get into their seats. Becky offers a smile and they play, with energy, the school fight song.

While this is happening, a student monitor looks at the notes left on the chart and submits the attendance record for her.

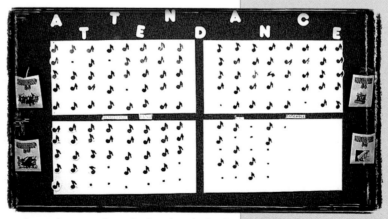

Becky Hughes is ready on the first day of school.

**Heidi Olive, a teacher in Nevada, knows that the first five minutes of class are critical.** She has either a preview or review activity posted. The format of the activity varies. Students might be asked to write a reaction to a quote or newspaper article, copy a timeline, brainstorm emotions felt in response to a piece of music, or answer questions on the previous night's reading assignment. **Whatever the opening activity, its primary purpose is to engage students the minute they walk through the door** and to provide her an opportunity to handle attendance and other housekeeping duties. The opening activity also provides a jumping-off point for the day's lesson.

It's obvious that structuring the opening of class is critical for student involvement the rest of the school day. It's like the opening of a movie—it needs to capture your attention and keep you in your seat. If there is no opening-of-class activity, the students will be out of their seats, waiting for the class to begin.

Starting on time is a common procedure in the adult world. Businesses open on time. Weddings, meetings, ball games, and television programs all start on time. At least, they are supposed to, just as classes are supposed to start on time.

## A Strange Sense of Attendance

In our nanosecond-driven world there are some teachers who are still taking roll at the beginning of each day or period, wasting five or more minutes of student learning time and arguing with the class as to who is absent.

Arguing? Yes. Students have a strange sense of attendance. They believe that if they are anywhere on campus, or even within a mile of the school site, they are present; whereas, most teachers consider a student absent if a warm body is not in an appropriate seat.

When this teacher comes to a name in the roll book that gets no response or sees that a seat is empty, the teacher says, "Ah, Ernie is absent," and is about to mark Ernie absent. Then a voice, maybe more than one, shouts out—without permission—"Ernie is not absent. He's coming down the hall. He'll be here." Or "I saw him in the library. There's a long line. He'll be here."

Now what is this teacher going to do? It's the teacher against the class. The class says that Ernie is present on the campus, but the teacher does not see Ernie in his seat. She marks Ernie absent, nonetheless.

And with four absences in the class, the scene repeats itself four times. Each time, the noise level rises and more on-task time is wasted.

Or, this teacher reads every name from the roll book and the students respond, "Here or Present." Then someone says, "Hey." The class giggles.

"Yo." The whole class breaks up. But the teacher, glancing up for a second, goes right on.

**The students quickly learn that the teacher does nothing when inappropriate behavior occurs.** The students could care less about the attendance process, so the noise level gets louder and louder. This is followed by frustrated demands to quiet the class down. And class hasn't even started yet.

By comparison, the effective teacher has a classroom in which the students all know how to begin.

**Please do not take roll at the very beginning of the class.**

> **Roll taking is not the responsibility of the students, so do not take up class time with the process.**

**GoBe**

**Attendance Keeper**

**Keeping attendance does not have to be a time-consuming task.** See the **Go**ing **Be**yond folder for Chapter 16 at EffectiveTeaching.com and read how Sarah Jondahl organizes roll taking.

## The Student Who Is Absent

*I have a procedure for roll taking and for students who are absent.* I have three students trained to take the roll on a rotating basis. They do this while the students are completing their opening assignment.

*If a student is absent, the roll taker completes a form that says, "Makeup work for Mr. Hockenberry," clips it to the work for the day that has already been prepared, and places it in an envelope along one of the walls marked with the appropriate period.*

*A returning absent student does not come to see me.* The procedure is that when absent students return, they obtain their work from the envelope and ask one of the three roll takers if something is not understood before coming to me for help. They seldom do, and class proceeds quickly with the lesson for the day.

Ed Hockenberry
Midlothian Middle School, Virginia

## Effective Roll Taking In an Effective Class

**T**he effective teacher starts the class immediately with an assignment, not roll taking. The effective teacher knows how to develop a classroom in which the students responsibly start working on their own. Effectively taught students know the following:

- How to enter the room quickly and courteously
- How to go to their seats and take out their materials
- Where to look for their assignments
- To begin their work immediately

**There are many ways to take roll; however, your first priority is to get the students on task.**

As soon as the tardy bell rings, your first task is to scan the room. It is not to take roll, but rather to look for students who are not at work. You quietly signal these students to get to work immediately. Use a firm smile and a hand gesture that clearly indicates that you want them to work.

They know where the assignment is posted, and they know what to do. You are maximizing academic learning time.

As soon as the class is at work, proceed to do whatever administrative chores are necessary. Taking roll is usually one of these.

### The Outcomes of Ineffective Roll Taking

- Each time the class yells out a response, the noise level gets higher.

- Confrontation builds up between the class and the teacher over whether or not a student is absent.

- Valuable minutes are wasted.

- Many students sit, bored, while precious learning time is wasted on a bookkeeping chore that really does not involve the class.

# Three Ways to Take Roll Efficiently and Effectively

**T**here are many other ways to take roll. **Regardless of which method you use to take roll, you should take roll quickly and quietly without disturbing the class.**

1. Look at your class and refer to your seating chart. Mark whoever is absent. Do not involve the class; they are on-task.

2. Have folders or something personal in a box at the door. When the students come in, they are to take their folders, go to their seats, and get to work on the posted assignment. After the students are at work, you look in the box. You see three folders left, note the names, and mark these students absent.

3. Similar to Becky Hughes' procedure on page 131, some teachers have each student's name on a clothespin. Clip these pins to a cutout, chart, or a seasonal object like a jack-o'-lantern or heart. When the students come in, they move their clothespins indicating they are in attendance. After the students are at work, you note which pins have not been moved and mark these students absent. Assign a student the task of transferring, at an appropriate time, the clothespins to the original position.

Other administrative tasks can be accomplished at the same time, such as indicating whether or not lunch will be purchased.

Each morning, the students take their cards out of the apple and place them on the magnetic board to show lunch preference for the day. At a glance, the teacher is able to take attendance and do the lunch count while the students are doing their morning warm ups.

**The research is emphatic.** The more time students are on task, the better their achievement and learning. The effective teacher knows how to get the students on task immediately, after which preparing the attendance count for the administration is done in private.

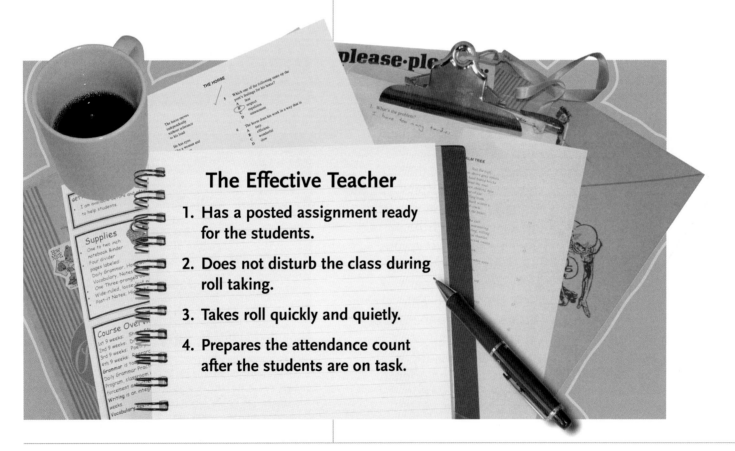

## The Effective Teacher

1. Has a posted assignment ready for the students.

2. Does not disturb the class during roll taking.

3. Takes roll quickly and quietly.

4. Prepares the attendance count after the students are on task.

## It's Really a Grade Record Book

An organized grade record book allows you to assess for the learning of every student at any given moment.

## THE KEY IDEA

A grade record book must show the results and progress of each student at all times.

There was a time when students would come to class and sit passively in rows, listening to a teacher. The only activity might be some reading and writing, done quietly and personally.

The students were never told the purpose of the lesson, nor did they have any clue as to why they were doing it. They would never dare to question the teacher's authority or ask, "Why do we have to do this?"

Tests were given at intervals governed by the grading period—not to assess for learning. The test questions were rather arbitrary because teachers never explained to the students what they were studying.

Then, the teacher gave a grade. Yes, the teacher was the Supreme Determiner as to what grades would be given to each student. Some teachers even proudly said, "I only give out one A and three B's." Although it was useless to argue about grades, there was lots of arguing from many of the students—and parents. The teacher actually had no idea what was being covered. Yet, "Will I be able to cover all of this before the semester is over?" was the major concern of numerous teachers.

**COVERAGE was the teacher's mission; not STUDENT LEARNING.**

With a teaching system such as this, a grade book was necessary only to record the attendance and the test grade given by the teacher. The grades were averaged for the report card, and life continued on for the ineffective teacher who was focused only on covering the textbook.

**GoBe**

### The Fallacy of Textbooks

Covering the textbook is not effective teaching. Read why in the **Go**ing **Be**yond folder for Chapter 17 at EffectiveTeaching.com.

## What Kind of a Grade Record System?

For the effective teacher, recording what and how well students are doing is essential in assessing and helping each student reach maximum learning capacity.

The question is, "Do I record grades and records in a traditional book or use a software program?"

The answer may be both. If you live in fear that the grade book will be lost, it's nice to have an electronic version. However, network systems sometimes go down, and computers can crash. It's comforting to know you have at least the minimum records in a hard-copy book. Many teachers use a software program, but keep a grade record book—just in case.

## A Traditional Grade Record Book

From Day 1, you will need a book in which to keep student records. It must be ready before you see a single class. This book is typically called a "grade book," and it comes in all different sizes, shapes, and configurations. **A grade book should more correctly be called a student record book or a grade record book.** A grade record book contains far more than grades. It is used to keep various records about each student.

**The problem with many grade books is they have only one or two lines on which to record information for a student.**

> **Record books organize essential information for immediate retrieval.**

Thus, you have these problems:

- You have only enough space to show one record, such as attendance.

- To record additional information, you have to turn to another page and possibly write all the names again. You are constantly flipping pages.

- If the number of students in your class exceeds the number of lines on a page, you have to repeat the information at the top of every page.

- The major problem comes when you need a progress report or a summary for the grading period. Because there is only one line to record all information for each student, you must sift through attendance, homework, projects, tests, and anything else you may record about the student to determine the student's progress. As a result, progress is not readily apparent at a glance.

If you are planning to buy your own grade record book, you must first determine how you will be grading and what records you will be keeping so you will know what to look for when you shop.

**It is imperative that you decide before you begin the school year just what you want to record.** People in other professions do the same thing:

- Accountants set up the categories on a ledger before entering numbers.

- Businesspeople title the columns on a spreadsheet before entering data.

- Statisticians name the columns in a baseball box score so the results can be entered in the right places as the game progresses.

- Brides-to-be design a chart to record information about the people coming to the wedding.

---

**Designed properly, a grade record book should let you see each student's RESULTS and PROGRESS immediately.**

---

You must determine what you want for each student; for example:

| | |
|---|---|
| Attendance | Project grades |
| Homework assignments | Extra-credit work |
| Classroom work | Class participation |
| Test grades | Classroom behavior |
| Skills mastered | Cumulative progress |

## Keeping the Three Basic Records

To keep good student records, you probably need three or even four lines after each student's name. Because most commercial grade books have only one or two lines after each name, you may have record-keeping problems if you use an inadequate grade book.

> The **three basic records** in a grade record book each require a separate line:
>
> 1. **Attendance**
> 2. **Scores**
> 3. **Running Total**

### First Line: Attendance

An attendance record is probably mandated by the administration, if not by the school board. Attendance is a fact of life in most of our everyday endeavors. Schools are paid, people are paid, and students are graded by their presence on a job or in school. So make the recording of attendance as efficient and as unobtrusive as possible. (See Chapter 16.)

**The four common attendance records you need to keep are "present," "absent," "unexcused," and "tardy."**

1. **Present.** Usually, nothing is noted in the space. This tells you that the student was in class on this day.

Grade books with one or two lines per student may not have enough space for all the information you wish to record.

2. **Absent.** Typically, an **A** is noted in the space, reminding you that the student was absent on this date. If the student brings a note that excuses the absence, you may want to draw a diagonal line through the **A̸**. This tells you that you have seen a note or received authorization from the office, excusing the absence. If you do not see a diagonal line, it means that you are still waiting to see the excuse.

3. **Unexcused.** If no note is presented explaining the absence, place a check (✔) or a breve (˘), the mark used to indicate a short vowel sound, above the **A**.

   An unexcused absence is simply one for which the student does not have a note of explanation, typically from a parent, a doctor, or another teacher. In some schools, you will determine if the absence is excused or not. In other schools, the attendance office will process this for you.

   How you treat an unexcused absence may be determined by school policy. Ask the administration. A school may allow only so many unexcused absences before administrative action is taken. A good school will notify the home at once if an unexcused absence or cut has been determined.

   Also, ask other teachers how they treat unexcused absences. **In most cases, an unexcused absence does not release a student from responsibility for missed work or assignments.** The student must make up the work.

   An unexcused absence might mean the teacher is not obligated to help the student make up the work; for instance, the teacher may have to explain to the student:

   > *You cut the class, so you must accept responsibility for having missed the lecture, movie, or activity. You must find the material you missed on your own. That's the consequence when you do not show up for class.*

4. **Tardy.** This is typically denoted with a **T**. If the student has a pass excusing the tardiness, erase the **A** you recorded for that student earlier. If the student does not have a pass, the student is tardy. Erase the **A** and write a **T**, or just write a **T** over the **A**. Find out what the school policy is concerning tardiness. You may be asked to refer the student to the office after a certain number of tardy arrivals.

For a stress-free way to take care of assignments missed during absences, refer to Ed Hockenberry's procedures on page 134.

### Second Line: Scores

You really need a second line to record the results of individual assignments, such as tests, projects, papers, worksheets, and homework. You can show results using whatever system you choose, in letter grade or numerical form. However, a numerical system is much better if you want to weight each score differently or if you want a running progress report.

### Third Line: Running Total

Teachers are bombarded with requests for results on students' progress. You will get calls from parents, requests from the counseling department or the main office, forms to complete for determining extracurricular activity eligibility, and students' questions about their own progress. **An up-to-date overview of the progress of each student must be available at all times.**

With a three-line grade record book, as you enter each score on line 2, add it to the previous score on line 3 and update the running total on line 3. The running total allows immediate access to any student's cumulative grade. **With a three-line grade record book, details of a student's progress are available at any time.**

With a three-line grade record book, you have a running progress report and can turn your grades in instantly. While all others are gnashing their teeth, "trying to get their grades in," you can have time to explore other interests, go to the gym, take in a movie, or rest with a good book because **you have a grade record book that shows the results and progress of each student at all times.**

## "The Three-Line Attendance and Grade Record Book"

Merle J. Whaley is a teacher who was frustrated with the one-line grade book supplied by his district. So he told his wife, "I want to make a grade book anyone could understand that would also show each student's progress immediately." After two years and many changes, *The Three-Line Attendance and Grade Record Book* became more than a dream.

He says, "I finally had a book and a method of doing grades that easily displayed a students' records and progress in seconds. With three lines per student, I could now have attendance or essential skills on the first line. The second line could be used for all of the student's scores, such as daily work, quizzes, projects, and test scores. The very important third line would show a running total for each student. **Now when parents call or visit the school, the progress is available in seconds.**"

Whaley's grade record book also has a tear-off top to each page. You only need to record the date or assignment ONCE at the top of one of the pages for all the students having the same activity. All unused tops are torn off and index tabs are applied so that you can have fast access to any class. For instance, many teachers will have several classes of 30, 40, or more students with the same activities. The tops of the pages are torn off to allow entering activities, dates, and possible scores one time, saving a tremendous amount of time on grade record book work. Each grade book has detailed examples.

Whaley has developed a software program that will print out the parent name, student, phone, and ID data. Without handwriting or typing the names for each grading period, the data are printed directly to his loose-leaf version of the three-line grade book pages or are printed on a label designed for the bound version.

All of his products are available from

Whaley Gradebook Co., Inc.

2521 Weslo Court    Grand Junction, CO  81505

Telephone:  970-241-7777    Facsimile:  970-241-0016

Internet:  www.whaleygradebook.com

Email:  office@whaleygradebook.com

With a three-line grade book, you can show each student's attendance, score, and running total.

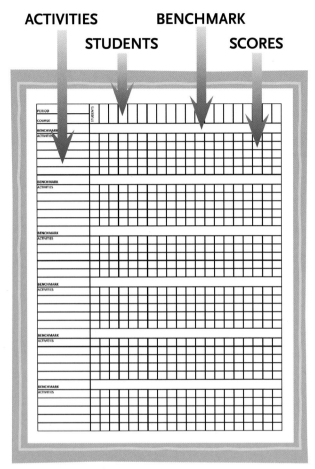

**ACTIVITIES**     **BENCHMARK**

**STUDENTS**     **SCORES**

Grade record book for benchmark scoring.

## An Electronic Grade Record Program

imes have changed. Assessment for student learning is now the forte of effective teachers. In fact, effective teachers gather in groups to discuss specific students who need help, just as a group of doctors would gather to assess and plan the best treatment for a patient.

Like a doctor's detailed record of a patient, a detailed record-keeping system is necessary to help each student succeed. For this to happen, an electronic grade record program may be what you need. You need a program you and your colleagues can access instantly that will provide on-the-spot feedback about a student.

The school or school district may already have a grade record program installed. If not, here are some resources where you can find dozens of such programs:

- www.educational-software-directory.net/teacher/gradebook
- www.gradebooks4teachers.com/

As you will see in Unit D, for a student to master what you want the student to learn, you will need a grade record program that allows you to see the student's grades on the activities that are tied to the benchmarks. For this you will need a grade record program for benchmark scoring.

If you are looking for a personal electronic grade record program, consider that you may want to record:

- activities (lab work, art work, technology work)
- writing assignments
- homework
- classwork
- participation
- projects (library research, term papers)
- performance records (singing, reciting, dancing)
- bonus points for enrichment activities
- scores tied to benchmark's test grades

Your electronic record program needs to be

1. user-friendly to learn and to enter data.

2. simple in how you can manipulate the data to help students stay on track.

3. able to provide instant and accurate presentation of grades for the entire class, by student, including current standing in the course.

4. able to accommodate online reporting from home.

5. connected to every computer if you have a networked classroom.

6. easily switched from individual to group instruction.

A good grade record program will allow you to diagnose students' weaknesses and tailor instruction to their needs.

It will also allow teachers, students, and parents to access records, grades, and assignments and to communicate with one another outside the classroom.

Obviously, the software must offer a layer of protection so that only invited members can enter the site. Many schools have grade record programs set up so the family at home can view only their child's scores and attendance.

Students like online grade record systems. For many students, visual references are easier to understand and remember.

What student hasn't repeatedly asked, "How am I doing?"

**Students tend to be more reflective and better problem solvers
when they can see their own record in private
and post their reactions or reflections online,
rather than being uncomfortable in the classroom.**

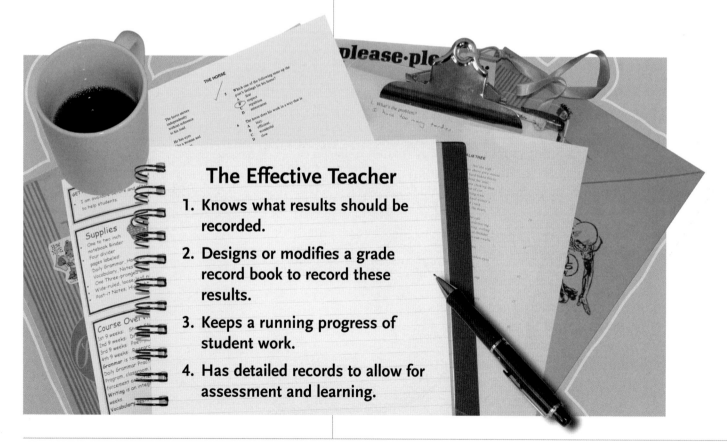

## The Effective Teacher

1. Knows what results should be recorded.

2. Designs or modifies a grade record book to record these results.

3. Keeps a running progress of student work.

4. Has detailed records to allow for assessment and learning.

## Discipline With a Plan

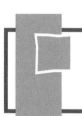

> If you do not have a plan,
> then you are planning to fail.

Have a discipline plan and then work the plan.

**W**hen it comes to handling behavior problems in the classroom, there are two kinds of teachers—**reactive and proactive.**

**The ineffective teacher or the teacher who doesn't yet know what to do is a REACTIVE teacher.** With no organized classroom structure (as described in the first 17 chapters of this book), this teacher **reacts** to every problem with yelling, screaming, punishments, threats, and coercion to whip the classroom into compliance. The reactive teacher goes home angry, tired, and stressed out.

**The effective teacher is a PROACTIVE teacher.** Because 80 percent of classroom problems are caused by ineffective teachers, the effective teacher has a proactive plan to **prevent** problems from occurring. **The effective teacher knows that the #1 problem in the classroom is not discipline; it is the lack of procedures and routines—the lack of a plan that organizes a classroom for academic success.** The proactive teacher knows how to prevent problems and thus have a successful classroom. This teacher can go home at the end of the day happy, with the knowledge that students have learned.

### I Did Not Even Have a System

*I was going insane and then I realized that I did not have a fair system or even any system in place . . . .*

*My students, after we had the plan in effect, commented on how quiet the room was and how easily they could do their work. The principal commented about the plan and said how pleased he was to see quiet, working, behaved students!*

*As for me, I was thinking of quitting teaching because I was so uptight—until you shared a plan with me.*

Sheila
Lethbridge, Alberta, Canada

> It is highly recommended that you read
> Chapters 18, 19, and 20 in one sitting.
>
> **A well-managed classroom will minimize your discipline problems.**

# Continuum of Discipline Plans

**You will never find a foolproof discipline system that works automatically.** If you have not implemented Chapters 1 to 17, 19 and 20, it's important to know that

this chapter used in isolation<br>will not solve your behavior problems in the classroom.

Discipline plans are like diet plans. Most diet plans do not work, because people are looking for quick-fix diet solutions without having to change their eating patterns.

It's the same with discipline plans. There are dozens of them, yet most do not work unless you are willing to commit and work at a classroom management plan that prevents problems from occurring in the first place.

There are many different discipline plans. They all have their good and bad points, but they are all plans. Today, we are serving a student population with diverse skills, languages, and needs, so it is obvious that one plan will not work in all situations. In fact, effective teachers may use two different discipline plans for two different kinds of classes and change plans year-to-year.

There is no such thing as a one-size-fits-all discipline plan. As part of your professional growth, you will probably move from one kind of plan to another. It's OK to change plans in the course of the school year.

**Discipline plans form a continuum.** They range from those in which the teacher is in charge, with rules, consequences, and rewards, to those in which the student is totally responsible and there are no rules, consequences, or rewards. **The important thing is that you have a hard copy of a plan for all to see and that you work that plan.**

As teachers become more proficient, they often progress from one type of plan to another. Initially, the teacher is totally in charge. They then move toward a discipline plan in which the teacher and each student jointly set limits; eventually, many teachers adopt a plan in which individual students are allowed responsibility.

## Typical Teacher and Student Roles in Various Discipline Plans

### Teacher Is in Charge (149)

Class is teacher-directed.
Teacher is hands-on.
Student is offered no choices.
Teacher provides consequences.
Teacher uses intervention and isolation.
Teacher tells what is to be done.
Classroom climate can be tense.
Classroom has limits without freedom.

### Both Student and Teacher Are in Charge (158)

Teacher and student work cooperatively.
Student is offered structured choices.
Teacher asks questions, discusses, and solves problems
    with student.
Teacher intervenes and agreements are reached.
Teacher and student together set limits by establishing a
    classroom code of conduct.
Classroom has freedom within limits.

### Student in Charge (162)

Class is student-centered.
Teacher is hands-off.
Student has many choices.
Teacher uses nondirective statements.
Student is responsible for conduct.
Teacher listens.
Student is taught responsibility.
Classroom climate can be chaotic.
Classroom has freedom without limits.

(Turn to the page numbers above to read the details for each type of plan.)

## Discipline Plan Where <u>Teacher Is in Charge</u> (page 148)

## Discipline Plans Have Rules or Guidelines

The basic structure for a discipline plan where the teacher is in charge has three parts:

1. **Rules:** What the student is expected to follow.

2. **Consequences:** What the student encounters if a rule is broken.

3. **Rewards:** What the student receives for appropriate behavior.

**To have a safe and effective learning environment, first establish firm rules that students are expected to follow.** The rules should be discussed so the students know that the rules are not orders or punishments. The purpose of rules is to set limits or boundaries, just as there are rules in games to maintain order.

**Clear rules promote consistency in the classroom.** Students prefer knowing the rules, consequences, and rewards rather than having a teacher who arbitrarily changes or makes up new rules to fit the moment. Ineffective teachers make up rules as a reaction to problems, which makes the rules feel punitive. Setting rules before a problem arises allows the class to have an understanding of the expected behaviors in the classroom.

- Rules immediately create a work-oriented atmosphere in which students know what you expect from them.

- After thorough deliberation, decide on your rules, and write them down or post them before the first day of school.

- Clearly communicate in both verbal and written form to your students what you expect as appropriate behavior.

It is easier to maintain good behavior than to change inappropriate behavior that has become established.

**What Can I Do?**

**It is ineffective to ask, "What can I do to this kid?"** It is much more effective to have a discipline plan (Chapter 18) and a classroom management plan (Chapters 19 and 20) to proactively take care of problems.

## The Two Kinds of Rules

**R**ules are used to set limits. Students expect teachers to give directions and set boundaries. Limits are important in school because different kinds of behavior are expected or tolerated by different teachers. For example, wandering around the room may be permitted by some teachers but not others.

**Students need to feel that someone is in control and responsible for their environment—someone who not only sets limits but also maintains them.** School must be a safe and protected environment where students can come to learn without fear.

**The function of a rule is to prevent or encourage behavior by clearly stating student expectations.** There are two kinds of rules: **General** and **Specific**. General rules are very broad; whereas, specific rules are precise.

### How Many Rules?

Have you ever noticed that your phone number, credit card, social security number, vehicle license number, and ZIP code are written in groups of five numbers or less? That's because people find it easier to remember numbers in groups of three to five.

- Limit your rules to a number that you and the students can readily remember—never more than five.

- If you need more than five rules, do not post more than five at any one time.

- The rules need not cover all aspects of behavior in the classroom.

- It is the teacher's prerogative to replace one rule with another at any time.

- As a new rule becomes necessary, replace an older one with it. The rule you replace can be retained as an "unwritten rule," which the students have learned. The students are still responsible for the one you have replaced.

**General Rules.** Encompass a wide range of behaviors:

- Respect others.

- Be polite and helpful.

- Keep the room clean.

**Advantage:** Addresses numerous behavior concepts and expectations in broad terms.

**Disadvantage:** Must be explained. For instance, students must be told that respecting others includes no hitting, no stealing, no tattling, and so on.

**General rules are more successful when used by effective veteran teachers who have learned how to encourage good classroom behavior over the years.** These teachers know how to calmly give the student a signal, a wave of the hand, or a stare and the student behaves.

**Specific Rules.** Typically focus on particular behaviors:

- In class when the bell rings.

- No offensive language.

- Hands, feet, and objects to yourself.

**Advantage:** Clearly state the expected student behavior without ambiguity.

**Disadvantage:** Need to limit rules to no more than five, as explained in "How Many Rules?" on the previous page.

**Specific rules are generally better for the newer teacher or the experienced teacher who is looking for a better discipline system.** You can always move from specific rules to general rules during the school year as students learn about your expectations for their behavior.

---

**These Are Not Good Rules**

- Academic procedures and performance should not appear on your list of rules. Such things as doing homework, writing in pencil, ink or typing, and turning in assignments fall into the realm of procedures (Chapter 20) and academic performance (Unit D). Your discipline plan should be concerned with behavior, not academic work.

- If possible, state rules positively. But recognize that sometimes a negative rule can be more direct, understandable, and incontestable:

  No cursing or swearing.
  No smoking.
  No fighting on the playground.

---

## What Should My Rules Be?

Some people call rules guidelines or expectations. Regardless, be sure you know the difference between a rule (Chapter 18) and a procedure (Chapters 19 and 20). **Use rules to state your specific behavior expectations, not what work you want performed.**

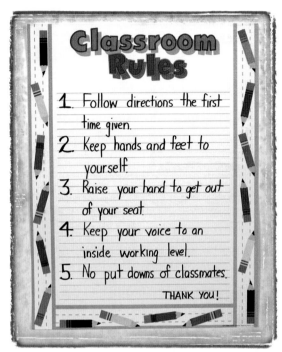

Classroom rules should be posted for the first day of school, with a copy ready for distribution to each student.

Here are some examples of specific rules that you may want to consider for your discipline plan.

**Universal Specific Rules**
1. Follow directions the first time they are given and thereafter.
2. Raise your hand and wait for permission to speak.
3. Stay in your seat unless you have permission to do otherwise.
4. Keep hands, feet, and objects to yourself.
5. No cursing or teasing.

**Specific Rules for Elementary Grades**
1. Wait for directions with no talking.
2. Eyes front when the teacher is talking.
3. Change tasks quickly and quietly.
4. Complete the morning routine.
5. Report directly to the assigned area.

**Specific Rules for High School**
1. Be in your seat when the bell rings.
2. Bring all books and materials to class.
3. No personal grooming during class.
4. Sit in your assigned seat daily.
5. Follow directions the first time they are given.

**Specific Rules for the Playground**
1. Swing only forward and backward on the swings.
2. Do not throw ice or snow at anyone.
3. Sliding paths must be clear before you start your slide.
4. Only two on the seesaw at a time.

**Specific Rules for the Cafeteria**
1. Follow correct traffic flow from serving counter to table, and from table to trash to exit.
2. Choose a seat and remain there.
3. Eat all your food in the cafeteria.
4. Raise your hand to be excused when finished eating.
5. Scrape food into bins with a rubber spatula and put utensils in the water.

## Discipline Plans Have Consequences

Rules must have consequences. Some students know they can break certain rules because the aftermath is consistent and predictable: Nothing will happen to the violator. The responsible adult may find this hard to accept, but many people—children and adults—believe they have done nothing wrong until they are caught.

> ### The Two Kinds of Consequences
>
> - Positive consequences or **REWARDS** result when people abide by the rules.
>
> - Negative consequences or **PENALTIES** result when people break the rules.

**Consequences are what result when a person abides by or breaks a rule.** Spend time discussing a fact of life: **Every action results in a consequence.** Consequences are not punishments. It is simply what happens when a person does something. For instance, if you overeat, smoke cigarettes, or park in a no-parking zone, there is a consequence for each action. Study hard, save money, or show kindness, and there is a consequence for each action as well. Help students understand that if they break a rule, they are not being punished. Rather, they have consciously made a choice to break a rule and accept whatever happens.

**A consequence is the result of a person's chosen action.**

**Consequences are not punishments.** At the most, they may be considered penalties. Students are used to penalties, however, because there are penalties in the games they play. The issue is **CHOICE**. People who cannot accept choice as part of responsible living cast themselves as victims. Victims blame others for their actions. Thus it is advisable to spend more time discussing consequences than discussing rules. Come to an understanding that their actions or choices result in consequences. Successful people accept that life is a series of consequences. And consequences can be positive or negative.

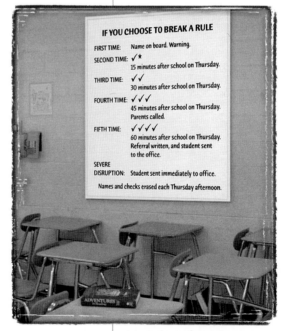

**IF YOU CHOOSE TO BREAK A RULE**

| | |
|---|---|
| FIRST TIME: | Name on board. Warning. |
| SECOND TIME: | ✓ ★<br>15 minutes after school on Thursday. |
| THIRD TIME: | ✓✓<br>30 minutes after school on Thursday. |
| FOURTH TIME: | ✓✓✓<br>45 minutes after school on Thursday.<br>Parents called. |
| FIFTH TIME: | ✓✓✓✓<br>60 minutes after school on Thursday.<br>Referral written, and student sent<br>to the office. |
| SEVERE<br>DISRUPTION: | Student sent immediately to office. |

Names and checks erased each Thursday afternoon.

A typical set of negative consequences posted by a teacher.

Rules must have consequences.

## Do Not Stop the Lesson

**I**f you stop a lesson to penalize a student, you disrupt the lesson, interrupt an important point you are making, or disturb people while they are working. **Do not stop instruction when carrying out a consequence.**

- When you see a violation of one of the rules, immediately implement the penalty.

- Implement the penalty quietly as you continue with the lesson and the class continues their work.

### Why Are You Picking on Me?

What do you say to the following three major questions asked by students worldwide?

> *Why are you picking on me?*
> *What did I do?*
> *Everyone else is doing it. Why look at me?*

Stand in front of a mirror and practice the following 100 times until you can say it calmly and automatically every time one of these questions is asked:

> *Because you CHOSE to break*
> *the rule.*
> *Because you CHOSE to break*
> *rule X.*

Do not argue. Do not ask the student if he or she is questioning your authority. Do not yell, scream, or raise your voice. Just calmly say every time:

> *Because you CHOSE to break the rule.*

After a few days, no one will ever ask, "Why are you picking on me?" because everyone will know exactly what you will say.

The key word in the phrase is *CHOSE*. Choosing means that one is responsible and accountable for one's actions. You are teaching your students responsibility and accountability.

> *The teacher is not picking on you.*
> *There are five rules in the classroom.*
> *The rules were discussed, agreed on, and signed. So when*
> *you CHOOSE to break one of the rules, you must*
> *accept the consequence.*

After a few weeks or months, if someone should ask you, "Why are you picking on me?" all you have to do is stand and smile at the student. The entire class will respond for you:

> *Because you CHOSE to break*
> *the rule!*

Here are some suggested ways for implementing penalties.

1. **Whiteboard.** Do not stop teaching. Just go to the designated area and write the student's name or place a check after the student's name.

   You may need to take a few seconds at the end of the period or day to remind those students of their penalty.

   Failure to work off the penalty automatically moves the student up to the next level of the consequences, or doubles the penalty.

2. **Ticket.** You may feel that putting a student's name on the board may be too embarrassing. Consider another method, such as handing out a yellow card, as it is done in soccer when a penalty is called. Or adopt the concept behind the traffic ticket. Come up with a method for giving the student a ticket. There is no need for a fancy form. A piece of paper with the **student's name** and the number of the rule broken is all that is needed.

   The ticket method is ideal for circumstances where you do not have a whiteboard, such as physical education and theatre classes, an assembly, or a field trip.

   You will need to keep a record of who has been given a ticket. This can be done in your grade record book, with a carbon, or with carbonless forms.

3. **Pattern.** Have students make patterns or cutouts to represent themselves for the bulletin board. When you see a rule violation, go to this board and "flag" the student's pattern. A flag could be the addition of a sticky note, removing the pattern, or turning the pattern over. If the pattern has been laminated, use a felt-tipped marker.

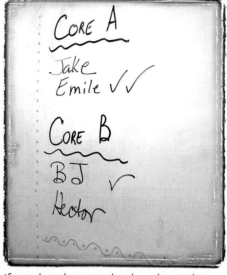

If a student chooses to break a rule, put the student's name or a check on the board or in a special location without interrupting the lesson.

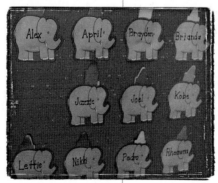

Patterns with pockets hold flags to indicate behavior.

## Discipline Plans Have Rewards and Positive Consequences

**E**veryone likes and expects special recognition, rewards, and incentives when good work is done. Perks, praise, honors, prizes, and awards are commonplace.

**Although rewards are a fact of life, today the wholesale bribery system of giving out endless supplies of stickers, candies, and other tangibles has got to come to a halt. Let's stop the "What's in it for me?" attitude prevalent in classrooms.**

In addition, the Child Nutrition and WIC Reauthorization Act of 2004 makes the use of food items to reward good behavior no longer acceptable; it can actually nullify your school's and district's efforts toward compliance with the Act.

**Self-discipline is what discipline is all about.** You can't teach self-discipline if the students are always looking for more treats, raffle tickets, and goodies from the Treasure Box.

> **The best reward is
> the satisfaction of a job well done.**

If you must use a reward, one that is popular for any subject or grade level is **30 minutes of free time on Friday** as a classwide reward. Everyone has to work together cooperatively the entire week for the reward. The 30 minutes of free time on Fridays is effective and simple because it is not a tangible *prize*—and your students will never grow tired of it. Besides, the time is used, mostly, for schoolwork. There are no popcorn parties, pizza parties, or videos to plan for and clean up after—just free time to work!

A typical set of rewards posted by a teacher.

Like rules and consequences, you will want to post your rewards. Indicate the time factor associated with the reward. Will the reward be given daily, weekly, monthly, at the end of the quarter, when?

Explain the simple system by which the reward is to be earned. The teacher does not give rewards; **the students earn rewards**.

The most common way of earning rewards, on a class basis, is to put a tally mark somewhere when you spot someone following directions or doing good. If you don't like tally marks, use marbles in a jar, raffle tickets, or red indicators on a drawing of a thermometer. When the class has earned a predetermined number of tally marks, your students can collectively have the reward.

---

**Discipline Plan for Room 16**
**Classroom Rules**

1. Have all appropriate materials and supplies at your table and be seated when the bell rings.
2. Respect the people, equipment, and furnishings of Room 16.
3. Adjust your voice level to suit the activity.
4. Follow directions the first time they are given.
5. Observe all rules in the student handbook.

**If You Choose to Break a Rule**

| | |
|---|---|
| First Time: | Name on board. Warning. |
| Second Time: | One check. 15 minutes after school on Thursday. |
| Third Time: | Two checks. 30 minutes after school on Thursday. |
| Fourth Time: | Three checks. 45 minutes after school on Thursday and parents called. |
| Fifth Time: | Four checks. 60 minutes after school on Thursday, referral written, and student sent to the office. |
| Severe disruptions: | Student sent immediately to the office. |

Names and checks erased each Thursday afternoon.

**Rewards**

Praise (daily)
Positive notes home (random)
Whole-class music time or free time (weekly)
"Raise a Grade" certificate (monthly)
Movie and popcorn party for class (every 9 weeks)
Various other positive perks (throughout the school year)
The joy of learning (each day of the school year)

**STUDENTS:** I have read this classroom discipline plan and understand it. I will honor it while in Room 16.

Signature_____     Date_____

**PARENTS:** My child has discussed the classroom discipline plan with me. I understand it and will support it.

Signature_____     Date_____

**TEACHER:** I will be fair and consistent in administering the discipline plan for Room 16.

Signature_____

******IMPORTANT******
PLEASE KEEP THIS SHEET IN YOUR BINDER AT ALL TIMES.
Thank you

---

## Discipline Plan Where Both the Student and Teacher Are in Charge (page 148)

### My Action Plan

**T**he most common form of a cooperative discipline plan is with a contract or some kind of an agreement from the student.

**Some elementary classes have "Power Centers."** This is a desk set aside for those children who must be sent to reflect on their misbehavior. They are told they can return to class activities when they tell the teacher, "I Have the Power," meaning I have the power to discipline myself and behave. If the child starts to waver, quickly ask, "Do you Have the Power?" Smile and you'll get a smile back.

Other grade-level classrooms have "Time Out Centers" which are similar to penalty boxes in hockey.

"My Action Plan" is a simple technique that not only addresses the specific problem, but simultaneously teaches the student **responsibility, problem solving, and self-discipline.**

Direct the student to a desk set aside with a pencil and a copy of "My Action Plan." (You can download a copy at EffectiveTeaching.com in the **Go**ing **Be**yond folder for Chapter 18.)

**Step 1.** Show the student a copy of "My Action Plan," and be prepared to work with the student on answering the three questions:

What's the problem?
What's causing the problem?
What plan will you use to solve the problem?

*What's the problem?* Indicate the rule or rules the student has violated.

*What's causing the problem?* The student is to list all the factors that are causing the problem to occur.

Work with the student in a **PROBLEM-SOLVING** mode here. Share with the student that the only way a person can solve a problem is first to isolate and identify it. You are not interested in degrading or scolding the student. You want to teach the student how to solve a problem, a technique that the student can use in future life.

***What plan will you use to solve the problem?*** The student is to write the action plan needed to solve the problem.

Have the student look at the factors causing the problem. Show the student that the way to solve a problem is to change or eliminate the factors causing the problem. Help the student see the logic of this.

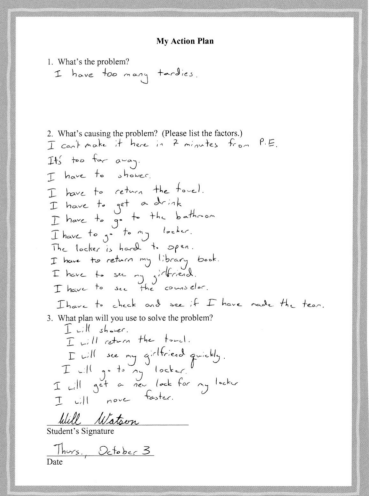

Have the student write a plan based on the causative factors listed under the second question. The student now takes **RESPONSIBILITY** for the plan. You did not tell the student what to do. The student, through problem solving, devised his or her own plan to correct the problem. You are teaching responsibility.

> **The three key concepts
> in the value of using "My Action Plan" are**
>
> 1. **Problem-solving**
> 2. **Responsibility**
> 3. **Self-discipline**

**Step 2.** **Have the student commit to responsibility by signing the action plan.**

If the problem is not corrected, go back and modify the third part of the action plan. It is much better to teach problem-solving, responsibility, and self-discipline than to yell, scream, and flunk. Yelling, screaming, and flunking benefit no one. Learning to be self-disciplined and responsible benefits all of society. Through persistence, have the student work on the action plan repeatedly until the problem is corrected.

**Commend the student when success occurs.**

**Step 3.** **For the student to carry through with his or her responsibility,** encouragement is needed from the home and the school to get the student to achieve **SELF-DISCIPLINE**.

Tips for calling home are in the **Go**ing **Be**yond folder for Chapter 18 at EffectiveTeaching.com.

---

**GoBe**

**More Help with Preventing Misbehavior**

Solving discipline problems is very complex. No perfect solutions have been found. Go to the **Go**ing **Be**yond folder for Chapter 18 at EffectiveTeaching.com for a quick refresher course in discipline basics.

## The Self-Manager Plan

SELF-MANAGER APPLICATION

Name: _____ Date Applied: _____

Parent's Signature: _____ Date Awarded: _____

| MANAGEMENT SKILLS | ALMOST ALWAYS | WORKING ON IT |
|---|---|---|
| 1. I am a good listener and I try to understand. | | |
| 2. I follow classroom and school rules. | | |
| 3. I do my work on time and as well as I can. | | |
| 4. I can work with a small group. | | |
| 5. I can work alone. | | |
| 6. I use playground equipment properly. | | |
| 7. I can take care of myself even when no one is watching. | | |
| 8. I have self-control. | | |

RESPECT FOR PROPERTY, SELF, AND OTHERS

| | | |
|---|---|---|
| 1. I cooperate with people | | |
| 2. I take care of my property and I respect the property of others. | | |
| 3. I go to and from class without problems. | | |
| 4. I use good manners while eating lunch. | | |

HELPING OTHERS

| | | |
|---|---|---|
| 1. I don't hurt other people. | | |
| 2. I am helpful to others. | | |
| 3. I am a good sport, I play fair and follow game rules. | | |

NOTE: To become a Self-Manager, ALL checks must be in the "almost always" column. A student's behavior may be verified by any teacher or staff member who has responsibility for his or her education.

Download this application at EffectiveTeaching.com in the Going Beyond folder for Chapter 18.

Jane Slovenske of Arizona uses a "Self-Manager Plan" in which students are taught to be responsible for managing their own behaviors. Students are presented with a Self-Manager application—a self-evaluation of responsible behavior, appropriate treatment of others, and prompt work completion to the best of their abilities.

**List of Appropriate Behaviors.** The class discusses a list of appropriate behaviors and standards for a Self-Manager. The class is then given an opportunity to revise the list. Once the list of behaviors is agreed upon, each student may complete an application to take home for their parents' review. When parents are in agreement with their child's self-evaluation, it is signed and returned to school.

**Teacher-Student Evaluation.** The teacher must agree with the student's evaluation. If the teacher disagrees, evidence must be provided to support this. Afterward, the student and teacher discuss their differences of opinion and come to an agreement. Jane says this is rarely necessary, because most students, with input from their parents, are honest about their performance. Students rated "almost always" in each category become Self-Managers.

Each qualifying student wears a badge that says, "I'm a SELF-MANAGER." Staff and students recognize and acknowledge Self-Managers by the badges.

**Student's Self-Evaluation.** About once every six weeks, all students, including Self-Managers, complete a self-evaluation. It is important that Self-Managers

maintain and reflect on appropriate behaviors. Remaining members of the class continue to have chances to refine their behaviors and become Self-Managers, too.

If a student loses or misplaces the badge, it can be replaced for a fee. This fee comes from their personal classroom checking accounts. Students earn "money" for their checking accounts by applying for a class job from a list of job descriptions. Only students who apply are given jobs. Checking account balances are used to pay fines for classroom infractions throughout the year.

**The class determines and agrees to privileges granted to those with a Self-Manager badge.** Types of privileges include walking ahead of the class to P.E., music, and art; sitting in beanbag chairs while the teacher reads aloud or during silent reading; not having to ask to use the restroom; and being first in line for dismissal.

**Self-Manager Help Group.** Self-Managers pair up with students who have not yet achieved Self-Manager status. Each Friday, after all students have received their weekly completion sheets, pairs of students review the list of missing assignments, work together to find it, and organize it for completion. This is strictly on a voluntary basis, but all students who are not Self-Managers must request assistance from a peer who is a Self-Manager.

Students and former students take great pride in this form of recognition. Many students have older siblings who were Self-Managers. They still have their Self-Manager badges and are proud to show them to their younger brothers and sisters.

Jane Slovenske's students manage their own behavior.

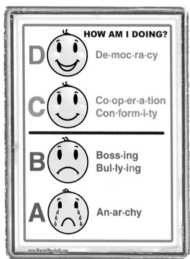

Posters are usually hung in the classroom so the students can see where they are on the levels of development. The posters can be smiley faces for primary grades, like the one shown.

## Discipline Plan Where the <u>Student Is in Charge</u> (page 148)

## The Raise Responsibility System

The ideal of discipline plans is to place the student in charge of his or her behavior. Marvin Marshall (<u>MarvinMarshall.com</u>) teaches **The Raise Responsibility System**. The plan teaches that democracy and responsibility are inseparable. Even though it is a noncoercive discipline system, it is not permissive. The system teaches four levels of social development.

- **Anarchy: Lowest level; absence of any social order;** only interested in themselves, as in the case of infants.

- **Bossing: Bossed to behave; bothers and bullies** with own standards; only obeys when more authority is exercised or threatened.

- **Cooperation/Conformity: Motivation is external**; acts appropriately, complies with teacher expectations, and follows procedures; also applies to outside influences, whereby a student conforms to negative peer pressure.

- **Democracy: Highest level; motivation is internal; takes the initiative** to develop self-discipline and act responsibly because it is the right thing to do; realizes most satisfaction from efforts.

**The Raise Responsibility System** has three stages of implementation:

1. **Teaching:** Proactive. Levels are taught at the outset, in contrast to waiting until misbehavior occurs. Most effective if students visualize what each level would look like and reflect on their level of chosen behavior.

2. **Asking:** Student recognition of own chosen level of behavior. The teacher asks a student to identify or reflect on the level. Defending oneself is completely eliminated. Student is separated from the deed. Ask, "What level do you think you are behaving at?" Discuss the level, not the behavior.

3. **Eliciting:** Redirects inappropriate impulses. Request, "Please take a moment and reflect on the level you have chosen."

## Effective Communication of Your Discipline Plan

N ow that you have thought out, constructed, and posted your discipline plan, all that is left is to communicate this plan to your students on the first day of school. How you communicate your plan will determine its success or failure.

| The Ineffective Teacher | The Effective Teacher |
| --- | --- |
| ■ May have no clearly defined rules. | ■ Has a discipline plan that does not degrade students. |
| ■ Communicates rules sporadically and as they are suddenly needed to stifle a situation. | ■ Communicates the plan at the start of school in a firm but controlled and friendly manner. |
| ■ Conveys rules in a gruff, angry, and condescending manner. | ■ Does not wince or convey disbelief in what is being said. |
| ■ Winces, shrugs, or conveys via facial expressions or body language disbelief in what is being said. | ■ Makes eye contact with each student while presenting the plan. |
| ■ Conveys that "I'm only doing this because the administration wants me to do it." | ■ Provides an understandable reason for the plan. |
| ■ Implies that "I was hired to teach the subject matter, not to maintain discipline." | ■ Provides a copy of the plan for each student and the home. |
| | ■ Enforces the plan consistently. |
| ■ Tells students, "If you don't want to learn, that's not my problem." | ■ Tells students that the administration supports the plan. |
| ■ Berates students with useless phrases to convey expectations of appropriate behavior, such as "Don't you know any better?" or "How many times do I have to tell you?" | ■ Reviews the plan with new students. |
| | ■ Has positive expectations that all students will abide by the plan. |
| | ■ Has self-confidence and faith in his or her capabilities. |
| | ■ Teaches students the concept of responsibility. |

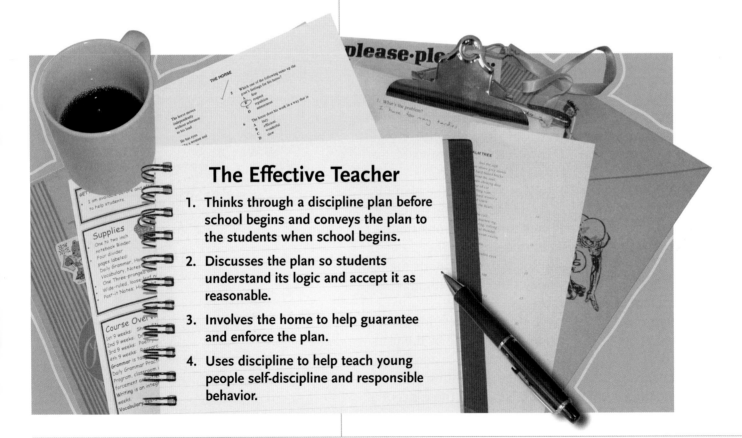

## The Effective Teacher

1. **Thinks through a discipline plan before school begins and conveys the plan to the students when school begins.**

2. **Discusses the plan so students understand its logic and accept it as reasonable.**

3. **Involves the home to help guarantee and enforce the plan.**

4. **Uses discipline to help teach young people self-discipline and responsible behavior.**

## The Problem Is Not Discipline

> The number one problem in the classroom is not discipline; it is the lack of procedures and routines.

## THE KEY IDEA

**A smooth-running classroom is based on the teacher's ability to teach procedures.**

ou have now arrived at the two most important chapters in this book. What you are about to read can provide you with a smooth-running, well-oiled learning environment. For this to happen, you must implement the practices and procedures described in Chapters 19 and 20. The information in these two chapters on classroom management will help you become a proactive teacher and will assist you in reducing the number of misbehaviors in the classroom.

> Effective teachers teach students how to responsibly follow procedures.
> Ineffective teachers use controlling tactics to coerce the students into compliance.

A vast majority of the behavior problems in the classroom are caused by the failure of students to follow procedures and routines. There are three main reasons why students do not follow procedures:

1. The teacher has not thought out what happens in the classroom.
2. The students have not been taught how to follow procedures.
3. The teacher spends no time managing the classroom with procedures.

Thus, the students cannot follow procedures that do not exist.

Coercion and compliance
will send you home
frazzled and angry.

**Why?**

Too many teachers do not teach.

They "cover" or "do" activities.
Then when things go wrong,
they discipline.

In short,
most classrooms are unmanaged.

## I Knew They Would Do That

*I was absent one day and called the school to tell my substitute something. No one answered so I began to panic! I called the teacher next door and asked her if my substitute was there. She told me that she had seen the substitute earlier, but had no idea why the substitute was not answering the phone.*

*When I returned to school the next day, the teacher met me in the hallway and said, "Remember when I told you that the substitute was in your room? Well, I was wrong. She thought that it was your planning period, so she was not in the classroom."*

*I began to panic all over again. But before I could say anything she said, "But, your kids were great! They had taken the attendance, posted it outside of your door, read the lesson plan that you left for the sub, and were working quietly when the substitute arrived!"*

*I was in shock! I was so proud of my students. They followed our daily procedures and continued to move right along!*

*After she told me that, the administrator came around the corner and said, "Mrs. Seroyer, I need to speak with you!" I thought that I was going to be in trouble because he found out that my students were in the classroom alone.*

*As he was talking, I was thinking, "Oh my goodness . . . I'm going to lose my job!" But finally he said, "Congratulations! When the sub arrived, your students had posted the attendance and were working so quietly that no one knew that they were alone!"*

*With a smirky smile of relief, I said, "I KNOW. We have PROCEDURES in place! I KNEW that they would do that!"*

Chelonnda Seroyer,
Bob Jones H.S., Alabama
(See page iii.)

## Could I Have the Plans Back?

*Due to illness, I called for a sub. When my students came in for homeroom, I wasn't there; nor was a sub. The students took roll, filled out the attendance Scantron, listened to the announcements, recited the pledge, and dismissed on the bell.*

*My first-period class came in next and the sub still hadn't arrived. The students took out their daily work and began working. When most had finished, one student went to the front, used the key and led the class through the answers. He then looked at the board for the schedule and had everyone take out their grammar homework. He used that key and went over the homework with them.*

*Now, about 20 minutes into the period, they still didn't have a teacher. The self-appointed leader wrote out a pass for another student and sent him to the office to check on the teacher situation.*

*When the office was notified, there was concern and distress. What had been going on for the last 20 minutes? The principal went back to the room with the student.*

*When I returned the next day, the principal told me when he entered the room, the students were seated and working on the current grammar lesson with the student leader working it on the overhead.*

*The principal asked the student for the sub plans and moved to leave the room.*

*The student leader then said, "Mr._____, could I have the plans back? I haven't finished teaching yet."*

*Procedures and organization have empowered my students and myself. I don't have problems with discipline and I look forward to coming to work and spending time learning with "my kids" since I've been using procedures.*

Terri L. Schultz,
Lakota School District, Ohio

# What Is Classroom Management?

Classroom management consists of the practices and procedures that a teacher uses to maintain an optimum environment in which instruction and learning can occur.

Classroom management and discipline are not the same. You manage a store; you do not discipline a store. You manage a team; you do not discipline a team. Likewise, effective teachers manage a classroom; they do not discipline a classroom. Teachers who view classroom management as a process of organizing and structuring classroom events tend to be more effective than teachers who view their role as disciplinarian.

Teachers who are effective classroom managers

- have planned procedures for classroom organization.

- have instructional procedures to maximize student engagement.

- systematically teach these procedures.

**It is not what teachers do to stop misbehavior that characterizes effective group management, but how they prevent problems in the first place.** Effective teachers implement a systematic approach toward classroom management with procedures at the beginning of the school year.

---

**Effective and Ineffective Classrooms: A Comparison**

**Effective Classroom:**
> The students are actively involved in meaningful work.
> The procedures govern what they do and they understand how the class functions.
> The teacher, who is also involved in work, is moving around the room, helping, correcting, answering, disciplining, encouraging, smiling, and caring.

**Ineffective Classroom:**
> The students are in their seats doing busywork or nothing.
> The only person who is observed working is the teacher.
> The teacher controls the class.

**Learning occurs only when students are actively engaged and in control of their own learning.** Are the students working in your classroom?

---

## The Person Who Works, Learns

**S**tudents readily accept the idea of having a set of uniform classroom procedures because it simplifies the task of succeeding in school. Procedures allow a wide variety of activities to take place during the school day, often simultaneously, with minimal confusion and wasted time. If there are no procedures, much time is wasted organizing and explaining each activity, even for recurring activities. The lack of procedures also leads to students' acquiring undesirable work habits and behaviors that are subsequently hard to correct.

**No learning takes place when you discipline. Learning takes place only when a student is at work.** Discipline temporarily stops misbehavior and disrupts the learning process.

**Effective teachers know that the more time students spend on task, called academic learning time, the more the students learn.** Who is working and learning in your classroom?

## The Difference Between Discipline and Procedures

**C**lassroom management should not be equated with discipline. **Discipline plans have rules. Classroom management plans have procedures.** Please DO NOT call a procedure a rule.

Procedures are not found in a discipline plan; nor should a procedure be a threat, a rule, or an order. Procedures lay the groundwork for student learning. **A procedure is simply a method or process for getting things done in the classroom.**

**Procedures and routines are different from a discipline plan.** Do not confuse procedures with discipline. There are two major differences.

Whoever is working is the only one learning.

**DISCIPLINE** concerns how students *BEHAVE*.
**PROCEDURES** concern how things *ARE DONE*.

**DISCIPLINE** *HAS* penalties and rewards.
**PROCEDURES** *HAVE NO* penalties or rewards.

A student is generally not penalized for failing to follow a procedure or rewarded if a procedure is followed.

### Example of a Procedure

There is a procedure for opening a lock on a locker. It's usually two turns to the right, one turn to the left, and a final turn to the right.

There is no penalty if the procedure is not followed. The lock just does not open. Likewise, there is no reward if the procedure is followed. The lock simply opens. To do anything in life successfully, you simply follow the procedures.

**Student success or achievement at the end of the school year is directly related to the degree to which the teacher establishes good control of the classroom procedures in the very first week of the school year.** Procedures set the class up for achievement to take place.

> **A rule is a DARE to be broken, whereas a procedure is not.**
>
> **A procedure is a DO, a step to be learned.**

## Why Procedures Are Important

**S** **tudents must know from the very beginning what they are expected to DO in a classroom work environment.** Discipline dictates how they are to behave; procedures and routines teach what they are to do or work at. Procedures and routines offer security. Students cannot get down to the serious business of learning unless they feel secure in the classroom. They want instruction and guidance on all the how-to's in class—how to head a paper, how to ask for help, how to sharpen a pencil, how to get to work, how and when to use the computer, and so on.

Since a **PROCEDURE** explains how you want something done, it is the responsibility of the teacher to have procedures clearly stated. A **ROUTINE** is what the student does automatically, without prompting or supervision.

Procedures are necessary for an effective classroom for several reasons.

- Classroom procedures are statements of student expectations that are necessary to participate successfully in classroom activities, to learn, and to function effectively in the school environment.

- Classroom procedures allow many different activities to take place efficiently during the school day, often several at the same time, with a minimum of wasted time and confusion.

- Classroom procedures increase on-task time and greatly reduce classroom disruptions.

- Classroom procedures tell students how the classroom is organized, thus reducing discipline problems.

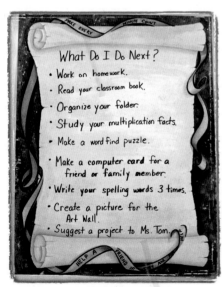

Students are less likely to act up in frustration, trying to figure out what the teacher wants, if the classroom procedures are clearly stated.

---

**PROCEDURE:**
What the teacher wants done.

**ROUTINE:**
What the students do automatically.

## Students Accept and Want Procedures

**E**ffective teachers manage with procedures. **Every time the teacher wants something done, there must be a procedure or a set of procedures.** For instance, have procedures for taking roll, exchanging papers, registering the students on the first day, taking turns speaking, and moving from task to task. If you don't, time that should be spent on learning will be wasted getting these tasks done.

Classroom procedures address such issues as these:

What to do when the bell rings
What to do when the pencil breaks
What to do when you hear an emergency alert signal
What to do when you finish your work early
What to do when you have a question
What to do when you need to go to the restroom

**Tell your students that classroom procedures are for their benefit. Following procedures will help them do their work with less confusion and thus help them succeed.** Knowledge of classroom procedures tells your students such things as these:

How to enter the classroom
What to do when they enter the classroom
Where to find the assignment
What to do when you want their attention
How a paper is to be done
Where you want the paper placed
What to do if they want to sharpen a pencil
Where to find assignments if they have been absent
What to do upon dismissal of class

Every classroom needs to have a set of procedures, which allow the class to operate smoothly. A smooth-running, effective classroom is free of confusion and is a pleasure to teach and learn in.

### No Need for Discipline

*I tell my new teachers that I am a lousy disciplinarian, but a good classroom manager.*

*If they will follow my advice and have a procedure for everything that they do, they should not need to discipline a student.*

Joan Blassengame Davis,
Hampton City Schools,
Virginia

Judie Gustafson of Manor, Texas, is a high school math teacher. On the first days of school, she gives her class an eight-page paper titled "Procedures." It begins as follows:

*Procedures are a part of life. We follow procedures for using a telephone book, boarding an airplane, approaching a traffic light, and attending a wedding. The reason we have procedures in life is so that people can function in society knowing the acceptable and efficient ways people do things.*

*There are also procedures in this classroom. These procedures establish our classroom culture.*

This is followed by procedures for use in the following situations:

- Entering the classroom
- Asking a question
- Listening to and responding to questions
- Sharpening your pencil
- Indicating whether you understand
- Responding to my request for your attention
- Turning in papers
- Working cooperatively
- Changing groups
- Maintaining your notebook
- Leaving the classroom
- When you are tardy
- When you need a pencil or paper
- When you are absent
- When someone knocks
- When you need help or require a conference
- If the phone should ring
- An emergency alert
- Progress reports
- End-of-period class dismissal

A smooth-running classroom is the responsibility of the teacher and the result of the teacher's ability to teach procedures.

**"** *My daughter hated school until this year. She loves school now.*

**Why?**

*Because of the way her teacher has organized the class.* **"**

_A parent

## Procedures Are Part of Life

**P**rocedures are important in society so that people can function in an acceptable and organized manner. Everyday life is full of procedures—for instance:

**Telephone directory.** At the front of a telephone book are procedures on how to make a long-distance call, make a foreign call, contact directory assistance, get emergency help, upgrade your services, and contact the business office.

**Airplane.** After the "discipline plan" is stated at the beginning of the flight, (and yes, there are penalties and fines associated with those rules) the flight attendants explain the procedures. These procedures include how to fasten the seat belt, how to use the oxygen mask, where to find the life vest, and how to find the aisle in case the cabin fills with smoke.

**Elevator.** If you are waiting to enter the elevator, step aside to allow passengers to exit before you enter. If you are already on the elevator when more passengers enter, step to the back of the elevator and make room for the new arrivals. Or, if your floor is the next stop, step out, allow new passengers to enter, and then reboard.

**Wedding.** At the conclusion of a wedding ceremony, a procedure is followed. The bride, groom, and wedding party leave. They are followed by the parents in the first row, who are followed by each row of guests from the front of the seating area.

**Procedures demonstrate how people are to function in an acceptable and organized manner.** When we say that someone is ill-mannered, it is because that person doesn't know or doesn't care about the local customs, culture, or procedures. To function successfully with classmates and other people, the best guideline is the old saying, "When in Rome, do as the Romans do."

> In the first few days of school, teach only procedures necessary for the smooth opening of class.
>
> Delay the other procedures until the appropriate activity arises.

<table>
<tr><td>

**Classroom Procedures That Must Become Student Routines**

</td></tr>
</table>

## Procedures Are Part of School Life

s in everyday life, procedures must be followed in the classroom. Here are some that nearly every teacher must teach.

**Procedure for Dismissal at the End of the Period or Day.** When the dismissal bell rings, are the students already standing at the door waiting to leave, or do they just get up and leave, even if you are in the middle of a sentence? You can always tell who is running the class—the students or the teacher—by how the students behave at the end of the period or day. (See page 178.)

**Procedure for Quieting a Class.** Do you know how to quiet a class in 15 seconds or less? It can be done easily! Do you yell, scream, and flick the lights—all to no avail? Or if you do succeed, does it take a long time to get the students' attention, not to mention years off your life span from stress? (See page 182.)

**Procedure for the Start of the Period or Day.** When the students enter, do they know what to do, where to sit, and what materials to have ready? Or do they sit and wait for the teacher to tell them what to do? (See page 197.)

**Procedure for Students Seeking Help.** Do your students raise their hands when they want your help, flapping their hands to attract your attention, calling your name at the same time, stopping work in the process, accompanied by muttering and complaining to their classmates because you do not respond instantly? (See page 186.)

**Procedure for the Movement of Students and Papers.** Do your students take forever to pass their papers in and even longer to change from group to group or task to task? And when they turn their papers in, do they throw them in a pile on your desk or punch each other in the back as the papers are passed forward? (See page 198.)

## The Three-Step Approach to Teaching Classroom Procedures

**M**ost behavior problems in the classroom are caused by the teacher's failure to teach students how to follow procedures. Telling is not teaching. Students must be physically engaged in the process if you want them to learn it.

---

### The Three Steps to Teaching Procedures

1. **Teach.** State, explain, model, and demonstrate the procedure.

2. **Rehearse.** Rehearse and practice the procedure under your supervision.

3. **Reinforce.** Reteach, rehearse, practice, and reinforce the classroom procedure until it becomes a student habit or routine.

---

**Step 1.** **Teach Classroom Procedures Clearly**

**Effective teachers know what activities need to be done and have worked out the procedures for each of them.** These procedures are posted or distributed to the students early in the school year or when the activity surfaces in class. Unless the students read well, primary grade teachers should explain the procedures verbally rather than post them.

**It is essential that you have the procedures for each opening-of-school activity ready on the first day of school.** Revise and hone these procedures year after year until they become models of efficiency. Remember that the effective teacher has a script for the first day of school. (See page 110.)

### Step 2. Rehearse Classroom Procedures Until They Become Routines

**All procedures must be rehearsed!**

Effective teachers spend a good deal of time during the first weeks of school introducing, teaching, modeling, and rehearsing procedures. Do not expect the students to learn all the procedures in one day, especially at the elementary school level. Behaviors must be taught, modeled, practiced, monitored, and retaught.

Watch a good music, drama, athletic, or foreign-language coach. Such people are masters at the rehearsal technique. They tell and show you a technique, even have you watch a video of the technique. Then they have you do it repeatedly while they watch you. Some people call this technique "guided practice."

Parents have their children practice the piano because the more they practice, the better they play. The reason coaches have their teams run the plays over and over again is that the more they run the plays, the better they will be able to execute the plays during the game.

**Rehearse**

- Have students practice the procedure, step by step, under your supervision. After each step, make sure the students have performed it correctly.

- Have students repeat the procedure until it becomes a routine. The students should be able to perform the procedure automatically without teacher supervision.

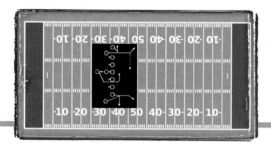

### Run the Play, Sing the Song

The reason many teachers cannot get students to do things is that they just tell the students what to do.

You must do what all coaches do, what all music teachers do, and what all effective second-grade teachers do: Have your students run the plays, sing the songs, and spell the words over and over again **until the procedures become routines**.

### Step 3. Reinforce a Correct Procedure and Reteach an Incorrect One

Again, watch a coach, because good coaches are the best teachers. As the coach guides a team, class, or student through practice, corrections are made instantly. The coach tells, shows, demonstrates, cajoles, and even loudly calls out commands until the task is done right.

And when it is done right, the coach responds with words of praise, hugs, pats, and smiles. But good coaches don't stop there. They reinforce the correct technique by having the student do the acquired technique over and over again, each time exhorting the student to do it better.

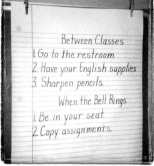

---

### Reinforce

- Determine whether students have learned the procedure or whether they need further explanation, demonstration, or practice.

- Reteach the correct procedure if rehearsal is unacceptable and give corrective feedback.

- Acknowledge the students when the rehearsal is acceptable.

---

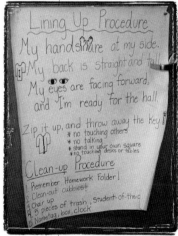

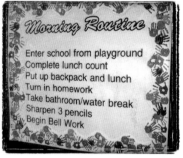

Post the classroom procedures if you want the students to follow them.

## Using the Three-Step Approach to Teach Procedures

**T**he following are examples of how some procedures are taught. You may not need or want them, but note how each procedure is taught. Then substitute your own procedure, using the **teach**, **rehearse**, **reinforce** technique just described.

- How to dismiss a class (page 178)

- How to quiet a class and gain the students' attention (page 182)

- How students are to ask you for help (page 186)

- How students are to pass in papers (page 198)

- What to do during transition (page 200)

- How to take lecture notes (page 290)

- How to complete a rubric (page 266)

## Procedure for Dismissal at the End of the Period or Day

### Teach

*Students, there is a procedure at the end of the period. You are to remain in your seat (or at your desks with the chairs pushed in) until I dismiss the class. The bell does not dismiss the class. You do not dismiss the class. The teacher dismisses the class. Thank you.*

You will want to explain the criteria for dismissal, such as how clean you want the desk or work area, and where and how you want the chairs and equipment to be positioned. Show and demonstrate this procedure. Have several students (never one, because it creates a show-off situation) demonstrate the procedure. Praise each so the students know that you are validating the correct procedure.

---

**GoBe**

**I Did Not Start
on the First Day of School**

It's mid-year and you've just been hired or you want to wipe the slate clean. Find help for starting again after the real first day in the **Go**ing **Be**yond folder for Chapter 19 at EffectiveTeaching.com.

## Rehearse

Be alert a few seconds before the bell rings on the first day of school. Anticipate that you will need to make an immediate correction if the procedure is not followed. If the class starts to file out, it is too late to correct the procedure. The failure to correct a procedure will only escalate the problem until the students dismiss themselves and are really the ones in control of the class.

**On the first day of school, remind the class of the dismissal procedure a few seconds before the bell rings at the end of the period or day.** This will reduce the hassle of correcting the class; however, if any students begin to leave at the bell, simply say,

*No, no, no. Tom, Joel, Anne, please return to your desks.*

Do not scold, yell, or demean. And do not use meaningless phrases or questions like "Listen to me" or "What did I say about the dismissal procedure?" You do not want a discussion, an argument, or a response. You want all students at their desks. Calmly, but in a voice of authority, tell the students who began to leave to return to their desks.

## Reinforce

**Every time a procedure needs to be corrected—**

1. **REMIND** the class of the procedure.
2. Have the class **EXPERIENCE** the procedure.

**Remind:** *Class, I would like to remind you of the procedure at the end of the period. You are to remain at your desks until I dismiss the class.*

**Experience:** *Look around the room. You are all at your desks (and your chairs are pushed in). This is the correct procedure, and I thank you for doing it correctly.*

*Well done. Please do it again tomorrow. Have a nice day!*

### For Whom Does the Bell Toll?

The school's bell, buzzer, or chime at the end of the period or day is a signal for teachers, notifying them that their instructional time has come to an end. The bell is of no concern to the students. The bell does not dismiss the class. You dismiss the class with a pleasant expression of farewell.

The effective teacher uses every moment of class time to engage the students in learning.

**Effective teachers have the students see, feel, and experience each procedure. The students see all the others remaining in their seats and experience the procedure correctly.** Ineffective teachers only tell students what to do. The students do not experience what should be done. That is why many teachers fail when they want students to follow procedures.

Rehearse the procedure every day to reinforce the procedure until it becomes a routine. By the end of the third or fourth day, the procedure will have become automatic.

Thereafter, all you need to do a few seconds after the bell rings is smile and say, "It's been nice seeing all of you. See you tomorrow. Have a nice day." This is much better than, "You're dismissed."

---

**Technique for Teaching Procedures**

1. Teach

2. Rehearse

3. Reinforce
   -Remind
   -Experience

(See page 175 for details.)

---

## Why Children Never Tell Mom They Are Going Out

Many parents shake their heads in frustration when their children leave the house and never say, "I'm going out, Mom." They just leave, showing no respect or manners.

If, each day, for 180 days, when the class is ready for dismissal at the end of the period or day, the teacher says, "Have a nice day" to dismiss the class, then **the teacher is modeling respect and manners**.

The students may not realize it, but they are getting a lesson in the appropriate behavior of well-mannered people. People acknowledge people as they leave a group or setting.

Adults should repeatedly model appropriate behavior so that a student may experience how to behave in society.

## How to Teach a New Student All the Class Procedures

You have invested a few weeks of practice and rehearsal toward classroom procedures. Your class is now a smooth-running, humming learning environment.

Suddenly, a new student joins the class. What do you do? Not to worry! First, understand that you cannot tell a new student the classroom procedures if you haven't first told your existing class. If your class is never sure what to do, there is no way you can ever orient and teach a new student. Second, if you have a class in which the students have learned the routines, you have developed a classroom culture. A culture is the prevailing way a group functions—for instance:

- When someone is waiting at a crosswalk, drivers stop to let them cross the road.
- On an airplane, people lower the window shades when the movie begins.
- At a wedding, people stand when the bride walks down the aisle.
- At a Chinese family dinner table, the prevailing culture is never to help oneself first. That would be considered selfish and uncouth. The hostess or host always says, "You first, please."

**You create a culture when students perform in a manner understood to be appropriate in your classroom.**

- When a new student joins the class, give the student a copy of the classroom procedures.
- Explain to the student what procedures are and why you have them.
- Tell the student that you will help with the procedures but that the student will probably be able to learn them by observing how the rest of the class functions.

For example, the bell rings at the end of the period and the new student stands up. Then, he notices that all the others are remaining in their seats. The student says mentally, "Oh, I'd better stay seated, too, like the rest of the class, and see what happens." The student has just learned the class procedure.

### The Greatest Gift

One of the greatest gifts a caring teacher can contribute to children is
to help them learn
    to sit when they feel like running,
    to raise their hand when they feel
      like talking,
    to be polite to their neighbor,
    to stand in line without pushing,
    and to do their homework when they
      feel like playing.

By introducing procedures in the classroom, you are also introducing procedures in preparation for living a happy and successful life.

### Procedures Are Everywhere

Procedures are everywhere in life.
Procedures also apply to schools,
at all grade levels
and all subjects.

**No matter what grade level
or subject you teach,
all procedures must be rehearsed.**

Calmly and without saying anything, raise your hand when you want the class quiet.

## Procedure for Quieting a Class

### Teach

*Students, I have a procedure when I want your undivided attention. You will see me stand here with my hand up. Or I may tap a bell because some of you will not be able to see my hand while you are working in a group. When you see my hand or hear a bell, the procedure is as follows:*

1. *Freeze.*
2. *Turn and face me; pay attention; and keep your eyes on me.*
3. *Be ready for instruction. I will have something to say.*

*Let me repeat and demonstrate what I said.*

Repeat and look for class understanding.

*Byron, please tell me the procedure when you see my hand or hear a bell.*

Byron does so.

*Yes, yes, yes. Thank you, Byron.*

Repeat this with several more students.

*Is there anyone who does not understand or know what to do if you see my hand or hear a bell?*

### Rehearse

*Good, let's rehearse the procedure. We will be working together this year, so let's get to know one another. Please look at the person to the right of you. You will have two minutes to introduce yourselves and get to know one another.*

After two minutes, hold up your hand or ring the bell, perhaps doing both this first time. Do not say a word when you raise your hand. Do the demonstration exactly as you will be doing it for the rest of the year.
Be patient and wait until the class does the three steps and pays attention.

Do not give up as you wait for the students to give you their undivided attention. Compliment them when you have their attention.

> *Thank you. You practiced the procedure correctly.*

> *Now please look at the person to the left of you. You may have two minutes to introduce yourself and get acquainted.*

After two minutes, hold up your hand or ring the bell. Compliment them when they have complied.

> *Thank you. You followed the procedure correctly.*

> *We are not finished with the rehearsal. You will often find yourself out of your seat—working in groups or alone somewhere in the room away from your seat. So let's try a different scenario.*

> *I would like two of you to stand by the pencil sharpener, two of you at the sink, two of you at the bookcase, and one of you at the computer.*

You then hold up your hand and watch for the seven students to pay attention.

### Reinforce

> *Thank you. That was the correct procedure when you see my hand or hear a bell. Please do the same thing each time you see my hand or hear a bell.*

You keep using the same language because you must use the same procedure if you want the students to exhibit the same routine. You can also use a technique called "Praise the Deed, Encourage the Student," described on the next page.

## Praise the Deed, Encourage the Student

**An effective way to praise is to praise what the person did, rather than the person, and then encourage the person to do the achievement or deed again.** The technique is called specific praise, or "praise the deed, encourage the student." Praise is nice, but it is not tangible or meaningful—for instance:

*Amber, you are a bright child.*

For a more effective kind of praise, point to something the student did well. Then encourage the student to do it again—for instance:

*Amber, please take out your last spelling test. What score did you get? Right, 19 out of 20 correct.*

*Great! Pat yourself on the back. Shake your own hand. Congratulate yourself. DO IT AGAIN ON THE NEXT TEST.*

Here are some other examples:

*Thank you, class. That was the correct procedure when you see my hand or hear a bell. Please do the same thing each time you see my hand or hear a bell.*

*Heidi, thank you for the excellent report at the faculty meeting. The next time I need assistance, I would truly appreciate your help again.*

*Julio, thanks for helping with the dishes tonight. Mom had a meeting to go to, and you helped out. The next time Mom needs assistance, I would be glad to have you help out again.*

The reason people are more likely to do well again is that they know that you saw them do something specific. They believe, "You were paying attention to me. You noticed me! And you thanked me for doing something I did personally."

Pep talks are invigorating but hollow. They become meaningless quickly because no one is sure to whom the message is directed. When you praise the deed and encourage the student, you help the student do two things:

1. Accept responsibility for having done the task.
2. Develop a sense of accomplishment.

The key words are **responsibility** and **accomplishment**, two things that all people must develop to be successful in life.

With gratitude to Barbara Coloroso,
author of *Kids Are Worth It*,
for suggesting this technique.

## She Quieted 100 People in Five Seconds

We were invited to our daughter-in-law's class to attend the annual International Day celebration. Students from three sixth-grade classes were gathered in a large room for the culmination of their study of the country of their ancestry or choice. The students were dressed in native attire and had information and food samples typical of their selected countries.

The three classes and an assortment of guests—parents, teachers, administrators, school board members, and friends—numbered about 100 people. As we were walking from display to display, talking with the students and tasting food, we suddenly heard the students call out, ". . . 3, 4, 5."

Then there was silence in the room, including those of us who had no idea what was going on. Everyone faced the teacher, Cindy Wong, and she spoke. Then everyone went back to what they were doing.

Later I asked Cindy what she did to quiet the room so quickly. She said, "Dad, it's a variation on your three-step technique. I have a five-step procedure because I teach younger students than you do, so I wanted to be more specific as to what I wanted.

"My five steps are these:

1. Eyes on speaker
2. Quiet
3. Be still
4. Hands free (put things down)
5. Listen

"The way it works is, I say, 'Give me five.' They go through each of the five steps in their mind.

"I have rehearsed them in this procedure, so when I say, 'Give me five,' it takes them no more than five seconds before I have their attention.

"In addition, all three sixth grade teachers have the same procedure. So, when another teacher, an aide, a substitute teacher, an administrator, or another student says, 'Give me five,' they have the students' attention.

"It's the consistent culture for all the sixth graders."

The Give Me Five plan in Spanish.

Cindy Wong and the Give Me Five plan posted in her classroom.

## Works With 800!

Susan Galindo from San Antonio, Texas, shared her Give Me Five story with us. She was at a Fiesta Event for the River City Christian School. There were over 600 mentally and physically challenged public school children (from 10 different school districts across south Texas) attending, and it was time for lunch under the big tent.

During lunch there was an awards presentation to several community members.

Susan kept trying to get the attention of the very loud and boisterous group gathered. After several unsuccessful attempts, she yelled out to the nearly 200 teachers who were also eating, "How do I get these kids' attention?"

A resounding unanimous reply from the teachers was, "Say, give me five!"

So she calmly said, "Give me five," and held up her hand. The whole group of 800 became quiet IMMEDIATELY.

The honored community members were quite impressed.

The "Give Me Five" hand signal is not the only way to quiet a class or group. Create your own technique or steal from the list that follows:

1. A principal holds up an orange card at an assembly and can quiet an entire student body in seconds.

2. Many teachers simply say, "May I have your attention, please?"

3. A Texas teacher says, S-A-L-A-M-E, which rehearses out to **S**top **a**nd **L**ook **a**t **ME**.

4. A football coach says, "Gentlemen, please."

5. A teacher in Arizona plays a table-top chime.

6. A pre-K teacher sings a song.

## Procedure for Students Seeking Help

**H**and raising is not effective when students want your attention. There are better methods for students to use to get your attention.

The class is at work and you are walking around the room helping. You see a hand up and say, "Pam." The whole class stops to look at you and Pam.

Pam says, "May I sharpen my pencil?"—a reasonable request.

You say, "Yes," or "No," and the class goes back to work.

A few seconds later, you see another hand up. You say, "Carlos," and the whole class stops to look at you and Carlos.

Carlos says, "I need your help"—an appropriate request.

You say, "Wait a minute," and the class goes back to work.

**Every time you speak, you interrupt the class.** These interruptions can occur frequently, often two or three times a minute.

You would be distracted if the principal beamed announcements two or three times a day, no less two or three times a minute. Before you complain that the principal creates too many interruptions during the day, consider how many times a teacher interrupts a class when the students are concentrating on their work.

---

### Student Methods for Getting the Teacher's Attention Without Interrupting the Class

**Hand signal:** The student signals with different numbers of fingers.

**Toilet tissue tube:** The student signals with a colored tube.

**Styrofoam cup:** The student signals with the position of a cup.

**Index card:** The student signals with a message on an index card.

**Textbook:** The student signals with an upright textbook.

---

### Hand Signal

With this technique the students signal the teacher with a predetermined number of fingers. The number of fingers raised corresponds to a predetermined request established by the teacher.

Post a sign on the wall with your hand signal chart. Then train your students to use the system.

- If they wish to speak, they are to raise the index finger.
- If they wish to leave their seat, they are to raise two fingers.
- If they need your help, they are to raise three fingers.
- If they need to go to the bathroom, they cross two fingers.

When you see a signal, silently respond to the signal with a nod or shake of the head or a gesture of the hand.

This is a variation of the hand signal procedure.

## A Difference in the Noise Level Alone

*Dear Rosemary,*

*We really enjoyed seeing you again at our symposia. The wonderfully creative and practical ideas you gave us will be put to good use. My husband is already using your hand signals in his grade 5 and 6 classroom, and he can't believe the difference it has made in the noise level alone.*

*Thanks again for all of the above and so much more.*

Debbie Fraser
Kinburn, Ontario, Canada

---

**To Obtain the Teacher's Attention, Raise—**

**One Finger:** "I wish to speak."
**Two Fingers:** "I wish to leave my seat."
**Three Fingers:** "I need your help."

**The important thing is that the class is not disturbed.**

### Toilet Tissue Tube

Use an empty toilet tissue tube and wrap one end with red construction paper and the other end with green construction paper. The tube is placed with the green end up on the student's desk.

The procedure when the student wants the teacher's attention is to turn the tube so the red end is up and to **continue to work**. When the teacher comes to help the student, the green end is turned back up.

### Styrofoam Cup

Tape a short length of string to the bottom of a Styrofoam cup. (Styrofoam cups are noiseless.) Tape the other end of the string near the edge of the desktop, and leave the cup dangling off the table.

The procedure when the student wants the teacher's attention is to place the cup on the desk and to **continue to work**.

### Index Card

Fold and tape an index card into a three-sided pyramid. On one side write, "Please help me." On another side write, "Please keep working." Leave the third side blank. Place the card on the table so the blank side is facing the student.

The procedure when the student wants the teacher's attention is to turn the card so that "Please help me" is facing forward. The student sees "Please keep working" and is reminded to **continue to work**.

### Textbook

High school teachers may appreciate this simple system. The procedure when the student wants the teacher's attention is to take a textbook and place it in an upright position and to **continue to work**.

## Instructional Procedures for Student Learning

**J**ust as there are classroom procedures that organize the structure of the classroom, there are Instructional Procedures that govern the academic work of the students.

Some basic instructional procedures include the following:

1. How to work in groups (page 209)
2. How to take lecture notes (page 290)
3. How to read the textbook (page 291)
4. How to do the homework (page 292)
5. How to summarize each day's learning (page 218)

These procedures apply to any subject or content area. Just as classroom procedures lay the foundation for structuring the classroom, instructional procedures lay the foundation for acquiring information and learning.

## What If Procedures Do Not Work?

**T**hey just won't stop talking. What about the kid who blurts out? What if . . . ? Here are the four most frequently asked questions about procedures:

1. **What if they do not do the procedure?** "I tell them, I remind them over and over again and they just will not do it" is the anguished statement made most often. Just telling someone will not get them to do it. A procedure must be rehearsed and rehearsed. (Review pages 175–177.)

2. **What if they forget the procedure? Students forget and blurt out in class.** We all forget. A student knows the procedure, but just forgets. There is no need to rehearse it again as there is a much better, quicker, and saner way. Just say,

   **"And what's the procedure, please?"**

Stand in front of a mirror and calmly repeat this statement over and over again a thousand times until it becomes an automatic response to you. This is the statement:

   **"And what's the procedure, please?"**

"And what's the procedure, please?" "And what's the procedure, please?" Repeat it a thousand times. Do it calmly and with a firm, but caring smile.

The next time you see a student do something that should not be done, the next time a student blurts out, simply go over to the student and with no anger or stress, and with a firm, but pleasant smile, just say,

   **"And what's the procedure, please?"**

The statement and body language are not confrontational. It's a question. After the student corrects himself or herself, acknowledge the response with a smile and go on with teaching.

3. **What if a new student comes into the classroom?** (Review page 181.)

4. **What do I do if all else fails?** Assuming you have mastered the skill of how to teach a procedure (page 175) and the student just will not cooperate and be part of the class procedures, you have the alternative of turning the procedure into a rule. Be sure you know the difference between a procedure and a rule (page 169). If you choose to convert the procedure into a rule, inform the student there will be a consequence. Follow through on this consequence the next time the procedure is not followed.

The decision is yours to make. With consequences comes enforcement and compliance, maybe even coercion. Think twice, because it may still be easier to try and teach the responsibility of doing a procedure.

## Helping the At-Risk Student

**S**tudents who are at-risk can be helped. Students who are labeled at-risk are really "at-promise" kids, a much more positive expectation of what you want the outcome to be. At-risk has nothing to do with the student's intelligence, gender, skin color, national origin, or socioeconomic background. At-risk means the student is in danger—at-risk—of failing or dropping out of school.

The reason a student is failing is typically because the student has not done the work, and failure to do the work results in failing grades in the classroom. Most at-promise students are failing because they have not been taught many of the academic procedures discussed in Unit D. These techniques offer at-promise students opportunities to succeed.

- How to take lecture notes (page 290)
- How to read a book (page 291)
- How to do the homework (page 292)
- How to work in groups (page 209)
- How to understand the assignment (page 227)
- How to study for the test (page 242)
- And a plethora of other things students are expected to DO in the classroom (Note the word DO, rather than behave.)

**GoBe**

**Procedures at Home**

Lena Nuccio-Lee was having problems with her two kids leaving clothes all over the floor. How she solved this problem is in the **Going Beyond** folder for Chapter 19 at EffectiveTeaching.com.

> **Here is the #1 solution for helping at-promise students.**
>
> **They need STRUCTURE!**

In a well-managed classroom students are taught how to **DO** things. They are taught structure—the structure of how to do things. We compound the disadvantage of students who are at-risk, when we place them in a classroom that lacks STRUCTURE (translation: disorganized and chaotic).

- The Effective Classroom has STRUCTURE.
- Procedures + Routines create STRUCTURE.
- Effective teachers manage and instruct with PROCEDURES and ROUTINES.

**Procedures give students and teachers structure.** Many students come from dysfunctional (unstructured) homes. The effective teacher provides structure so students have something familiar and secure they can rely on.

**Having special procedures is reassuring to a student—it gives the student something to fall back on.** Procedures don't have to be elaborate, but they need to have a certain regularity—consistency. They can be as simple as knowing where to line up for an elementary student and knowing where to go quickly in the face of danger for a secondary student. It's ironic that teachers have a lounge where they can retreat, but students do not have a safe haven where they can retreat.

Once you have procedures in place, you can have responsible students.

> **The only way to have responsible students and to help students who may be at-risk is to have procedures and routines for which the students can feel responsible.**

**GoBe**

**You're Worth It**

Teaching is not easy. It is hard work, with rewards that are life altering. In the **Go**ing **Be**yond folder for Chapter 19 at EffectiveTeaching.com are some reminders of your value and worth to the world.

## Procedures to Rehearse With Students

| | |
|---|---|
| Entering the classroom | Moving about the room |
| Getting to work immediately | Going to the library or tech center |
| Listening to and responding to questions | Structuring headings on papers |
| Participating in class discussions | Returning to a task after an interruption |
| Keeping your desk orderly | Asking a question |
| Checking out classroom materials | Walking in the hall during class time |
| Indicating whether or not you understand | Responding to a fire drill |
| Coming to attention | Responding to an earthquake |
| Working cooperatively | Responding to a severe weather alert |
| Changing groups | Saying "thank you" |
| Keeping your notebook | When you are tardy |
| Going to the office | End-of-period class dismissal |
| Knowing the schedule for the day or class | When you need a pencil or paper |
| Keeping a progress report | When you are absent |
| Finding directions for each assignment | When you need help or conferencing |
| Passing in papers | When you finish early |
| Exchanging papers | When a schoolwide announcement is made |
| Returning student work | When visitors are in the classroom |
| Getting materials without disturbing others | If the teacher is out of the classroom |
| Handing out playground materials | If you are suddenly ill |

Procedures and routines established early in the school year free up the rest of the year to devote to teaching and learning in the content areas.

**Remember, it is the procedures that set up the class for success to take place.**

> " *You seemingly waste a little time at the beginning to gain time at the end.* "
>
> _Lim Chye Tin

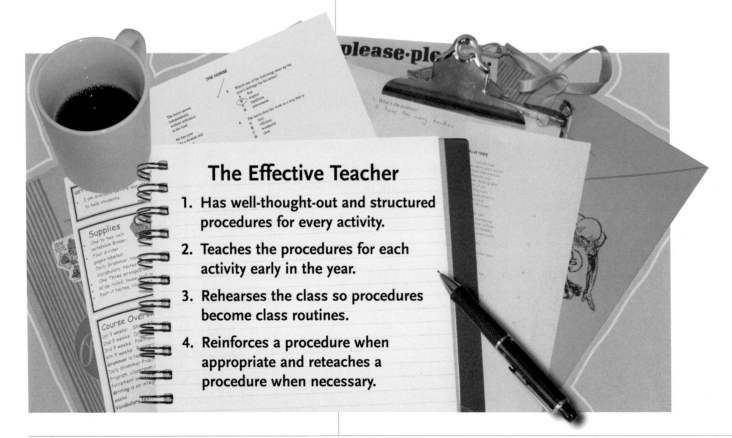

## The Effective Teacher

1. Has well-thought-out and structured procedures for every activity.

2. Teaches the procedures for each activity early in the year.

3. Rehearses the class so procedures become class routines.

4. Reinforces a procedure when appropriate and reteaches a procedure when necessary.

## Organized and Predictable

**Effective teachers have invisible procedures.
Observers in the classroom don't see them,
but they know they exist.
That is why effective teachers' classrooms run so smoothly.**

### THE KEY IDEA

**Student learning improves in a well-managed classroom.**

When you walk into a room, you do not pay attention to the floor. But if it were missing you would. It's the same with classroom management. Teachers who have a well-managed classroom have invisible procedures. The class just flows along smoothly with student learning. That's because effective teachers spend time during the first week of school organizing and structuring their classrooms for student learning.

The most important factor that must be established the first day and first week of school is **CONSISTENCY**.

**Consistency means the classroom is organized and predictable.** There are no surprises; the teacher and the students know how the class is structured and run. The students know what to do. **They know the procedures**.

For instance, the students know the procedures for

- Coming to attention (page 182)
- Entering the classroom and starting work (page 126)
- Asking for help (page 186)
- Walking down the hall (pages 213 and 329)
- Riding in buses or cars (page 218)

> " *Power comes when you make life predictable for people.* "
>
> _Howard Stevenson

---

**More Procedures**

Unit D has more instructional procedures.

Note taking (page 290)
Reading a textbook (page 291)
Homework (page 292)

---

**A Place of Acceptance**

School is a sanctuary for many kids.
They do not come to school to be yelled at
    and screamed at.
Kids come to school to belong.
They want to be accepted
    and they want to learn.

---

In the instructional realm, they know the procedures for

- Bellwork (page 214)
- Taking lecture notes (page 290)
- Working in a group (page 209)
- Studying for a test (page 242)
- Distributing materials (page 208)

**As a result of these procedures, the teacher is not constantly yelling or ordering the students what to do.** The students know what to do and are learning in a well-organized classroom.

## Procedures Produce Permanent Change

**S**tudents who know what to do in the classroom produce results, and results produce learning and achievement. This is because students take responsibility and ownership for the tasks that need to be done, resulting in fewer behavioral or discipline problems and increased academic learning time.

Procedures result in **PERMANENT** behavior changes.
Handling behavioral problems only results in **TEMPORARY** behavior changes.

Stated in a similar manner,

Effective teachers **MANAGE** their classrooms with procedures and routines. Ineffective teachers **DISCIPLINE** their classrooms with threats and punishments.

A teacher with no opening morning routine is inviting disaster in the classroom the first day and every day of the school year.

In Chapter 19 we shared classroom procedures that include

- Class dismissal
- Quieting a class
- Students wanting teacher's help
- Helping at-risk students

In this chapter we will present classroom procedures for

- Starting a class
- Movement of paper
- Transition
- The pencil problem

In this chapter we will also address instructional procedures for

- Dividing into groups
- Structuring group activities

Remember, there are specific steps for teaching a procedure—Teach, Rehearse, and Reinforce. If you need to review this technique go back to Chapter 19.

You'll create many more procedures that apply to your classroom environment. The more procedures you have in place, the more you will maximize the time students have to learn.

## Procedure for the Start of the Period or Day

**E**ffective teachers always have the procedure for the day posted or ready for distribution when the students arrive. This procedure should be implemented consistently so it becomes a routine for the students.

This is an example of a procedure for the beginning of the school day. It is used by one particular teacher, but it may not apply to many other teachers. Examples are helpful because effective teachers can look at an example and modify it to use in their own grade levels or for a particular subject matter. Preparation is critical:

- A carpenter will have all the tools accounted for before beginning the job.
- A surgeon will have the instruments ready before beginning the surgery.
- A chef will have all the food items and kitchenware ready before taking the first order.

---

**Procedure for Teaching a Procedure**

Teach
Rehearse
Reinforce

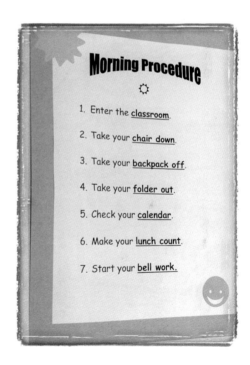

**Morning Procedure**
☼

1. Enter the <u>classroom</u>.

2. Take your <u>chair down</u>.

3. Take your <u>backpack off</u>.

4. Take your <u>folder out</u>.

5. Check your <u>calendar</u>.

6. Make your <u>lunch count</u>.

7. Start your <u>bell work</u>.

## Procedure for the Movement of Paper

If your students are sitting in columns and rows, it is more effective to have them pass their papers across the rows to the side of the room than up the row to the front of the room.

**Students should pass their papers across the rows, not up the rows.**

Why? Here are the problems with passing papers up the rows to the front of the room.

1. If papers are passed up the row, you cannot see what is happening behind each student's back as you stand at the front of the room waiting for the papers.

2. Some students tap, poke, shove, and hit the back of the student in front to announce that the papers are coming up the row. Others wave the papers in the face of the student in front. No matter what is done, the student in front is irritated, words are spoken, and the disturbance in the class increases.

3. When papers are passed from hand to hand, some papers may fall to the floor. It follows that the more students who handle the papers, the more likely it is that papers will fall, which detracts from valuable learning time.

4. There are frequently more students up a given row than across rows, therefore more students handle a stack of papers.

5. Thus, passing papers up a row takes longer to accomplish and is frequently accompanied by student agitation.

Routines are the hallmark of an effective classroom.

**We've established that there are advantages to passing papers across rows to the side of the room.** Now we need to establish a procedure:

**Step 1.** Have the students place their papers on the desk next to theirs, starting with the student at one end of the row.

**Step 2.** The next student is to add his or her paper to the stack and place the papers on the next desk. Do not have the students pass the papers from hand to hand. This will eliminate flicking of papers as they are passed.

**Step 3.** As the students pass the papers from desk to desk, monitor the procedure, making adjustments and corrections when necessary and praising students when appropriate.

**Step 4.** Walk to the side of the room and look across all the rows to monitor the procedure. This tactic allows you to see across the rows, whereas you cannot see behind the backs of students when you stand in front of the room while they are passing papers forward.

**Step 5.** Pick up the papers, or ask a student to pick up all the papers. If the students are sitting at tables instead of chairs in a row

- Have the students place their papers at the head of the table (point to the designated spot).

- Have students or an aide pick up the papers or do so yourself.

It is not a good procedure to have the students place their papers in a basket on the teacher's desk. This procedure involves too much movement and often results in a mess. Sometimes papers are claimed to be turned in when in reality they are still in the student's possession. **Whatever procedure you choose to use for collecting papers, rehearse the procedure the first time you collect papers.**

## The Procedure for Transition

**T**here will be transitions all day long. You can't prevent it. Times and schedules are mandated. Students go from one activity to another, from one class to another, from one teacher to another. There's recess, break time, lunch time, assembly time, club time, and a host of other things happening at school. Transitions can also include quickly moving from reading books to completing worksheets, from watching a video to participating in a discussion—from writing to recitations, from cleanup to preparations for class dismissal.

You want transitions in your classroom. Nothing would be so boring as to sit in one chair for seven hours doing one task day after day. No matter the transition, a procedure will help make it happen smoothly, without turmoil or commotion. **Effective teachers have procedures that quickly facilitate transition time.**

Students do not perform well when given an abrupt order to do something else. To help students ease into a transition, you must prepare them for it. It's best to say, "In two minutes I will want you to . . ."

Transition is difficult for some students to handle because it requires a student to do three things at one time:

1. Close one task.

2. Prepare for another task.

3. Refocus on a new task.

> **The key to a good transition is clarity and simplicity of instruction.**
>
> **Keep it short, simple, and easy to do.**

**Step 1. Close.** Give the student a time warning. "In two minutes, I will say 'change'" (or a word of your choice).

**Step 2. Prepare.** "When I say 'change,' I would like you to close or put away . . ."

**Step 3. Refocus.** "Then get your history book out, turn to page 222 and start with question 3." In addition to verbal instructions, always write the page number and question number on the board. Remember that you are asking someone, a young person perhaps, to do step 3 while they are trying to process steps 1 and 2.

**When the transition begins, do not talk during the transition time.** Talking distracts the students' ability to switch properly. If constant directions are being given, then your transition instructions are not short, simple, and easy to do.

Watch carefully and if someone is not shifting properly, give a firm smile and a hand signal or point to the directions on the board. The student will understand.

Harry K. Wong

**Everyone Returns on Time**

If you have ever heard Harry Wong speak, then you know his audiences number in the hundreds and thousands; yet, he can successfully motivate everyone to return from a break on time.

He does not say, "OK, let's take a break." What happens is people take a long break and saunter in gradually, standing in the aisles and talking until another set of instruction is issued.

He does not say, "Let's take a 20-minute break." No one clocks the interval and people just gradually come back in when they see others begin to return.

Instead, Harry says, "Here's the procedure for the break." And there are always playful chuckles from the audience when they hear the word "procedure," but they understand.

> "Please do not leave until I finish explaining the procedure. At 10:55 A.M., please be back in your seat—not walking in or standing in the aisle. Please be in your seat at 10:55. And when I raise my hand, I would like it quiet so that I can begin immediately on 'How to distribute materials in one minute and get everything back in one minute without anything being broken or stolen.'"

Then he asks, "May I see a show of hands if there is anyone who does not understand the procedure?" No hands go up. What's he doing? He's using a very common procedure used by all effective teachers. **He is asking for validation that they understand the procedure.**

In 20 minutes, or at 10:55 A.M., he stands on the stage facing a thousand people, raises his hand and smiles as the crowd comes to a hush in under five seconds.

Try this at a faculty meeting, in Sunday school, or at any club meeting. **The transition technique works.**

## Procedure to Solve the Pencil Problem

**D**on't get upset. Don't spend time muttering about the lack of responsibility these days. Don't waste another precious moment of learning time in the classroom.

**Don't fight it.**
**Just give them a pencil.**

Notice the two cans pictured. One can is labeled, "New Pencils" and has sharpened pencils in it.

The other can is labeled, "Used Pencils."

Put the cans at the entrance to the classroom. As students enter, they can select a sharpened pencil to use during the class period or school day. At the end of the class or day, the students

Can the problem. Have pencils available for those who need one.

return their pencils to the "Used Pencils" can as they exit the room. Appoint a class helper to sharpen the pencils for use the next day or period.

There will be no more whining, "I forgot my pencil. I can't do my work, today."

This is just one way to handle the pencil problem. As part of an end-of-day procedure, some elementary teachers have students put a sharpened pencil in their mail cubby and retrieve it upon entering the next morning. With their pencils sharpened the day before, the students are ready to write as soon as they enter the classroom.

### Transition Tunes

Robin Barlak teaches pre-school Special Education in Ohio. The students in her class sing their transition procedures. They sing the following tunes:

- good-morning song
- snack song
- clean-up song
- good-bye song

Her students eagerly anticipate each sing along time.

Robin Barlak

The concept is simple: If the student doesn't have a pencil, have one available to use. You design the procedure that works for you and your students to achieve that goal.

The same procedure applies to pencil points that break during class time. Instead of the constant grinding of the pencil sharpener, use your "New Pencils" pencil can for the replacement pencils. The students put the pencil with the broken point in the "Used Pencils" can and take one for use from the "New Pencils" can. It's a procedure that only involves the student with a broken pencil point and not the entire class.

**District Emergency**

**Code A**
- Evacuation or prepare for evacuation
- Transportation plan implemented
- Reunification plan implemented
- "Boogie Buckets" – if available
- Teachers must have class roll in posse
- All students need to be accounted for

Posted in a classroom in a Texas high school.

### Code Red

**There is no more important procedure than to have one for an emergency drill.** This may be for an impending weather problem such as a tornado or hurricane, severe thunderstorm, or for an earthquake. It may be for an intruder on campus or for campus violence.

Perhaps you have been in a store and you've heard seemingly innocuous messages like "Code 99 in Women's Shoes" come over the sound system. These are in-house codes used to call someone for assistance or to alert the employees of an emergency.

In some schools, "Code Red" comes through the speakers and is used to tell the teachers to put a procedure into place pending further information.

To guard against upsetting students and parents, letters explaining the drill should be sent home before the students are even rehearsed in the procedure.

Tell the students, "We don't expect anything terrible to happen to you. This is just to keep you safe."

"Drop and cover" is a signal to get out of the line of fire and protect yourself. It's what law enforcement people recommend if anyone is near gunfire.

In California, where an earthquake can strike instantly, the students have two seconds to duck under a desk when the teacher yells, "Duck and cover!"

In Saskatchewan, Canada, teacher Laurie Jay has the class roster Velcroed next to the door jamb. She is ready to grab the class roster when the class leaves for a fire drill or if they have to evacuate quickly.

**Be prepared. Emergencies come without warning. The better you and the students are prepared for an emergency, the greater the chances are of coming through it unharmed.**

## Compete Only Against Yourself

The message to your students is this:

- There is only one person in the world you need to compete against and that is yourself.

- Strive each day to be the best person possible.

- Your mission in life is not to get ahead of other people; your mission is to get ahead of yourself.

- While you are competing against yourself, you are expected to work with everyone else in this classroom cooperatively and respectfully.

- You are responsible not only for your own learning but for the learning of your groupmates as well.

## Procedures for Groups

**D**evelopmental psychologist Jean Piaget is credited with saying that kids learn best by doing and then thinking about what they've done. **Hands-on, minds-open learning is one of the best methods to engage students in their own learning.**

Analyzing data from The National Assessment Report on 14,000 eighth-grade math and science tests, Educational Testing Service found the following:

> **Students whose teacher conducted hands-on learning activities outperformed their peers by about 70% of a grade level in math and 40% in science.**[1]

An added value of having students involved in group activities is they are getting the training in leadership, group decision making, and conflict management they'll need to be successful in later life.

> **The better the students work together, the more learning that takes place.**

Group learning is a structured situation. There are procedures to learn so that during the activity, the students clarify opinions, compare impressions, share solutions, and develop skills for leadership and teamwork. A group of people who care for and are committed to one another are going to achieve the goal of an activity more quickly than if each were to attempt the task alone.

[1] Wenglingsky, Howard. (2000). *How Teaching Matters: Bringing the Classroom Back Into Discussions of Teacher Quality.* Educational Testing Service.

# How to Divide Your Class into Groups

The question is not how to divide the class but rather how quickly and smoothly the class will divide itself when the students are asked to do so.

Some teachers have no problems dividing their students into groups. When told to, the students do it rapidly and with ease. Other teachers have problems getting their students to divide into groups. When told to do so, the students whine, complain, and even refuse to work with other people. Why?

**Effective grouping is dependent on two major factors:**

1. The class climate

2. The explanation

### The Class Climate

Quite simply, if the students dislike the class or the teacher, or are not successful, grouping will be difficult. **It is important that all the determinants of successful student cooperation be in place before the class is divided into groups.**

The box to the right lists determining factors that may affect student cooperation. When students do not cooperate, the ineffective teacher helplessly wonders, "What am I supposed to do?" and looks for a quick fix to resolve the crisis. There are no quick fixes in education. Implicit in the "Factors of Success" list is a fact that **it is the teacher who is responsible for the success of the classroom.** The effective teacher knows this.

**GoBe**

**How to Motivate Your Students**

The lack of structure in classrooms often interferes with the learning process. Ways you can motivate your students to learn are in the **Go**ing **Be**yond folder for Chapter 20 at EffectiveTeaching.com.

## Factors of Success

The number in parentheses before the item indicates the chapter in this book where more information can be found.

(6) Enhancing positive expectations

(7) Using first-day-of-school activities

(8) Dressing for success

(9) Involving the home

(9) Using invitational learning

(10) Using the five appropriate words

(11) Implementing effective classroom management strategies

(12) Having the classroom ready with a positive atmosphere

(13) Introducing yourself properly

(14) Arranging and assigning seating

(15) Posting and starting assignments immediately

(16) Taking roll quickly

(18) Investing time on teaching the discipline plan

(19) Rehearsing procedures and routines

(21) Sharing the purpose of the lesson

(22) Giving tests that have purpose

(23) Explaining that students can govern the grade they earn

The Explanation

**How quickly students move into groups depends on how explicitly the teacher explains why groups will be formed and how.**

"OK, divide into groups of four" is not how groups are set up. Vague directions like this are sure to provoke comments like these:

> *Can I work with Andrew?*
> *Do I have to work with Charlotte?*
> *How long do I have to stay in this group?*

There is no need to solicit class input on grouping, because there will be no permanent groups in the class. Simply use this as a guide and tell your students the following:

- **Number of People in a Group:** *The class will be divided into groups many times. Each time there is a need for a group, the size of the group and the people in the group will depend on the nature of the activity. Some activities may take two people; others may take four, eight, or whatever. In fact, whatever number is needed, that will be the number of people in the group.*

- **Length of Time in a Group:** *Each time the class is divided into groups, the length of the group activity will depend on the nature of the activity. Some activities may take two minutes; others may take two days or two weeks. When the activity is finished, the group will be disbanded.*

Teaching young people to work well in groups will not happen overnight. Teaching the procedures for group work occurs incrementally and requires time, patience, and constant reinforcement. The societal shift from teaching students to "think for themselves" to a Y Generation era of people thinking with each other in teams sets well the stage for group activities in the classroom.

---

### They Knew the Names of Only Six Students

Here is part of a letter we received after presenting a workshop to a group of student teachers at a local college.

*One of the student teachers tried something in her class to test out one of your ideas. She handed out a blank seating chart to her ninth grade class and asked all the students to fill in the seating chart, giving first and last names. Only about 80 percent of the kids seemed to have more than two-thirds of the names correct. Many of them knew only first names, and there were even a few students who could name only 6 or 8 students sitting right around them out of a class of 35.*

The letter was dated May 20, so these student teachers were in a classroom that had been together for nine months. In addition, there were two teachers in the room: a cooperating teacher and a student teacher. Yet at the end of the year, few of the students really knew one another.

When you have a situation like this, students will misbehave. They will refuse to work together and will be reluctant to participate in group activities.

When students refuse to work together, the teacher may be to blame.

Students inherently like to work—and play—together. So the problem is not student participation or interaction. It is inadequate instructions. **When the directions, whether verbal or written, do not state what is to be done and what is to be accomplished, the students will create their own version.** The teacher must structure and write the activity for maximum understanding before the activity begins.

> **How smoothly students move into groups depends on how clearly the teacher explains the mechanics and responsibilities of the group assignment.**

## How to Structure Group Activities

Corporations spend hundreds of millions of dollars to find and train people to work together. Likewise, the effective teacher invests time to teach and train students to work together.

---

**Group Structure**

1. Specify the group **NAME**.

2. Specify the group **SIZE**.

3. State the **PURPOSE**, **MATERIALS**, and **STEPS** of the activity.

4. Teach the **PROCEDURES**.

5. Insist on **INDIVIDUAL ACCOUNTABILITY** for the work of the group.

6. Teach **EVALUATION METHODS** the students can use to determine how successfully they have worked together.

---

> **" The idea that people working together toward a common goal can accomplish more than people working by themselves is a well-established principle of social psychology. "**
>
> _Robert Slavin

Materials are pre-arranged in trays for quick distribution and collection. The trays are numbered to corresponding group numbers. One student is responsible for the tray and its contents.

**GoBe**

**Distributing Materials**

A student can distribute materials and have everything returned in a few minutes. Read how it's done in the **Going Be**yond folder for Chapter 20 at EffectiveTeaching.com.

1. **Specify the Group Name.** Learning together is epitomized by the concept of a support group. There are support groups for people trying to lose weight, stop addictions, overcome fears, and learn parenting skills. Support groups exist for single parents, senior citizens, abused children, battered wives, and war veterans. Networking groups, start-up groups, even CEO groups support each other in expanding their businesses.

> Consider calling your groups **support groups** and each member of the support group a **support buddy**.

A support group is formed by people, with like needs and goals, who join together to care for and help one another solve problems and achieve success. Support groups in the classroom are formed for the same reason.

2. **Specify the Group Size.** The size of the group is a factor of how many jobs are needed to complete the activity. For instance, in a group of four—

   **Student 1** is responsible for getting the materials and returning them to the appropriate place when the day or period is over.

   **Student 2** is responsible for seeing that the steps of the activity are followed.

   **Student 3** is responsible for making observations, recording data, and taking minutes while the activity progresses.

   **Student 4** is responsible for overseeing the writing of the group report.

3. **State the Purpose, Materials, and Steps of the Activity.** The students must be assigned an activity that is structured enough so they will know what is to be done and how to do it. See the activity on page 210 for an example of how to do this.

4. **Teach the Procedures.** Here are four procedures for you to consider with your students:

- **You are responsible for your own job and the results of the group.** (In the working world, you are responsible for your own job and the results of the people you work with.)

- **If you have a question, ask your support buddies.** Do not ask your teacher. (In the working world, you do not raise your hand for help. You seek, ask, research, and Google because you are expected to act on your own initiative.)

- **You must be willing to help if a support buddy asks you for help.** (In the working world, you are expected to apply teamwork skills.)

- **If no one can answer a question, then agree on a consensus question and appoint one person to raise a hand for help from the teacher.** (In the working world, negotiating and reaching agreements are the keys to success.)

5. **Hold the Individuals Accountable for the Work of the Team.** The teacher acts as consultant to the group after setting the objectives, assignments, and procedures. Problems are turned back to the group for resolution.

The support groups are to cooperatively write reports and give team presentations. The students are accountable for the quality of their group work and the results of their work.

**The support group will get a group grade and that grade will be each individual's grade, so it is important that each member of the group support the others' achievement efforts and contribute equally to the group's success.**

Group procedures are posted in this classroom.

### Sample Activity

In this activity, you will be working in **support groups** of four. Your teacher will choose the members of the **support group**. The reason you work in support groups is because when you discuss new ideas with your classmates, you understand the ideas better.

Sometimes you will work with your friends, and sometimes not. No matter who your support buddies are, your responsibility is to help one another understand and complete the activity. This is why you are called **support buddies**.

Your teacher will explain what jobs need to be done. Either the teacher will choose or you will be asked to choose who does which job.

You need to work together and talk about your assignment so that each member of the support group understands what your group has done and why. When it is time for your support group to report to the class, your teacher will call on only one member of your group. That member will explain the support group's results, so make sure that you all know what is happening before you get called on. When your support group looks good, you look good!

### How Do Propellers Work?

#### Background

Some airplanes and helicopters fly because of propellers. As the shape and pitch (angle) of the blade change, different results are obtained.

#### Problem

How many different ways can you design a propeller blade?
How does each design perform?
What is your evaluation of each design?

#### Support Group Jobs

**Equipment Manager:** Your job is to obtain the materials needed for the activity and to make sure that they are returned to the appropriate place at the end of the designated time.

**Facilitator:** Your job is to make sure that the group is following each step of the activity carefully and correctly.

**Recorder:** Your job is to observe, take minutes, and record data. You need to see that the support group has the proper forms to record the results of the activity as they occur.

**Reporter:** Your job is to coordinate the writing of the group report.

#### Materials

Binder paper, scissors, and a paper clip

### Activity Steps

1. Cut a piece of binder paper across its width into 2-inch strips.
2. Cut and fold the paper as shown in Fig. 1.
3. Hold and release the paper as shown in Fig. 2.
4. Try different versions of the helicopter.
5. Observe and record each result.

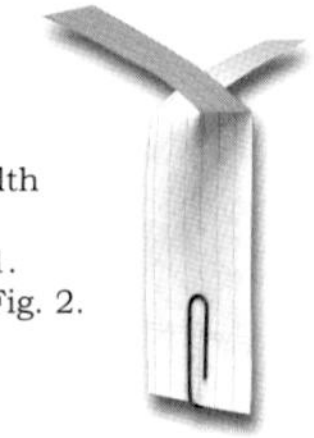

### Support Group Procedures

Move into your groups quickly and quietly.
Stay with your group in your area.
Do your job.
Help each other.
Follow the Activity Steps listed above.

### Support Group Responsibilities

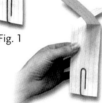

Fig. 1

Fig. 2

1. The **facilitator** needs to make sure that everyone has read and discussed the activity before beginning to work. Do not start until everyone knows the purpose of the activity, what needs to be done (Activity Steps), and what everyone needs to do (Support Group Procedures and Responsibilities).

2. The **equipment manager** needs to see that the materials are collected.

3. The **recorder** needs to see that a record page is set up on which to record what is to be observed. This can be a form for taking minutes, a table for recording numbers, or a chart for writing observations. Do not start until the record page has been set up.

4. The **facilitator** takes the group through the activity steps, as a moderator would take a meeting through its agenda.

5. At all times, the members of the **support group** must cooperatively and respectfully help each other by following the Activity Steps and the Support Group Procedures.

6. The **support group** must help the recorder record the results of the activity.

7. The **reporter** coordinates the writing of the group report. Make sure that everyone in the support group can explain the activity:
   its purpose,
   steps, and
   results.

When everyone can explain the purpose and results of the activity, all the members of the group should sign their names to the group report.

Thank you!

LEARNING
is an individual activity
but not a solitary one.

It is more effective
when it takes place within
a supportive community of learners.

6. **Teach Evaluation Methods Students Can Use to Determine How Successfully They Have Worked Together.** Tell your students to write down the group procedures. See the activity on page 211 for a list of the procedures. After each procedure, have students state whether the support group followed the procedure most of the time, sometimes, or not at all.

For each procedure, have the support groups discuss how they can improve their team skills. The procedures that must be discussed are those that received a rating of "most of the time." By reviewing them, and being aware of why they followed certain procedures *most of the time*, students can apply their successful ways of working together toward improving those procedures that were rated lower.

The more time students work together
and the more responsibilities students take for their work,
the greater the learning that takes place.

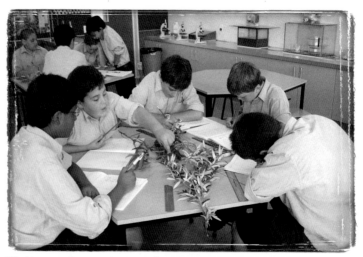

Working together equals greater learning.

# A Plan in Place

Sarah Jondahl

**S**arah Jondahl, a teacher in California, was ready the first day of her teaching career with a **specific, consistent classroom management action plan in a binder.** Although the binder took months of work to compile, her *plan* resulted in her success from the very first minute of her teaching career.

Sarah's plan includes a letter she sends to her students prior to the first day of school. It tells a little about her background and sets her students' expectations for lots of work and learning. It also contains the class' first homework assignment.

She scripted or planned the first day of school as follows:

**Greet Each Student at the Door**

- Direct them toward their assigned seats (alphabetical)
- Tell children to read and follow the instructions written on the board (the bellwork)

**Introduce Herself**

**Teach Classroom Procedures**

- **Teach Classroom Rules, Consequences, and Rewards**
- **Communicate the Expectations of the Classroom**

**Two major problems in a classroom are movement and noise.** Sarah had these solved on her first day of school. She planned out exactly how her students were to enter the classroom in the morning, come in from recess, line up to leave the classroom, get ready for lunch, walk in the halls, and get ready for dismissal. She then taught and rehearsed her students in how to be successful with the procedures.

**GoBe**

**Hallway Procedure**

With a schoolwide procedure in place, the movement of students in halls is very efficient. Read how it's done in the **Go**ing **Be**yond folder for Chapter 20 at EffectiveTeaching.com.

## An Elementary Teacher's Experience

*I am a single parent, and it is sometimes difficult to leave for work on schedule, but I was on time. Alas, my good fortune was not to continue because traffic came to a halt on the freeway due to an accident. As I sat in my car waiting to resume my commute, I tried to imagine the scene in my classroom. I could not call to let anyone know I would be late. What would 25 unsupervised fifth graders do? What would I find upon my arrival? Would the gym teacher be annoyed because we were all going to be late for gym?*

*What I found in my classroom was a beautiful reward for 20 years of loving students and striving to make them responsible and self-sufficient. To my amazement, I found an empty classroom and the following note left on my desk.*

*Dear Ms. Gould,*

*We took the attendance, did the lunch count, completed our morning math warm-ups, and went to gym.*

*Love,*
*Your Class*

*I cannot agree with you more on the importance of clearly defined procedures and routines. My students are proof of this.*

Sue Gould Flynn
Williamsville, New York

Today, Sarah is an experienced teacher and she says, "My classroom management plan is based on establishing procedures I learned from the book, *The First Days of School*. Having procedures in place from day one and teaching my students about these procedures made the educational experience in my classroom extremely effective."

Teachers like Sarah Jondahl will succeed in any kind of a school, because it truly makes no difference what grade level or subject you teach, whether you teach in a public, private, or charter school, whether your school is traditional or year-round, or whether your students are urban or rural. **All effective teachers have procedures to assist in managing a classroom and maximizing learning time.**

### Sarah's Sample Procedures

These are some of the procedures and routines Sarah has ready to teach on the first day and first week of school. **Steal from her list of ideas as you plan for your classroom!**

### Entering the Classroom

Students enter the classroom quietly and calmly, put their belongings away quickly according to the morning routine, and do the "bellwork."

### Bellwork

Each morning there is a "bellwork" assignment on the board or overhead projector. Students enter the classroom and get started on the assignment.

### Quieting the Class

The teacher raising her hand quiets the class.

### Taking Class Roll

A student is taught the procedure of how to be the "Attendance Keeper." This student places an "Absent" folder on that desk of the student who is absent. A glance around the room can quickly establish who is absent.

## Class Motto

Every morning the class says the classroom motto, which is posted on the wall in the front of the room. Everyone stands and says the motto together to start off our day.

## Collecting Seat Work

Work is collected according to the configuration of the desks. If the desks are arranged in rows, students collect their seatwork by passing the papers across their rows. Students seated at tables collect their work by placing their finished papers in the middle of their table. The student whose job is to collect papers walks around the room and picks up each table's stack of papers and puts them in the finished work basket at the front of the room.

## Turning in Work

There are two baskets placed in the front of the room. One basket is labeled "class work" and the other is labeled "homework." Children place their work in the appropriate basket.

## Notes From Home

Students place any notes from home in the basket labeled "Notes from Home."

## Restroom Breaks

Individual students are allowed to go to the bathroom four times a month without having a tally pulled. They use their daily agendas as their pass and have the teacher sign and date when they are going. Only one student may use the restroom at a time. Students are excused as a class to go to the restroom during lunch and recess.

## Going to Lunch

Students form two lines by the outside door, one for "home lunches" and one for "school lunches." The students buying their lunches line up in alphabetical order. Students are picked up after lunch on the blacktop as they wait in the area of their classroom number. (Numbers are painted on the blacktop.)

### A High School Teacher's Experience

*I arranged for a substitute teacher and left lesson plans in my grade book (world history and P.E.). Unfortunately, the substitute teacher went to the wrong room and arrived with 10 minutes remaining in first period. He found the students on task, working on their assignment. They had opened the classroom through another classroom, recognized the lack of a teacher, taken the roll book from my desk, taken the roll, found the lesson plan in the book, and proceeded with the lesson for the day.*

*There's more! On the day that I was absent, we were on an assembly schedule. The substitute teacher did not know of the schedule change. During my prep period, he left the campus to run an errand, planning to return by regular fifth period.*

*Unfortunately, while he was gone, fifth period happened. As I arrived the next day, this is what I was told. "When you didn't arrive, Mr. Wall, we took the roll for you. When you still weren't here, we did our calisthenics. Then we went outside to do our activities. When it started to rain, we came back in and played our game in the gym."*

*It wasn't planned, but my daily procedures had taken hold of my classes, and the students never missed a beat. Procedures and routines work!*

Bob Wall
Susanville, California

### Cafeteria

Students follow the cafeteria procedures as well as the classroom rules. Students clean up their sitting areas after they are done. Students should be on their best behavior by saying "Please" and "Thank You."

### Working in Learning Groups

Students are placed in teacher-chosen groups at all times. They are reminded of the procedures for Support Groups.

1. You are responsible for your own work.

2. You are to ask a "support buddy" for help if you have a question.

3. You must help if you are asked for help.

4. You may ask for help from the teacher after the entire group agrees on a question.

### Selecting Monitors

Students are chosen to do things in class by picking a Popsicle stick from the can labeled "Pick a Stick." Each student's name is written on the bottom of a Popsicle stick. The sticks are all placed in a can. The teacher draws a stick to pick students for a variety of things.

### Pinning Up Class Work

Students pin up their work on the clothesline at the front of the classroom. Whenever an activity that requires glue or paint is completed, the clothesline is used to hang the paper to dry. At the end of the day, students remove their dried papers and stack them in the "Class Work" basket.

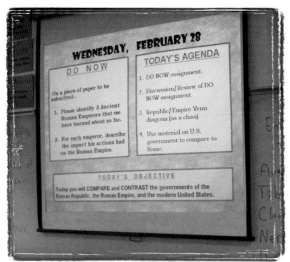

Even without the teacher present, the students know how this classroom runs.

### Keeping the Noise Level Down

A traffic signal is used to remind students of the noise level for the classroom. A large cutout stoplight is hung in the front of the room with three black circles and a hook on each circle. Green, yellow, and red circles have been cut to fit over the black circle. The red circle is hung from its hook to indicate *silent* time, the yellow circle for *whisper* time, and the green circle for *talk freely* time.

Classical music is played during class time. Children keep their noise levels lower than the sound of the music.

### Sending Notes Home

Notes to go home to parents at the end of the day are placed in the cubbies. This is the cubby keeper's job to do. Students are responsible for sharing all of the notes with parents each evening.

### When a Student Is Absent

When a student is absent, an absent folder with a yellow sticker is placed on that student's desk. Copies of all papers passed out during class or any notes that need to go home are placed inside the folder. When the student comes back to school he/she knows to complete the missed work in the yellow folder. The absent work is placed on the shelf in the front office of the school for parents to pick up after 3:00 P.M.

### Changing Groups/Transitions

The teacher gives a verbal announcement of "five minutes left" before changing centers, lessons, activities, etc. When it is time to change, a variety of methods are used:

1. Play music.

2. Snap/clap rhythm pattern led by teacher.

3. A bell is rung.

Students know what these different signals mean and make the change quickly and quietly.

Red No Talking.

Yellow Talk in Whispers.

Green Talk in an Indoor Voice.

The traffic light technique in Kristen Dardano's school library.

### If the Teacher Is Out of the Classroom

Students remain on task while the teacher is out of the room. Classroom rules and procedures are followed as they continue their work. The classroom aide or a teacher next door is available for help if needed.

### Daily Closing Message

At the end of the day the class reads the daily closing message, a short summary of the day's events. One child is chosen to read this message to the class as everyone else follows along. The daily closing message is prepared by the teacher during the day and then photocopied for each student to share with their parents that evening. This communication tool is a great way for teachers to keep parents aware of upcoming events, important information, and the children's day in school.

### Saying "Thank you"

At all times remember to say "thank you" to one another. Along with *thank you*, "please" should also be used at all times.

### End-of-Class Dismissal

The bell does not dismiss the class; the teacher dismisses the class. Students are dismissed when called upon, either individually or by groups.

### Transportation

Students follow the school's rules and classroom's procedures even when riding in vehicles on school outings. When walking to or from the school bus or a car, the procedures for the halls are followed. Students stay seated while on the bus or in the car and respect the property. Seat belts are worn at all times. Low voices are always used in the vehicle. There is no eating in the car or bus unless the driver says it's OK.

**Teacher success can be traced to the ability of the teacher to manage the classroom. Sarah Jondahl is an example of a successful and highly effective teacher.**

---

**GoBe**

**Create a Classroom Management Plan**

Sarah's classroom management action plan is the heart of the eLearning course featured on ClassroomManagement.com. Learn more about this course in the Going Beyond folder for Chapter 20 at EffectiveTeaching.com.

## The Class Runs Itself

Once you establish structure and responsibility, you can have the most exciting classroom in school, doing all the challenging and fascinating things students love to do. You will also be able to leave school knowing that if you were not in class tomorrow, the class could responsibly run itself.

---

**The ineffective teacher** begins the first day of school attempting to teach a subject and spends the rest of the year running after the students.
**The effective teacher** spends most of the first week teaching the students how to follow classroom procedures.

---

**When students know how the class is run, they will be more willing to do whatever you want them to do.** You can then have an exciting and challenging classroom that maximizes student learning time because procedures and routines manage the classroom.

---

### I'm Managing My Attitude, Too

*I had a disastrous first year as a teacher. I could not control my students and, as a result, I was asked to not return to teach.*

*Well, I got another job the second year in an alternative high school. That summer I got a copy of **The First Days of School** and I began to map out a plan. On the first day of school I started to work that plan.*

*Now, it felt really weird because it just didn't match my personality. However, the students seemed to be responsive and so I kept on the plan. What happened is that the very positive student response drove me to work the plan even harder. Soon I had the lowest referral rate in the school.*

*Now, these were students who had to leave their regular home school and come to my alternative classroom. In fact, one of them is now in prison. But they enjoyed my class.*

*They made astonishing progress and they liked my class. Several of them even went back to their home school and became star performers.*

***What happened is that gradually I realized that not only was I managing my classroom, I was also managing my teaching and managing my attitude.***

—Marjory T.

## The Effective Teacher

1. Structures the class with procedures and routines.

2. Teaches classroom and instructional procedures.

3. Has a classroom that can run itself.

*Third Characteristic*

**_Lesson Mastery**

The effective teacher knows
how to design lessons to help
students achieve.

# Unit  Third Characteristic _Lesson Mastery

The effective teacher knows how to design lessons
to help students achieve.

## Learning Basics

Learning has nothing to do with
what the **TEACHER COVERS**.
Learning has to do with
what the **STUDENT ACCOMPLISHES**.

## THE KEY IDEA

**The greater the structure of a lesson and the more precise the directions on what is to be accomplished, the higher the achievement rate.**

**W**e owe it to kids to teach them what they do not know and to teach it well. Politicians, the press, parents, and even the students are all clamoring for engaging curriculum. Learning. The future of humanity depends upon it. Students come to school for one reason only—to learn.

Remember we stated that Chapters 19 and 20 on procedures and routines are the most important chapters in the book. You must get your classroom organized for learning. **Unit D is the most important Unit in the book. It will show you how to get your students to learn and achieve.**

Assuming you have mastered the skill of positive expectations and classroom management, you are now ready to teach the knowledge and skills students come to school to learn.

> **But you can only teach the knowledge and skills
> if you have built a caring relationship and
> have created a safe, organized classroom.**

The effective teacher knows how to

- **Teach** for student learning (Chapter 21)   INSTRUCTION – What the teacher does to teach for learning
- **Test** for student learning (Chapter 22)
- **Assess** for student learning (Chapter 23)   ASSESSMENT – What the teacher does to assess for student learning
- **Enhance** student learning (Chapter 24)

Children come to school to learn.

**The effective teacher is learner focused.**  The student is the learner and a learner must learn!  For this to happen, the teacher must be an effective instructor.  **Good instruction is 15 to 20 times more powerful than family background and income, race, gender, and other explanatory variables.**[1]

---

**Student learning must be at the heart of all decisions made in the school.**

---

The research is very specific about student learning.

- Mike Schmoker says, "Lay out a sound set of standards and then actually teach these standards and there will be an immense increase in levels of achievement almost immediately."[2]

- Robert Marzano reported on a study of what affects student achievement and says, "It is what gets taught!"[3]

- Andrew Porter of the University of Pennsylvania says, "What gets taught is the strongest possible predictor of gains in achievement."[4]

**Schools exist and teachers are hired for one reason only:  to help students learn and achieve.**

---

[1] Hershberg. T. (December 2005).  "Value-Added Assessment and Systemic Reform:  A Response to the Challenges of Human Capital Development."  Phi Delta Kappa *Kappan*.

[2] Schmoker, Mike.  Author of *Results: the key to continuous school improvement*.  (1996).  Alexandria, Va.: Association for Supervision and Curriculum Development.  Retrieved from an email correspondence with authors April 2007.

[3] Marzano, Robert.  (2003).  *What Works in Schools: Translating Research into Action*.  Alexandria, Va.: Association for Supervision and Curriculum Development.

[4] Porter, Andrew.  (October 2002).  "Measuring the Content of Instruction:  Uses in Research and Practice."  *Educational Researcher*, 31(7) pp. 3–14.  Updated from an email correspondence with authors August 2007.

Teachers are charged with getting the students to comprehend and achieve. There is no one right way to do this. Just like classroom management, there is no one right procedure for getting the students to do what you want them to do. There are many options, but they are based on core information. That's the purpose of Unit D—to teach you some fundamentals and understandings all teachers need to know about mastery learning.

This chapter shows how to write assignments in which students demonstrate that learning, comprehension, or mastery has taken place.

## What Is an Ineffective Assignment?

> **The bottom line in education is student learning. If the students do not do their assignments, no learning will occur.**

It is commonplace for teachers to give assignments and expect students to complete the assignments. However, not all students complete their assignments, often because they either cannot understand the assignment or they fail to see the reason for doing it. In both cases, the assignment may be poorly designed.

For instance, the teacher says,

> "The assignment is Chapter 7, and there will be a test on Friday covering everything in Chapter 7."

*Chapter 7*? The students have absolutely no idea what this means. Neither do the parents, whom the teachers incessantly proclaim should be more involved.

**An ineffective assignment results when the teacher tells the class what will be covered.** Not only is "Chapter 7" an ineffective assignment, it is not an assignment at all. It is simply an announcement of a chapter number.

The following are also ineffective assignments:

| | |
|---|---|
| Open your books to page 143 | Long division |
| Pages 404–413 | Do this worksheet |
| Questions 9 to 19 | Watch this video |
| *Moby Dick* | Break into groups |
| Write a paper on the Byzantine period | |

**It is difficult if not impossible for a student to get the work done when the assignment does not spell out what the student is to learn.** There are no standards, no objectives, and no activities done for a specified reason. It's like shooting arrows blindfolded hoping that one will hit a non-existing target.

**When the students have no idea what is to be learned, and the teacher has no idea what is to be taught, no student learning can take place.**

This explains why students come to class every day and ask, "What are we going to do today? Or they ask that really nerve-racking question, "Are we doing anything important today?" Don't blame the students, because they truly do not understand the assignment. Some students call this "mystery learning."

Ineffective teachers stumble from day to day, wondering what to do next. Their students ask, "Why are we doing this?" Or they declare, seemingly in unison, "We're bored." When this happens, no learning takes place and behavior problems ensue.

Common sense dictates that if you do not teach it, students won't learn it. If a salesperson does not up-sell the product, the customers aren't going to buy it. If the pitcher does not throw the ball, the batter will have nothing to hit. And, if you don't send invitations to a wedding, the guests are not going to come!

**Stop asking,** "What video am I going to show? What activity am I going to do? What worksheet am I going to give out?"

The only one doing any work in these questions is the teacher. And when the test scores come back disappointing, as they surely will be, this teacher will become angry and blame the students: "Well, I covered the material. If they don't want to learn it, it's not my fault."

**Here's what you should be asking:**
- What do I want the students to learn?
- What do I want the students to accomplish?

Convey to the students what you want them to learn or accomplish so that they can take control of their own learning. **When the students know what they are to learn, it becomes "mastery learning," rather than "mystery learning."**

**Learning has nothing to do with what the TEACHER COVERS.
Learning has to do with what the STUDENT ACCOMPLISHES.**

**The role of a teacher is not to COVER. The role of a teacher is to UNCOVER.** The effective teacher uncovers the lesson by telling the students, up front, what the students will accomplish.

## The Four Steps to Creating an Effective Assignment

Look at the word "assignment." It means that someone will be assigned a task, and at the end of the task a result or a product should be evident. For instance, you say to an assistant, "Please type this letter and then give it to me so that I can sign it." The letter may go back and forth a couple times, but the assistant has been given a clear assignment and the expectation is a completed and correct letter.

---

**The Four Steps to Creating an Effective Assignment**

1. Determine what you want the students to accomplish. (page 228)
2. Write each accomplishment as a single sentence. (page 234)
3. Give the students a copy of the same sentences. (page 241)
4. Post or send these sentences home with the students. (page 243)

---

**Stop Covering and Start Accomplishing**

**Stop asking,** "What am I going to cover tomorrow?"

**Start asking,** "What will my students learn, achieve, and accomplish tomorrow?"

One of the most frequently used and useless phrases in education is, "I have so much to cover. How am I going to finish it by the end of the year?" Notice that the word *I* is used twice and the word *student* is never used.

**Getting the students to learn is the teacher's top priority.** Teaching is not "coverage" because coverage has nothing to do with learning. Why? Because the students do not know what the teacher wants them to accomplish. Worse yet, the teacher probably does not know what he or she wants the students to know.

Learning has nothing to do with what the teacher covers. **Learning has to do with what the student is able to accomplish. Learning occurs only when a student demonstrates accomplishment.**

Here's another example: You go to the bakery to inquire about cakes for your wedding. The baker produces a binder of pictures showing various wedding cakes. After one is selected, you say, "On Saturday, July 18, I want that cake delivered to the church fellowship hall at 3 P.M." The baker has been given a clear assignment: a specific product is to be delivered at a specified time and place.

**Similarly, good classroom assignments specify what the students are to do or learn. The finished product is what the teacher wants produced as evidence of having completed the assignment.**

**Step 1. Determine what you want the students to accomplish.** The question that must be asked repeatedly is, "What do I want my students to learn?" not "What am I going to cover?"

This is a question best answered by the school or district curriculum guide. This guide pairs what the student is to learn with state standards. **Standards identify what is essential for students to master. Most states have standards.** In Virginia, they are called Standards of Learning (SOL); in Arizona, they are called Arizona's Instrument to Measure Standards (AIMS).

**Standards form the core or backbone of the curriculum. With standards in place, schools then can create guides for the curriculum. These guides tell the teachers what the students are to master and recommend methods to teach the content.** When you are hired, ask for the curriculum guide for your teaching assignments.

**GoBe**

**You Teach the Students, Not the Textbook**

Teaching is not covering the textbook. Neither is the textbook the curriculum. More on this concept is in the **Go**ing **Be**yond folder for Chapter 21 at EffectiveTeaching.com.

## What Is a Standard?

Standard is derived from the French word, *etandard*, the pennant around which soldiers would rally or go forth from. It represented the unifying symbol of solidarity for the soldiers' purpose or mission.

The term **standard** has become the measuring rod of quality used in many fields. When buying a car, we look at the performance *standards*. We buy from companies that produce goods and services at the highest *standards*. We expect the food and drug industry to meet the highest quality *standards*. The buildings we work in and roads we drive on are expected to be constructed to rigorous safety *standards*. We tell students that we want them to act with the highest *standards* of behavior.

There is nothing we dislike more than having to return a defective product. Many companies proudly state that they meet ISO 9000 specifications, a set of worldwide standards companies strive to qualify for. ISO, International Organization for Standardization, consists of a set of standards that monitors the manufacturing process to produce quality goods and reduce defects.

We expect and demand high standards to protect and enhance our lives. This is why most every enterprise has standards, **including education**.

Here are typical subject level standards from state education guides:

**Elementary Geometry, Minnesota**
Classify simple shapes by specified attributes and identify simple shapes within complex shapes.

**Seventh Grade Physical Education, California**
Explain the effects of nutrition and participation in physical activity on weight control, self-concept, and physical performance.

**High School Language Arts Literacy, New Jersey**
Write multi-paragraph, complex pieces across the curriculum using a variety of strategies to develop a central idea (e.g., cause-effect, problem/solution, hypothesis/results, rhetorical questions, parallelism).

Standards do not deprive you of creativity. Rather, they form the base point from which to design the lesson. Builders can design and construct homes in an unlimited number of ways, provided they do not violate the city's standards. The city checks to see that the plans meet codes or standards for the proper use of plumbing, electricity, structure, roofing, and other construction factors. If you were to buy a home, you would want to know that your home was built to code, which signifies that it meets the standards.

The building industry has standards.

> **Standards are the basis for learning.**
> **Standards are the basis for creativity.**
>
> **Standards describe what to teach, not how to teach it.**

## What Is a Curriculum?

**The curriculum is the course of study and experiences that states what the students are to learn.** It is the teacher's guide of what to teach and what the students are to learn.

A curriculum is a school document that identifies the content to be taught and the suggested methods to be used. It is like a menu in a restaurant that lists the different wholesome food items available and how they are prepared. It is then up to the chef to create the recipes so diners can enjoy the food.

The curriculum is created by a committee of teachers, administrators, and curriculum specialists. This group takes the state standards and designs curricular and instructional strategies that best convey the content to the students. This work is assembled into a curriculum guide. Its purpose is to guide the teachers so that students can achieve high levels of proficiency in the content areas.

The district curriculum guide should

1. Identify the content (facts, concepts, topics, themes, skills, etc.).

2. Suggest instructional methods to be used (discussion, case studies, role playing, rehearsals, real-life experiences, cooperative learning, experiments, etc.).

3. Suggest activities to teach the content or illustrate the method to be used.

Therefore, if you have not already been given the curriculum guide, ask for it. You must have a guide as you teach, just as you must have a map as you travel. **It is not your position to develop a personal curriculum for your classroom. It is your charge to deliver the district curriculum.**

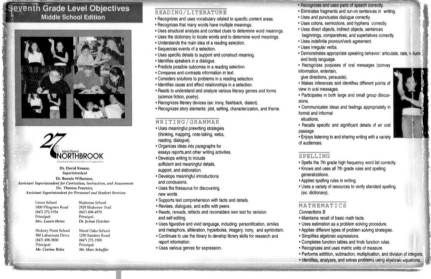

The Northbrook School District 27 in Illinois has its curriculum posted on its website.

Too often, new teachers have little or no access to information about what exactly they are to teach their students. Too many are handed a key to the classroom and sent off to teach, without adequate information about curriculum and available resources, and often without knowing what their students are expected to learn before going on to the next grade.

A research group at Harvard, The Project on the Next Generation of Teachers, discovered that

> **Few teachers began teaching with a clear, operational curriculum in hand, and even fewer received curricula that aligned with state standards.**[5]

This recipe for discouragement and failure on the part of new teachers and their students can be alleviated if a district has a curriculum guide for each subject and grade level and then shows new teachers how to implement the curriculum guide.

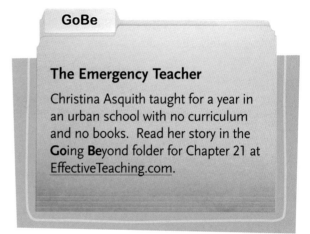

**GoBe**

**The Emergency Teacher**

Christina Asquith taught for a year in an urban school with no curriculum and no books. Read her story in the **Go**ing **Be**yond folder for Chapter 21 at EffectiveTeaching.com.

Lafourche Parish Public Schools

*Shaping the future, one child at a time.*

**Mathematics Curriculum Work Plans**

*A teacher affects eternity. He can never tell where his influence stops.*
—Henry Adams

**A Curriculum Work Plan**

**Many school districts have well-organized curriculum guides.** Lafourche Parish Public Schools in Louisiana have **curriculum work plans**. These are correlated to the Louisiana Comprehensive Curriculum standards. The Lafourche Work Plans have each student objective aligned with state standards. Each objective is accompanied by several suggested activities—so the Work Plan is really a teachable curriculum.

Each Work Plan provides teachable objectives, a list of all available resources, technology connections, teaching activities, remediation activities, enrichment activities, sample assessments, and suggested activities.

A teacher is not required to use the activities in the Work Plan; they are merely suggestions. However, just think how much more successful a teacher could be in a district that supplies its teachers with a **Curriculum Work Plan. This is teaching for mastery learning, not mystery learning!**

[5]Kauffman, D., S. M. Johnson, S. Kardos, E. Liu, and H. G. Peske. (March 2002). "Lost at Sea: New Teachers' Experiences With Curriculum and Assessment." *Teachers College Record, 104*(2), pp. 273–300.

## Are You Teaching for Accomplishment or Just Telling the Students What to Do?

**Ineffective teachers do not teach for learning; they tell students what to do.** Often the work that is assigned is used to kill time. Unfortunately, there are teachers who thumb through the teacher's manual, saying to themselves:

*What can I find to keep them busy?*      *What can I do to kill the period?*      *What fun activity can I find?*
*What can I use to keep them quiet?*      *What worksheet can I give them?*      *What can I do to make students like me?*

As a result, an ineffective assignment tells students what to do; for example:

Read Chapter 24.                                    Complete this worksheet.
Do the problems on page 34.                         Write a paper on Mexico.
Do this activity.                                   Sit quietly and read pages 23 to 30.
Answer the questions at the end of the chapter.     Read the instructions on page 1.

These are not accomplishments. They are jobs. They tell the student what to do. They do not tell students what is to be comprehended, learned, or achieved. When a student is told what to do, no sense of accomplishment or responsibility is associated with what the student is to learn. Assignments like those in the example cause students to say:

*What are we doing today?*                          *What's our assignment?*
*Are you going to show us a video today?*           *Why do we have to do this?*
*Are we doing anything important today?*            *I'm finished; what do I do now?*

The student may be finished, but did the student learn anything? In an ineffective classroom, students just sit around waiting for the teacher to tell them what to do.

Effective teachers teach for student accomplishment and responsibility. When an assignment helps a student understand what is to be accomplished, it is also teaching responsibility. Students who are responsible and are working for learning and accomplishment will ask questions like these:

*How am I doing?*          *What do you think of this?*          *Will I be first chair?*          *Is this good enough for an A?*

Questions like these tell you that the student is constantly and responsibly working to improve.

> **Teach for accomplishment, using structured assignments with objectives,
> and not only will the students demonstrate competence,
> but you will be regarded as a competent teacher also.**

## "Your Assignment Is Chapter 24"

*Why didn't someone tell me how to give an assignment? I thought giving an assignment was telling the students what chapters to read.*

*"Students, your assignment for this week is Chapter 24. And the test this Friday will cover everything in Chapter 24."*

*When I gave them the test a week later, I was horrified at all the poor test scores. And I started to blame the students for their poor achievement.*

- *They were not studying "hard enough."*
- *They were not spending "enough time" on their homework.*
- *They were not reading "carefully."*
- *They were not "focusing."*

*I had assigned, lectured on, led discussion on, and given them study time on the chapter. I even had a worksheet of questions for homework. It had to be the students' fault.*

*Little did I know that when the students went home to do their homework, the parents would ask, "What's your assignment?"*

*The students would respond, "Chapter 24."*

*Both the parents and the students were at a loss as to what the assignment was. What does "Chapter 24" mean? What is the student supposed to learn? How is the parent to help?*

*It never occurred to me that the problem was me. I did not know how to give an assignment.*

*I now know how to give assignments that help students achieve. It was not until years later that I learned this.*

_A high school teacher

> **The greater the structure of a lesson and the more precise the directions on what is to be accomplished, the higher the achievement.**

**Step 2. Write each accomplishment as a single sentence.** To teach for accomplishment, you must have a series of single sentences that clearly and precisely state what is to be accomplished. These single sentences are called **OBJECTIVES** or **LEARNING CRITERIA**.

> **OBJECTIVES** are what a student must achieve to accomplish what the teacher states is to be learned, comprehended, or mastered.

## The Objective of the Lesson Is the Aim of Learning

> Objectives help students anticipate, focus, and understand the purpose of a lesson.

**F**ocusing on objectives makes a huge difference in student learning. The research of Kevin Wise and James Okey showed that "the effective classroom appears to be the one in which the students are kept aware of instructional objectives and receive feedback on their progress toward these objectives."[6] In other words, if students know what they are to learn, you increase the chances that they WILL learn.

**Objectives are classroom learning targets. The students know what they are aiming for; thus, they know what they are responsible for learning.**

When both the student and teacher are moving toward the same target, goal, or objective, learning can occur.

> **The students must be given a set of objectives at the beginning of their assignments telling them what they are responsible for accomplishing.**

---

### Only One out of 12

Wise and Okey wanted to know what teaching strategies were most important in helping students achieve. They looked at these 12 possible factors:

- Audiovisual
- Grading
- Inquiry/discovery
- Focusing on objectives
- Hands-on manipulation
- Modifying the textbooks and instructional materials
- Presentation mode of teacher
- Questioning strategies
- Testing
- Teacher direction
- Wait time
- Miscellaneous

They found that **focusing on objectives** had the biggest influence on student achievement.

---

[6]Wise, Kevin, and James Okey. (1983). "A Meta-Analysis of the Effects of Various Science Teaching Strategies on Achievement." *Journal of Research in Science Teaching*, pp. 419–435.

**Objectives give purpose to a lesson.** Students get more done when they see **where they are going** and **what they are doing**.

Objectives are important for the teacher too, because they specify what the teacher is to teach. Effective assignments occur when teachers teach with the end results in mind.

Objectives serve two purposes:

1. The lesson objectives tell the students what is to be accomplished.

2. The lesson objectives tell the teacher what is to be taught.

**As the students and the teacher are moving toward the same goals, there is a greater chance for learning to take place.**

Each objective must begin with a verb that states the action to be taken; it must show an accomplishment. The most important word to use in an assignment is a verb, because verbs help clarify whether or not an accomplishment has taken place.

> **To teach for learning, use words, especially verbs, that state how to demonstrate that learning has taken place.**

Verbs are "action words" or "thinking words." The chart on the next page lists some verbs that can be used. The verbs have been organized into levels like floors in a building. The chart is based on the work of Dr. Benjamin Bloom of the University of Chicago, and is known as Bloom's Taxonomy.[7] His taxonomy arranges verbs into six related groups:

1. Knowledge
2. Comprehension
3. Application
4. Analysis
5. Synthesis
6. Evaluation

> **"** *To begin with the end in mind means to start with a clear understanding of your destination.* **"**
>
> _Stephen Covey

**GoBe**

**Bloom's Taxonomy Revision**

A revision to Bloom's Taxonomy with two major changes is being used by some educators. Details are in the **Go**ing **Be**yond folder for Chapter 21 at EffectiveTeaching.com.

[7] Bloom, Benjamin S. (ed.). (1956). *Taxonomy of Educational Objectives: Cognitive Domain.* New York: Longman.

## Thinking Words to Use in Assignments

Bloom divided useful verbs into six categories. **All the verbs in a group invoke a specific kind of thinking skill needed to complete an assignment.** The verbs tell what the student is to do.

**6 Evaluation**

appraise, choose, compare, conclude, decide, defend, evaluate, give your opinion, judge, justify, prioritize, rank, rate, select, support, value

**5 Synthesis**

change, combine, compose, construct, create, design, find an unusual way, formulate, generate, invent, originate, plan, predict, pretend, produce, rearrange, reconstruct, reorganize, revise, suggest, suppose, visualize, write

**4 Analysis**

analyze, categorize, classify, compare, contrast, debate, deduct, determine the factors, diagnose, diagram, differentiate, dissect, distinguish, examine, infer, specify

**3 Application**

apply, compute, conclude, construct, demonstrate, determine, draw, find out, give an example, illustrate, make, operate, show, solve, state a rule or principle, use

**2 Comprehension**

convert, describe, explain, interpret, paraphrase, put in order, restate, retell in your own words, rewrite, summarize, trace, translate

**1 Knowledge**

define, fill in the blank, identify, label, list, locate, match, memorize, name, recall, spell, state, tell, underline

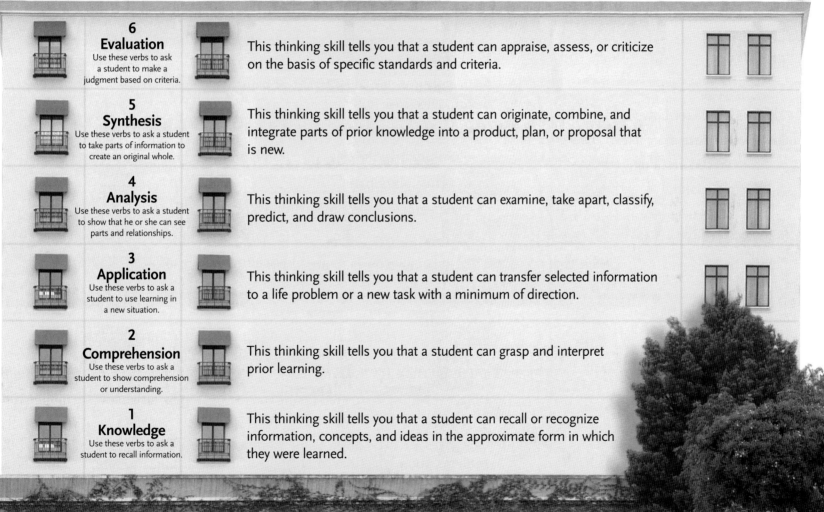

## Levels of Student Thinking Desired in an Assignment

The level of thinking you want from a student in an assignment is based on the level from which you select the verb to use. The type of thinking required at each level becomes more complex as you go from knowledge to evaluation.

**6**
**Evaluation**
Use these verbs to ask a student to make a judgment based on criteria.

This thinking skill tells you that a student can appraise, assess, or criticize on the basis of specific standards and criteria.

**5**
**Synthesis**
Use these verbs to ask a student to take parts of information to create an original whole.

This thinking skill tells you that a student can originate, combine, and integrate parts of prior knowledge into a product, plan, or proposal that is new.

**4**
**Analysis**
Use these verbs to ask a student to show that he or she can see parts and relationships.

This thinking skill tells you that a student can examine, take apart, classify, predict, and draw conclusions.

**3**
**Application**
Use these verbs to ask a student to use learning in a new situation.

This thinking skill tells you that a student can transfer selected information to a life problem or a new task with a minimum of direction.

**2**
**Comprehension**
Use these verbs to ask a student to show comprehension or understanding.

This thinking skill tells you that a student can grasp and interpret prior learning.

**1**
**Knowledge**
Use these verbs to ask a student to recall information.

This thinking skill tells you that a student can recall or recognize information, concepts, and ideas in the approximate form in which they were learned.

## What Objectives Accomplish

Objectives or criteria are written to accomplish two things: assign and assess. (Chapter 23 discusses assessment.)

1. **Assign.** Objectives give direction or tell a student what is to be comprehended or mastered in an assignment.

2. **Assess.** Objectives tell the teacher if additional study is needed to master an objective.

Each objective should be stated as a single sentence. Here are examples of typical objectives:

- Name, in order, the parts of the digestive system.
- Summarize the class discussion on important study skills.
- Plan a pizza party.
- Categorize the contents of the box.
- Create a new ending for the story.
- Judge the effects of global warming.

## When and How to Write Objectives

Objectives state what you want students to accomplish. **The students must know before the lesson, assignment, or activity begins what they are responsible for learning.**

Objectives must be written before the lesson begins because objectives tell the teacher what is to be taught and what they are to assess for learning.

Objectives are to be given to the students when a lesson begins so the students know what they are responsible for learning and what they will be tested on.

---

**Why Do Students Get Low Grades?**

**Students will achieve more if they know what**

- **Procedures (do)***

and

- **Objectives (learn)**

**they are responsible for.**

*See Unit C

---

Writing objectives is easy. There are only two things to do.

1. **Pick a verb.** Refer to the list on page 236, and use the verb you select as the first word in a sentence.

   Only you know which verb to pick because you know what you want or need to teach. Only you know the level of competence and readiness of your students. Only you know what you want to prepare your students to do next.

   Refrain from choosing verbs all from one category, because this would challenge your students at only one level of thinking.

---

**Objectives Begin with Verbs**

Verbs are **action words** that do two things:

1. Verbs tell the student what is to be accomplished.

2. Verbs tell the teacher what to look for to see if the student has accomplished what the teacher specified.

---

2. **Complete the sentence.** The verb tells the student what action is to be taken and the rest of the sentence tells the student what is to be accomplished or mastered.

   Make sure the sentence is precise and easily understood by you, the students, and their parents.

**Applying Bloom's Taxonomy to the Study of Antarctica**

1. **Knowledge:** Who was the first person to reach the South Pole?

2. **Comprehension:** Describe the difference between the Arctic and Antarctic regions.

3. **Application:** Give an example of one piece of modern technology that, had it been available to the explorers, would have made a difference in their trip.

4. **Analysis:** Compare the weather at the South Pole on December 1 and June 1 in any given year.

5. **Synthesis:** Pretend that you made the journey. Write an entry in your diary describing your emotions on the day you reached the South Pole.

6. **Evaluation:** Should Antarctica remain a continent free of development and left with its natural habitat? Justify your position.

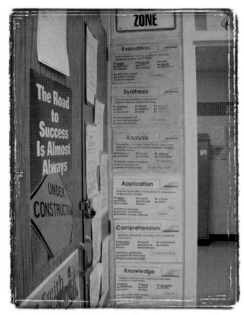

A list of verbs is posted in the classroom so the students and teacher can keep track of verbs that have been used.

Words like the following are not good action verbs because it is difficult, if not impossible, to determine from them what the student is to do. They are also not on Bloom's list. **Do not use these verbs when you write objectives.**

| | | | |
|---|---|---|---|
| appreciate | enjoy | beautify | love |
| be happy | like | celebrate | understand |

It is important that a layperson can easily read and understand an objective. **The more understandable the sentence, the greater the chance that the student will do what is intended.**

Objectives should be clear, concise, explicit, in student-friendly language, and aligned to the tests. Do not write complex objectives like the following, taken from a published elementary science program:

> *Given two different molds growing on the same plate, the student will describe the inhibiting reaction at the interface of the molds.*

Write precise objectives that state what you want the student to accomplish. The above objective could have been written in a straightforward and simpler way for all to understand:

> *Describe what happens when two molds grow together.*

Objectives do not have to be written; they can be stated verbally. This is a useful approach in the primary grades and certain special education situations. You need not present all the objectives at one time, either. For elementary students, it may be more appropriate to state the objectives one or two at a time.

**Most importantly, you must continually look at the objectives to make sure the class is on course.**

## How to Write an Objective

**Step 1.** Pick a verb. (See the chart on page 236.)

**Step 2.** Complete the sentence.

> Examples:
>> **List** four collective nouns.
>> **Create** a different system to catalog CDs in a library.

Can you explain why "Chapter 5" is not a good assignment?
Can you explain why "List four collective nouns" is a good assignment?

For instance, if you are driving, you refer repeatedly to your map. If you are building a house, the contractor, inspector, and you refer frequently to the blueprints. And if you are at a conference, you refer to the program to determine the topic of the next session and where it will be held.

Schools typically have an open house about a month after school begins. When the parents ask you, "How do I tell what my child's assignment is?" tell them how you give assignments.

When you show the objectives to the parents, use the analogy of a map, blueprint, shopping list, or agenda. This will help them understand what you are teaching. The better they understand what you are teaching, the better they can help their children do what they need to learn.

When the objectives of a lesson are matched to the district and state standards it is called *alignment*. What the student is to learn and how you teach it fit together smoothly.

**Step 3. Give the students a copy of the objectives.**

The assignment on the next page, used with great success for years, is presented as an example only. Ignore the subject and focus on how the objectives for the assignment are written as "study guidelines." Then apply the example to your own subject matter.

> **Students can be in control**
> **when they know**
> **what objective they are responsible to learn.**

## The Optimum Length of an Assignment

The shorter the assignment, the MORE likely the student will complete it. The longer the assignment, the LESS likely the student will complete it. Except for term papers and other special projects, there are optimum lengths for assignments.

- No high school assignment should exceed five days.

- No junior or middle school assignment should exceed four days.

- No intermediate school assignment should exceed three days.

- No primary school assignment should exceed a day or, occasionally, two.

- No special education assignment should exceed 15 minutes.

## The Digestive System

The digestive system breaks down food into usable forms for the cells.

**YOUR STUDY GUIDELINES**

Just as you would use a map to guide you to a destination, use these sentences to guide you in your study of this unit.

1. Define all the vocabulary words.
2. State the function of the digestive system.
3. Give examples of the different types of nutrients.
4. Differentiate and give examples of nutritious and nonnutritious foods.
5. Compare mechanical and chemical digestion.
6. Draw the digestive system, and state the function of each part.
7. Explain how nutrients get into the blood.
8. Devise a healthy diet for a weeklong trek into the mountains.
9. Assess the effectiveness of different weight-loss programs.

## How to Use Study Guidelines to Help Students Achieve

1. The first time you give students the assignment, explain to them the concept of "study guidelines." They are guides that you have prepared to help them complete the assignment. You want to be their guide and help them be successful.

2. Use the analogy of a map, program, agenda, or shopping list to explain the use of study guidelines. For example, explain to the students that just as a traveler would use a map as a guide to a destination, each sentence serves as a map to guide them in their study of this unit. The study guidelines are to be presented as "user friendly," not intimidating.

3. Tell students that the best way to use the study guidelines is to place them next to whatever source they are studying, such as their textbooks, worksheets, or notes. They are to use the study guidelines, just as their parents might use a road map as a guide while driving.

4. Tell students that the central concept for the lesson is between the two horizontal lines at the top. They are to focus on this as the key idea for the assignment (as opposed to meaningless assignments like "Chapter 24," "decimals," or "The Middle East").

5. Point out the numbered sentences on the study guidelines. It's not necessary to use the term objectives, but you might choose to do so. Explain to the students that these sentences tell exactly what they are responsible for, and that they must master these specifics if they are to understand the key idea.

6. Tell students that each sentence will be the subject of a series of questions on the exam. The students will be tested for their comprehension and mastery of each sentence or objective. (See Chapter 23.)

**Study guidelines assist students and parents in clearly defining the expectations for success in and mastery of the concepts presented in the lesson.**

**Step 4.  Post or send the objectives home with the students.**

### The Objective Is the Object of the Lesson

- Write the objective on the board.  Students are more likely to buy into the lesson and are more likely to participate in activities if they understand why they're doing it.

- Begin a lesson by pointing to the objective so that everyone knows where they are going.

- Refer to the objective during a lesson to allow the students to check for their own understanding.  This helps them recognize when they don't understand the lesson.

- Bring closure to a lesson with the objective to assist the students in focusing on their learning.

## What About Students Who Need Additional Directions?

bjectives are fine for average to above-average students who can be entrusted with a responsibility and will "take the ball and run with it."  These students will grow up to be teachers, retailers, or executives and will be able to translate a plan or a project into concrete results.  **They are people who know how to solve problems and achieve on their own.  They do not have to be told what to do!**

There are many students (and adults), however, who want to be told what to do.  These students are not necessarily below-average students.  They may be students who have no background in your subject, or who face a linguistic or cultural barrier.  For these students, write specific questions or procedures for each objective.  **This is an example of how to differentiate instruction.**

**Increase Achievement**

Simply tell students what they will be learning before the lesson begins and you can raise student achievement as much as **27 percent**.[8]

Study guidelines tell students up front what they need to know for achievement.

---

[8]Hattie, John A. C.  (2009).  *Visible Learning:  a synthesis of over 800 meta-analyses relating to achievement.*  New York:  Routledge.  Retrieved from an email correspondence with authors in October 2008.

---

**YOUR STUDY GUIDE FOR MAGNETISM**

"Nature of a Magnet"

Your textbook has these four objectives at the beginning of the chapter:

1. Explain how magnets are similar to objects with electric charges.
2. Use examples of the action of magnets to explain what magnetic poles are.
3. Explain how you can locate a magnetic field.
4. Use two magnets to demonstrate the effect of magnetic poles on each other.

I have prepared this study guide to help you learn these objectives. This guide breaks the objectives into smaller questions or tasks. As you work through them, please:

■   Write the page number where you found the answer in the left margin. This will help you find it again when you go back to study.

■   Note the number in parentheses before each question or task. This tells you which objective it is matched to.

Thank you.

PAGE

( 2 )   What is a magnetic pole?

( 1 )   In what three ways are the magnetic force and electrical forces alike?

( 4 )   Demonstrate these combinations for attracting and repelling:

N with N _____

S with N _____

S with S _____

( 2 )   What is a temporary magnet?

( 2 )   What is a permanent magnet?

( 2 )   Why does rubbing one end of a steel needle with a magnet magnetize it?

( 3 )   What is a magnetic field?

( 2 )   List five items that are attracted by a magnet.

( 2 )   List five items that are not attracted by a magnet.

( 4 )   How can you show that a magnet has two poles?

**I hope you are not *repelled* by this lesson!**

Rather than giving the page number, have the students write the page number in the left margin as they complete the task or question. This way, they can quickly go back to the source of the answer for review.

## Example

This example is based on objective 3 from the Study Guidelines on page 242.

### Objective

Give examples of the different types of nutrients.

### Accompanying Questions

1. Name the different kinds of nutrients.
2. Define and give examples of proteins.
3. Define and give examples of carbohydrates.
4. Define and give examples of fats.
5. Explain why proteins are important for your body.
6. Explain why carbohydrates are important for your body.
7. Explain why fats are important for your body.

### Accompanying Task

For students who really need lots of direction, next to each question, give the page number or location where the answer may be found.

## The Key to Having Students Do Their Assignments

**The Three Major Factors When Writing an Objective**

1. **STRUCTURE:**  Use a consistent format.
2. **PRECISENESS:**  Use succinct, clear sentences.
3. **ACCOMPLISHMENT:**  Tell what is to be achieved.

To maximize the frequency with which your students will do their assignments and to maximize your effectiveness as a teacher—

1. Write assignments for accomplishment based on objectives, not "coverage."

2. Write the objectives so succinctly and clearly that even outsiders, such as parents, can understand the assignment.

3. Give students the objectives in advance so they know what they are responsible for accomplishing.

> " *Education is not a process of putting the learner under control but one of putting the learner in control of his or her own learning.* "
>
> Allison Preece
> University of Victoria
> British Columbia, Canada

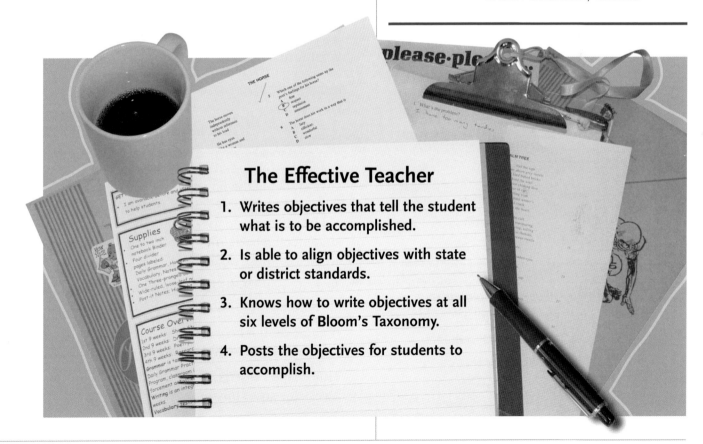

## The Effective Teacher

1. Writes objectives that tell the student what is to be accomplished.

2. Is able to align objectives with state or district standards.

3. Knows how to write objectives at all six levels of Bloom's Taxonomy.

4. Posts the objectives for students to accomplish.

## THE KEY IDEA

The purpose of a test is to determine if a student has mastered the objectives.

> **When you have measurements, you have performance. When you have no measurements, you have excuses.**
>
> _Peter Drucker

## The Purpose of a Test

The major reason for giving a test is to find out if the students have accomplished the objectives of the assignment.

**O**bjectives must be written before the unit or lesson begins because objectives tell the students what they are to learn and tell the teacher what is to be taught.

The test must be written before the lesson begins, because the test will be used to assess for student learning.

Give students the objectives at the beginning of the lesson so they know what they are responsible for accomplishing. Students like to have lesson objectives because they tell them what they are to learn. Objectives also tell students the basis upon which they will be evaluated, because the test is aligned to those objectives.

**Tests do not determine objectives; objectives determine tests.** Students like objectives because they see in bite-size chunks the purpose of a lesson.

If a test cannot be written to assess for learning, then the objectives have not been written correctly to measure for learning.

This chapter discusses the construction of tests and how tests are used to assess for accomplishment of the objectives.

# When to Write a Test

> **Both the assignment and the test are to be written concomitantly—in tandem—at the beginning of the assignment.**

The assignment and the test must be written together because they are interrelated and must therefore correlate with one another. Tests are to be used to monitor and assess for learning. Tests should NOT be used merely to verify teacher coverage of materials. **Tests SHOULD be used to determine if a student has or has not accomplished and comprehended the stated objectives of the lesson.**

**These are not valid reasons for writing tests:**
- Passage of time
- Material covered
- Curve grading
- Period to kill

**Passage of Time.** Learning has nothing to do with time intervals, such as the length of a grading period, the due date for deficiency notices, or because "two weeks have passed and it's time for a test." If grades are needed for report cards, you should structure the assignments, not the test, to fall within the grading period.

**Material Covered.** Tests should not be written at a particular juncture simply because "enough material has been covered." Your criteria, not the volume of material, should determine when to test your students.

**Curve Grading.** It is a mistake to state arbitrarily, "I want each test to be worth 50 points so that I will have a sufficient point spread to grade the class on a curve." The purpose of testing is not to compare one student to others. Tests are used to help the teacher determine what an individual student needs to learn.

---

### When You Assess, You Help

**Schools must change from a testing culture to an assessment culture.**

> **The purpose of a test is to assess a student's performance of the lesson objectives,** NOT to provide the teacher with the basis for a grade.

When you test for grading purposes, you are labeling students. When you assess for accomplishment, you are helping each student achieve success.

> **Tests are given for the students' sake, Tests are not given for the teacher's benefit. Tests are not given to grade students. Tests are given to assess for student learning.**

## What We Know About Grades[1]

Research has revealed this about grades:

- **Grading and reporting aren't essential to instruction.** Grades are not related to teaching or learning well. What is essential is how the teacher continually monitors and assesses for the learning progress of the student. This will be the subject of Chapter 23.

- **Grades have some value as rewards but no value as punishments.** Teachers should never use grades as weapons, because this offers no educational value, and it adversely affects student-teacher relationships.

- **Grading and reporting should always be done in reference to learning objectives, never on a curve.** Grading on a curve pits students against one another and converts learning into a game of winners and losers.

---

*Grades are only as good as the assessment system from which they are drawn. Grades are clear if clear standards and objectives are used. Narrative comments don't change this fact.*

Grant Wiggins
"Toward Better Report Cards."
(October 1994).
*Educational Leadership*, p. 29.
ASCD, Alexandria, Va.

**Period to Kill.** The number of questions on a test is not to be determined by the length of the class period. The length of a test is determined by each task, or the number of questions necessary to assess what each student knows and can do; in short, whether each individual has accomplished the objectives of the lesson.

## When to Give a Test

**C**all your assignments whatever you want: lessons, chapters, units, or topics. But to determine achievement for each assignment, you must administer a test.

- Each assignment must have a set of objectives that state the specifics of student accomplishment to be demonstrated.

- Each assignment must have a set of questions written for each objective.

- The test must be written at the beginning of the assignment, concurrent with the writing of objectives.

- The test is to be given when the students have finished the assignment.

## How to Write a Test

**E**very question must correspond to an objective. That makes it very easy to write a test. **All you do is write a set of questions for each of the objectives.**

> **The objectives govern what questions and how many questions are to be written for a test.**

---

[1] Adapted from Guskey, Thomas R., and Jane M. Bailey. (2001). *Developing Grading and Reporting Systems for Student Learning.* Thousand Oaks, Calif.: Corwin Press.

## Show Examples of Your First Assignment and Test

One of the most frightening times for students is when the first assignment is due or when the first test is to be taken. Often, this is a result of ineffective teachers who fail to post examples of an ideal assignment or how a typical test looks. Students are lost because there are no models or examples. They find out what should have been done or what should have been studied after the fact. Consequently, many students are so disillusioned by an initial failure that they give up.

**The following are ineffective instructions for assignments:**

> Complete the worksheet.
> Answer all the questions at the end of the chapter.
> Watch a video on *Macbeth*.
> Do all the problems on page 57.
> Write a summary of the chapter.

**The following are ineffective instructions for tests:**

> The test will cover everything since the last test.
> The test will cover everything we've covered this week.
> There will be some multiple-choice questions, some true-false, and maybe some fill-ins.
> The test will be worth about 50 points.

**The effective teacher uses these techniques for assignments and tests:**

- **POSTS** many good examples of past assignments and tests so the students can see what they are to do and what the tests look like.

- **EXPLAINS** how a finished assignment should appear and how the test questions are correlated to the objectives of the assignment.

Not only do the students see excellent models, but they recognize positive expectations through your encouragement, and realize that everyone can achieve success.

The effective teacher posts examples of tests and explains how they are constructed. This way, students know how to study and what to expect.

<table>
<tr><td>

**What Objectives Govern**

1. Objectives govern what students are to learn or turn in for the assignment.

2. Objectives govern how the teacher writes the test.

</td></tr>
</table>

**The purpose of a test is to determine how well each student has mastered the objectives of the lesson.** For the sake of illustration, a written test will be used here. However, it need not be a written test. It can be a musical number to be performed, an oral response, or the creation of a project or product. **Regardless, the test must be correlated to the objectives of the lesson.**

**Step 1.** **The basis of every test is the objectives for each assignment.** Have these available as you write the test.

**Step 2.** Look at the first objective. Write a set of questions for the objective. Avoid writing only one question. If the student guesses at the answer, you will not know if the student has mastered the objective.

### Two Examples

| | |
|---|---|
| **Objective:** | **Objective:** |
| List the steps of the scientific method. | Change words ending in y to plural form. |
| **Test Question:** | **Test:** |
| Which of the following are steps of the scientific method? | pony |
| | battery |
| a. observe, experiment, hypothesize | key |
| b. experiment, study, conclude | party |
| c. hypothesize, think, observe | decoy |
| d. collect data, state principles, draw conclusions | sky |
| | play |

**Step 3.** Use any type of question. The questions do not even have to be on a written test. The questions can be oral or physical types, whereby the teacher asks the student to perform a skill or produce a finished produc

**Step 4.** Repeat steps 1–3 for each of the remaining objectives. When you have written a set of questions for each objective, you have finished writing the test.

This is an example of a test that might have been written for a chapter or lesson on OBSERVATION. It has four key parts:

1. **Concept.** The key idea or major point of the lesson.

2. **Objectives.** The tasks the student is responsible for accomplishing.

3. **Questions.** Questions correspond to the objectives. Note the parentheses to the left of each question. The first number shows which objective the question corresponds to.

4. **Remediation.** Look at the parentheses again. The second number shows the part of the textbook where the answer to the question may be found. (The next section, "The Test as a Corrective Tool," explains how to use this information to help the student study.)

This is an example only.
Ignore the subject and focus on how the objectives and test questions correlate.
Apply the example to your own subject matter.

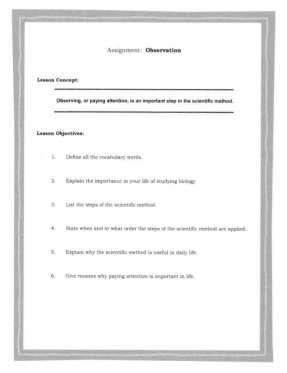

Assignment: **Observation**

**Lesson Concept:**

Observing, or paying attention, is an important step in the scientific method.

**Lesson Objectives:**

1. Define all the vocabulary words.

2. Explain the importance in your life of studying biology.

3. List the steps of the scientific method.

4. State when and in what order the steps of the scientific method are applied.

5. Explain why the scientific method is useful in daily life.

6. Give reasons why paying attention is important in life.

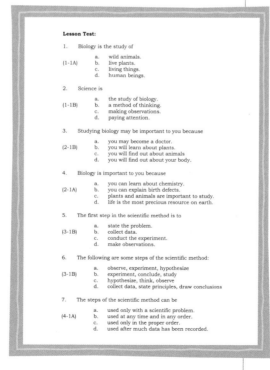

**Lesson Test:**

1. Biology is the study of
   (1-1A)
   a. wild animals.
   b. live plants.
   c. living things.
   d. human beings.

2. Science is
   (1-1B)
   a. the study of biology.
   b. a method of thinking.
   c. making observations.
   d. paying attention.

3. Studying biology may be important to you because
   (2-1B)
   a. you may become a doctor.
   b. you will learn about plants.
   c. you will find out about animals
   d. you will find out about your body.

4. Biology is important to you because
   (2-1A)
   a. you can learn about chemistry.
   b. you can explain birth defects.
   c. plants and animals are important to study.
   d. life is the most precious resource on earth.

5. The first step in the scientific method is to
   (3-1B)
   a. state the problem.
   b. collect data.
   c. conduct the experiment.
   d. make observations.

6. The following are some steps of the scientific method:
   (3-1B)
   a. observe, experiment, hypothesize
   b. experiment, conclude, study
   c. hypothesize, think, observe
   d. collect data, state principles, draw conclusions

7. The steps of the scientific method can be
   (4-1A)
   a. used only with a scientific problem.
   b. used at any time and in any order.
   c. used only in the proper order.
   d. used after much data has been recorded.

8. The scientific method can be used
   (4-1B)
   a. to make observations.
   b. to experiment and collect data.
   c. to state a conclusion.
   d. to accomplish all of the above.

9. The scientific method is used in daily life to
   (5-1B)
   a. solve problems.
   b. make observations.
   c. make discoveries.
   d. do all of the above.

10. Observations can be used in daily life to
    (5-IC)
    a. define science.
    b. help you stay alive.
    c. explain the word biology.
    d. list the rules of the scientific method.

11. In the business world, your boss will want you to
    (6-1C)
    a. conduct experiments.
    b. talk about science.
    c. write about science.
    d. pay attention.

12. When you don't feel well, your body is telling you
    (6-IC)
    a. to see a doctor.
    b. to work harder.
    c. to pay attention.
    d. to be careful.

13. Paying attention is a valuable life skill. It can help you
    (1-Key Idea)
    a. solve problems and make decisions.
    b. memorize the scientific method.
    c. appreciate life.
    d. find a job.

14. Paying attention is an important step in
    (1-Key Idea)
    a. the scientific method.
    b. the study of biology.
    c. the study of science.
    d. causing problems.

## It's Simple to Record Your Grades

1. Using an alphabetical listing of students, assign each student a number, beginning with 1, in your record book.

2. When new students join the class, add their names to the bottom of your class roster and assign them the next available number.

3. On all tests, papers, projects, and reports turned in during the school year, students must write their unique number.

4. For consistency, choose one place on papers where this number must be written as a class procedure and routine.

5. For multiple-choice, true-false, and fill-in answers, give your students an answer form so that all answers are in the same place.

6. After the papers are collected, ask a student to arrange the papers in numerical order.

7. Do not grade tests one at a time, while watching television and snacking. Spread the forms on a large table, perhaps 10 across, and correct the answers three to five questions at a time as you move across the forms.

8. Put the papers back in order ready to be recorded in your grade book. Then ask an aide, spouse, or trusted friend to record the grades for you if you are short on time.

The test you have just constructed in Steps 1–4 is a **criterion-referenced test**. The kind of test most teachers unknowingly write is the **norm-referenced test**. There is a major difference between the two types of tests:

- **A criterion-referenced test** requires that each question be written to a prestated criterion or objective. Since the students know what criteria they are responsible for, a percentage grade system should be used. The only person a student competes against in a criterion-referenced test is himself or herself. The student knows, for instance, the standard for an A is set at 93 percent.

- **A norm-referenced test** is used to determine placement on a normal distribution curve. Students are "graded on the curve," after a norm-referenced test. Norm-referenced tests are used to determine competitive ranking, such as for position on a team, entrance into a school, or placement on an organizational chart.

Norm-referenced tests have their place, as when you are trying to determine class rank or who will be on the first team. **When you are teaching a lesson, however, you are not teaching for rank. You are teaching for accomplishment, and you want everyone to succeed.**

> **The primary role of a teacher is not to grade a student. The teacher's main role is to help every student reach the highest possible level of achievement.**
>
> **To teach for accomplishment, use objectives and a criterion-referenced test.**

## You Already Know Before the Test Where Most of the Students Will Fall on a Curve

Benjamin Bloom noted the test scores of thousands of third graders and then followed them for several years. What Bloom found was that students' third-grade scores could be used to predict, with 80 percent accuracy or better, their scores in the eleventh grade. Achievement ranking, therefore, is highly consistent.

Achievement ranking is also highly subjective, to the extent that it is dependent on the nuanced art of norm-referenced test construction. It is comparable to a figure-skating competition with specific rules, or *criteria* for judging. Skaters who perform well under those criteria are more likely to win the competition. Likewise, students who perform well on norm-referenced tests in the third grade are likely to perform well on similar tests in the ninth grade. Conversely, students who perform at or only slightly above average on norm-referenced tests will likely maintain that level of performance all the way through elementary, middle, and high school. Norm-referenced tests, therefore, do not measure ability—what a student can do. Norm-referenced tests are analogous to a score board in a basketball arena; they keep points.

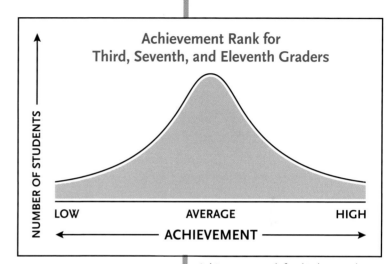

Achievement rank for third, seventh, and eleventh graders is highly consistent. The shaded area in the curve is the same for all 3 grade levels.

When a teacher says, "I need points so I can grade the class on a curve," this is not a valid reason for giving a test. According to Bloom, the teacher should already be able to predict where most of the students will fall on such a curve, which ultimately renders that curve pointless.

When students come into a class, most already presume who will be in the fast or the slow reading group, who will do well and who will do poorly in math—who will be treated as winners and who will be treated as failures. This is not what education is about. It's time to change our attitudes and students' presumptions about testing and grading.

### A test should be used to do two things:

1. The TEACHER should use the results of each test item to assess for student learning and, if necessary, remediate and correct for student mastery.

2. The STUDENTS should be graded on a percentage system. This way they are competing only against themselves to reach a level of achievement or success.

> If the student **MASTERS** an objective, do not assign more work to the student. Give the student enrichment materials, or ask the student to help another student. Enrichment work could include puzzles, games, software, or leisure reading.
>
> If the student **DOES NOT MASTER** an objective, give the student remediation or corrective help.

**GoBe**

**I'm Still Not Sure**

Brad Volkman's students can mark at the bottom of their daily quiz, "I'm still not too sure." See how Brad helps these students in the **Go**ing **Be**yond folder for Chapter 22 at EffectiveTeaching.com.

## The Test as a Corrective Tool

**A**ssume that you have returned from a visit to the doctor. Your friend or spouse asks you, "What happened at the doctor's office today?"

You say, "The doctor is running a test on me."

This does not mean that the doctor is going to grade you on a curve. It means that the doctor is awaiting the results of the medical tests. When the results are studied, the doctor then determines what needs to be done to correct your illness.

A criterion-referenced test is to be used, in the same way, as a diagnostic instrument. **A test tells you if the student needs corrective help.**

**If you do not correct and remediate, learning gets worse as the year progresses.**

It's no different from everything else in life. If you do not correct an illness such as a cold, or a bad habit such as smoking, your body or your life just gets worse.

After 10 chapters or units of study, many students have retained only 10 to 20 percent of what has been covered. The poor performance occurs because the ineffective teacher rolls through the school year, covering the chapters and giving tests for points to record in a grade book. After the test, the teacher blithely moves on to the next chapter without concern for students who do not comprehend the chapter.

So, what do effective teachers do instead?

Students who are lost or left behind need proper remediation to get them back on track.

# If a Student Misses a Question

**I**f a student misses a question, help the student take corrective action. Assume that the student answered question 6 incorrectly on the test shown on page 251.

6. Following are some steps of the scientific method:

|  |  |
|---|---|
|  | a. observe, experiment, hypothesize |
| (3-1B) | b. experiment, conclude, study |
|  | c. hypothesize, think, observe |
|  | d. collect data, state principles, draw conclusions |

 **3-1B**

**3 = OBJECTIVE**

**Objective correlation:**
The first number tells you which objective the question correlates with. This tells you that the student has not learned or mastered objective 3.

**1B = REMEDIATION**

**Answer source:**
The second number, 1B, tells you that the correct answer may be found in Chapter 1, Section B, of the textbook. Tell the student to review this section, or give the student another form of the same information; learning may be more effective in a different style.

Tests are to be given for the students' sake, not the teacher's. The purpose of a test is not to accumulate points to grade the students. **The purpose of a test is to help the teacher assess what the student has or has not learned.**

## A Symbol of Failure

*Most studies suggest that student performance does not improve when instructors grade more stringently and, conversely, that making it relatively easy to get a good grade does not lead students to do inferior work.*

*It is not a symbol of rigor to have grades fall into a "normal" distribution; rather, it is a symbol of failure—failure to teach well, to test well, and to have any influence at all on the intellectual lives of students.*

Alfie Kohn
"Grading: The Issue Is
Not How but Why."
(October 1994).
*Educational Leadership*, p. 41.
ASCD, Alexandria, Va.

## Formative and Summative Tests in Our Daily Lives

| Formative Tests | Summative Tests |
|---|---|
| Spring training | Opening day of the season |
| Dress rehearsal | Opening night |
| Training wheels on bike | Riding alone on two wheels |
| The bunny hill | The giant slalom |
| Driver's ed | Getting a driver's license |
| PSAT | SAT |
| Student teaching | The first day of school |

### GoBe

**Your Students Can Outperform 98 Percent of the Regular Students**

Benjamin Bloom shows how a teacher can achieve 98 percent mastery. Read how it's done in the **Go**ing **Be**yond folder for Chapter 22 at EffectiveTeaching.com.

## Do You Grade All Tests?

**T**here are two kinds of criterion-referenced and norm-referenced tests: FORMATIVE TESTS and SUMMATIVE TESTS.

- **Formative tests** are like drills and practice tests. They are given during the formative, developmental, or teachable period when the student is in the process of mastering an objective. You may not want to grade these tests. These simply let you and the students know how well you are teaching and they are learning the objective.

  **Formative tests are used to determine what remediation is needed for a student to master the content, skill, or objective.**

- **Summative tests** are given at the end of a unit when you want to sum up what the student has learned, and then to determine a grade.

**Tell students up front which tests they are taking for practice and which tests they are taking for evaluation.**

After giving a summative test and determining that a student did not master a certain objective, a corrective activity must be assigned. A corrective activity is one that is presented to the student in a differentiated form or with an alternate explanation so the student can grasp and learn the objective through a different approach.

After the student has completed the corrective activity, another formative test or a summative test should be given to determine mastery. **It should be the same kind of test as first given, but the questions must be asked in a different way.**

Some authorities, including Bloom, believe that you should test and retest until mastery is attained. Others believe that testing twice is sufficient because much of the content covered in class is spiraled, and the student will be exposed to the content again later on in the school year.[2]

[2]Guskey, Thomas R. (1996). *Implementing Mastery Learning*. Belmont, Calif.: Wadsworth.

The purpose of formative testing followed by corrective activities is not unique to education:

- A doctor does a laboratory test, prescribes medicine, and then repeats this procedure until the patient is cured.

- A baseball player watches a video of his or her swing, makes corrections at bat, and repeats this procedure until the batting average improves.

- A chef tinkers with a recipe, making changes until a perfect sauce results.

**The effective teacher tests and corrects, tests and corrects, because the teacher wants all the students to achieve.**

The ineffective teacher delights in giving out only a few A's. Teachers do not give grades; students earn grades. Also, the ineffective teacher is satisfied with grading people on a curve and labeling half the class as "below average" or "failures."

> **The purpose of teaching is to help all students succeed, not to label students as failures.**

---

### Teach to the Objectives

| The Ineffective Teacher | The Effective Teacher |
|---|---|
| Covers chapters | Teaches to the criteria |
| Finds busywork for the students | Has students learn toward the criteria |

**In the classroom of an effective teacher, students are focusing on the same objectives as the teacher.** The preparation and presentation of all lesson materials, reading assignments, worksheets, multimedia, lectures, and activities must be done for one reason only—to teach to the objectives.

---

Through testing and correcting, the effective teacher is seeking 80 to 90 percent mastery for each assignment. If each assignment reaches 80 to 90 percent mastery, after 10 chapters or units of studies, most students will have attained 80 to 90 percent mastery.

The students are successful and happy and the teacher spends much of the time encouraging the students to do even better.

Julie Johnson

Next, Julie holds up something that is **real world** and the students match the shape. Then she has them find something in the classroom to **match** their word cards.

## They Beg Me to Test Them

Julie Johnson teaches in Minnesota and what she does in her classroom applies to all grade levels. These are her steps for lesson preparation:

1. She **decides what** she wants her students to learn.
2. She **shows them** what they are to learn.
3. They **practice** together what they are to learn, which is called "guided practice." Then they practice on their own, which is "independent practice."
4. Then they are **tested** on the same material they practiced while they were simultaneously learning.

Julie succeeds because her students know what they will be learning and how they will show her that they have learned it; in other words, how they will be tested. She says, "There is no secret as to what is expected of them. When I do this they all succeed."

Julie says that *test* is not a bad word. It is something her students look forward to. It is their chance to

Julie first **teaches** her students what each **word card** is and what it looks like. Then she holds up **models** of a shape and they hold up the card that identifies the models.

show her what they have learned. They can't wait for their turn to be tested because, after all the instruction and practice, the test is the easiest part—at least that's what the students say.

They beg her to test them. They even stand in line waiting for their turn to show her what they have learned. Using this lesson structure, Julie shares how she taught a Minnesota Math Standard in Geometry:

Classify simple shapes by specified attributes and identify simple shapes within complex shapes.

She aligned the state standard into two simple objectives:

1. Identify, describe, and classify two-dimensional shapes.
2. Identify shapes that are a part of more complex shapes.

**During each step, Julie is assessing the class. She checks to see how the students are doing and whether they are meeting the objectives of each step, while teaching, correcting, and practicing as they progress.**

**She knows what she is teaching and the students know what they are learning.**

# Begin With the End in Mind

**Y**ou've planned many things backward, such as a wedding, a party, or a vacation. You begin by setting the date for the event, then plan backward with a schedule listing what is to be done leading up to the event.

Good lesson design works much the same way. The end product for the student is achievement of the objectives. To reach that point, the teacher plans two things:

1. What **method to use to assess** for the achievement of the objective

2. What instructional **strategies to use to teach** the objective

While this technique seems so common sense, there are many teachers who construct lessons by identifying a thing (like weather) and thinking of fun activities to do about weather (like making cotton cloud pictures). After a week of weather-related activities, it's test time. The teacher recalls all of the activities and creates a test based on topics covered. This piecemeal approach leaves students and the teacher wondering what students are supposed to learn, and what the teacher is supposed to teach. Achievement is never the focal point for the teacher or the students.

Grant Wiggins and Jay Tighe[3] have formalized the lesson design process with a term called **Backward Design. Backward Design contends that instead of planning a lesson around favorite activities, a more effective lesson should start with the results you want to achieve.** Then, plan backward to what you want to accomplish.

The backward design process includes these steps:

**Step 1. Identify Desired Results.** What do you want your students to know and be able to do? These are your lesson objectives.

## Lessons in High School

*When I begin a new unit or a topic, I project an outline of my unit on a screen, and it stays up there during the teaching of the unit. On the outline are the lesson objectives. My students see what lesson objectives they are responsible for learning.*

*I teach to the outline. The students are learning to the objectives, and I am teaching to the performance of the objectives, on the outline. When I finish the outline, I give them the test. And every single question that I write on the test is written to the objectives on the outline.*

***You see, if you don't know what you want your students to learn, how can you write a test or assess to see if they've learned it?*** *My student achievement results are awesome, but then why not? Both teacher and students know what is to be learned. All questions or skills are correlated with the known objectives. That's why my students, too, call it the 'no-mystery approach.'*

_A high school teacher

---

[3]Wiggins, G., and J. Tighe. (2004). *Understanding by Design.* Alexandria, Va.: Association for Supervision and Curriculum Development.

The purpose of teaching is to help all students succeed.

**Step 2. Determine Acceptable Evidence.** This would be the "test." Assess for student performance of the objective with oral questions, observations, dialogues, or with the more traditional quizzes and tests.

**Step 3. Plan Learning Experiences and Instruction.** What activities, materials, and resources will be used to help the student learn and reach the desired results?

## How to Create a Lesson Plan

**Y**ou know how to write an assignment and a test. Now, it's time to put these together into a lesson plan.

---

### Lesson Plans Are Learning Plans

Although it may be difficult to break from tradition, you may want to consider calling your lesson plans **"learning plans;"** for that's what you are planning. You are planning for student learning.

---

Football coaches have a game plan. Executives have a business plan. Pilots have a flight plan. Likewise, **effective teachers have a lesson or learning plan**. These plans are like diet plans, travel plans, and personal finance plans. They are constantly being modified and improved. **Thus, learning plans are rarely neat, and never complete.** Learning plans are a continuous process and go on for pages. Keep your plans visible on your desk. It's not a secret. It's a plan you want every student to follow successfully.

Most schools do not provide learning plans. They provide curriculum guides that will tell you what the students need to accomplish. It's up to you to create the learning plans to guide students to their ultimate destination.

**If you do not know where you are going,
how will you know when and if you get there?**

**This is a simple step-by-step procedure for starting a learning plan:**

1. Turn a sheet of 8½- x 11-inch paper landscape or sideways.

2. Along the left side of the page, write what you want the students to learn or perform. These represent the OBJECTIVES for the lesson.

3. Write the test by matching or aligning the objectives to the questions being asked on the assessment. Both the objectives and the test are ready before the lesson begins.

4. Along the right side of the page, write all the resources (lectures, activities, questions, videos, worksheets and the like) you will use to teach the lesson objectives. **List only resources that are matched to the lesson objective.**

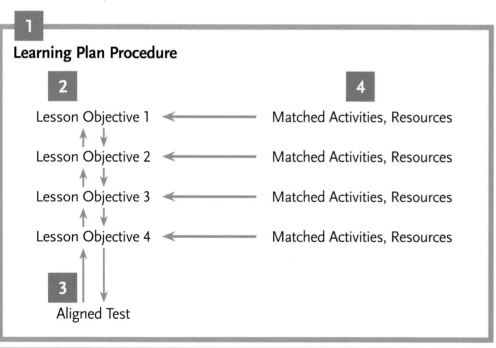

**Learning Plan Procedure**

**What Students Must Know**

The National Association of Secondary School Principals reported that to maximize learning and minimize disruptions, students must understand clearly what is expected of them. They need to know four things:

1. What they are to learn
2. How they are to learn it
3. How they are to demonstrate what they have learned
4. How the quality of their learning will be evaluated

Lorin Anderson
"Timepiece: Extending and Enhancing Learning Time." (1993).
National Association of Secondary School Principals, Reston, Va.

The learning plan shown on the previous page has the three components of the Backward Design strategy for constructing a lesson.

1. **Objectives.** The objectives state the purpose of the lesson. Effective teachers state the objectives at the beginning of each lesson, even before the students ask what they'll be learning. Every lesson meets particular objectives derived from state standards.

2. **Tests.** Whatever kind of test you give, the students must provide you with acceptable evidence that they have mastered the lesson objectives.

3. **Activities.** This is the heart of the learning plan. The better you instruct, the better your students will meet the objectives. Your instruction will depend on how well you make use of resources to help you engage your class.

It's all right to have videos, worksheets, and activities. In fact, you must have these. **However, the question you must ask first is, "What do I want the students to learn?"** Then start looking for the appropriate matching videos, worksheets, and activities that will enhance your teaching toward that goal.

The Internet is loaded with resources to help you create exciting, teachable lessons. Search "teacher lesson plans" and you'll have pages of links to use. In addition, attend conferences, workshops, and college classes. Read the journals. Most importantly, meet on a regular basis with your team to exchange ideas. This is the subject of Chapter 24. Working together will generate a wealth of strategies and spark your own creativity.

Without a learning plan, without a lesson plan, without a guide of some form, you are not maximizing the time you spend with your students. Teaching is a very precise skill. Learning plans will allow you to hone your craft and give your students the chance to soar and achieve.

Testing is a positive way to ensure that everyone stays on the course of learning.

**GoBe**

**Lesson Plan Links**

Bookmark these links to use as you beef up your learning plans. Find them in the **Go**ing **Be**yond folder for Chapter 22 at EffectiveTeaching.com.

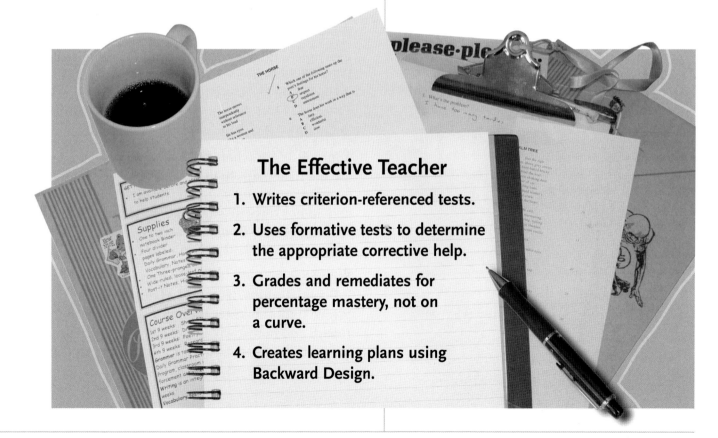

## The Effective Teacher

1. Writes criterion-referenced tests.

2. Uses formative tests to determine the appropriate corrective help.

3. Grades and remediates for percentage mastery, not on a curve.

4. Creates learning plans using Backward Design.

# 23

## THE KEY IDEA

The purpose of a scoring guide is to assess for student learning.

In a quest to find the ultimate hamburger, Harry and Rosemary used a Hamburger Tasting Rubric that included criteria for meat, preparation, bun, add-ons, and presentation.

## The Value of a Scoring Guide

Effective teachers give students a scoring guide that spells out how students can earn points or a grade for accomplishing a lesson.

**A**s a student, did you ever raise your hand and ask the teacher, "How will you be grading us?"

**Everyone wants to know up front how they will be scored, judged, and graded.** Did you ever have a teacher who passed papers back to you with points deducted for some omission without first informing the class that it was an expectation? If so, you probably muttered under your breath, "That's not fair. You didn't tell us how we were going to be graded on this."

**Your job as a teacher is to create success for your students. Scoring guides are the road maps to that success.** Students know up front what the expectation is, and you know in advance how you're going to grade it. Scores should not surprise students. Based on set criteria in the scoring guide, students should be able to accurately estimate their final grades based on how well they know they've performed.

**Scoring guides also improve communications with parents and other influential adults.** Parents, guardians, aunts, uncles, grandparents, care givers, tutors all know the expectation for completion of a paper, project, or report, and how it will be scored. They can use the scoring guide as an aid to help the child succeed.

Students love to be in classrooms where they know what to expect—how learning will be structured and how they will be graded.

- These are the classrooms with procedures in place and with students who are held accountable for those procedures.
- These are the classrooms with scoring guides in place and with students who are responsible for their own learning progress.

Students love teachers who share with them the expectations for success in the class.

## Scoring Guides Improve Student Learning

You've given your students an assignment with objectives (Chapter 21). These objectives help students to know the content they are responsible for learning. Objectives give students focus and enable them to check for their own understanding. As a result, they are more likely to buy into the lesson and become engaged in their learning.

The objectives are displayed in the classroom so the students see their goals during the entire lesson.

You have a test prepared (Chapter 22). The students know that the test or performance required is correlated to the objectives of the lesson. They know how to prepare for the test, just as you know how to prepare for the Department of Motor Vehicles driving test. There are no surprises or trick questions.

Now give the students a scoring guide (Chapter 23). This is presented to the students at the beginning of the assignment along with the objectives.

> Give the students a scoring guide that spells out how their assignment will be scored or graded.

## Parts of a Scoring Guide

**A** scoring guide has three parts. Each part indicates the factor evaluated or what counts for a piece of work.

- **Criteria:** Name the category or trait that will be scored.
- **Point Values:** Keep this simple. A scale of values from 0 to 4 fits most performance levels.
- **Performance Expected:** Define and give examples of performance levels and corresponding point values. This helps students judge and revise their own work before handing in their assignments. It gives them learning expectations and performance goals.

Typically, scoring guides are formatted as a series of columns and rows.

Each row represents a characteristic or trait for assessment as part of the lesson.

- Criteria are related to the objective of the lesson.
- Objectives can have multiple criteria for assessment.

Columns are each headed with a point value that the students can earn, such as 4, 3, 2, 1, and 0 or NS (no score).

Each square on the grid represents the intersection of a criteria and a point value, just as two points meet on a graph.

- A description of the expectation for receiving the point value is paired to the criteria.

Learning is a definable process and one that all students can experience. Our charge as teachers is to communicate this process to students in very concrete terms.

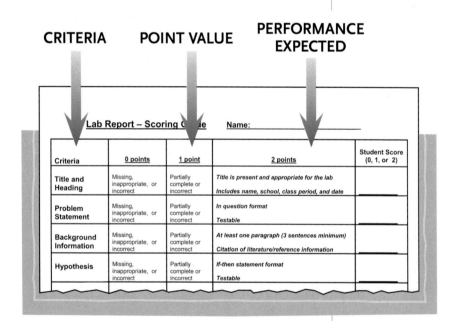

**CRITERIA     POINT VALUE     PERFORMANCE EXPECTED**

Lab Report – Scoring Guide     Name: _____

| Criteria | 0 points | 1 point | 2 points | Student Score (0, 1, or 2) |
|---|---|---|---|---|
| Title and Heading | Missing, inappropriate, or incorrect | Partially complete or incorrect | Title is present and appropriate for the lab / Includes name, school, class period, and date | |
| Problem Statement | Missing, inappropriate, or incorrect | Partially complete or incorrect | In question format / Testable | |
| Background Information | Missing, inappropriate, or incorrect | Partially complete or incorrect | At least one paragraph (3 sentences minimum) / Citation of literature/reference information | |
| Hypothesis | Missing, inappropriate, or incorrect | Partially complete or incorrect | If-then statement format / Testable | |

## Keep It Simple

**Scoring guides are most often called *rubrics* in education circles. However, you shouldn't be attached to calling them rubrics in front of students.** Do not baffle them with education jargon. At the beginning of a lesson, give the students a scoring guide and call it a "scoring guide."

**A scoring guide is a clear, simple, understandable term because it informs students what is expected of them and how they can earn a *score*.**

Students understand the concept of a scoring guide. They keep scores in the many games they play and they know scores determine whether they will win or lose certain games.

**What you see is a picture scoring guide.** It was developed by Kathleen Monroe, a first grade teacher in San Jose, California.

Kathy has the four pictures drawn up ahead of time. She shows the four pictures to her class and asks the students which one they think is the best. She asks, "How would you describe it?" This particular year, the class answered "Perfect!" She gives that picture a "4."

"Which one is the next best?" she asks. They agree on the word, "Good," and she gives it a "3." Kathy does the same for the remaining two pictures.

The four pictures are posted with their word descriptions and point values. The word descriptions change from year to year. She uses whatever the class says that year.

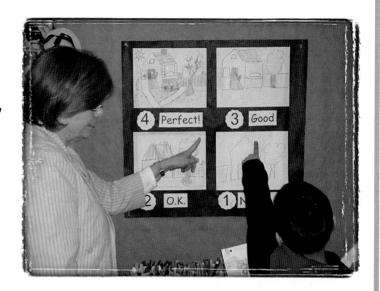

When the students are drawing their illustrations, they are invited to go up to the scoring guide posted in the room and decide if they have drawn a 4, 3, 2, or 1.

Does Kathy get terrific drawings from her students? Of course, she does! A scoring guide helps students determine what is expected of an assignment.

> **Effective teachers give their students a scoring guide that spells out how they can earn points or a grade for accomplishing a lesson.**

## Helping Students Make Progress to Improve

### Feedback Increases Achievement

Telling students the objectives before the lesson begins can raise student achievement as much as **27 percent**.

Additionally, providing students with specific feedback about their progress can raise their achievement as much as **37 percent**.[1]

> **A scoring guide defines achievement so students can work for accomplishment.**

**W**hen a doctor runs a test on you, like a blood test, hearing test, or eye exam, the purpose is not to grade you and then send you home. Rather, the doctor **assesses** the results of the test so the proper medicine or treatment to improve your health can be prescribed. **The goal is progress toward a healthier you.**

Similarly, effective teachers use assessment data collected from projects, tests, reports, and the various assignments to gauge a student's academic progress, with the intent of ensuring the student is making **progress toward accomplishing the objectives of the lesson.**

**For progress to be made there must be constant assessment for learning.**

Scoring guides are used in competitive sports such as gymnastics and figure skating. The judges are not subjectively grading the athletes. Rather, they have a predetermined guide that governs how points are earned after the athlete completes certain skills, moves, or criteria.

These scoring guides are known to athletes, their coaches, and their teachers. Together, they work to improve their skill and level of performance so they can be assessed high on the scale.

With safety harnesses attached, the coach pulls or lifts the cable to control the movement of the athlete while assessing and teaching at the same time—over and over again, working toward PROGRESS and ACCOMPLISHMENT.

[1]Hattie, John A. C. (2009). *Visible Learning: a synthesis of over 800 meta-analyses relating to achievement.* New York: Routledge. Retrieved from an email correspondence with authors in October 2008.

Likewise, when students are given scoring guides ahead of time, they can see how they will be scored and can earn better scores by doing better work. All the while, the teacher is involved in assessing for student progress and helping to improve each student's scores.

**To help students reach the highest possible level of achievement, the effective teacher is constantly assessing for student learning. This helps students go where they need to go and it helps them determine how best to get there.**

## A Level Playing Field

*The purpose of any educational feedback is not to rate, rank, humiliate, and sort students. The purpose of feedback is to improve student learning. When you ask most students, "Why did you get that grade?" the universal and truthful response is, "I don't know." When teachers use scoring guides, then students can use those scoring guides to improve their performance from the lowest level of achievement to success far beyond today's standards.*

*When teachers use scoring guides for evaluation, they are adopting a moral and ethical principle that every student deserves fair and consistent evaluation. After all, when kids play games, the rules are consistent, the dimensions of the field are the same, and the height of the goal, length of the field, and shape of the ball are all consistent. If we failed to provide that consistency, parents, teachers, and students would shout, "THAT'S NOT FAIR!"*

*The ethical imperative for scoring guides as a method of student assessment is that we should aspire to the same level of fairness and consistency in the classroom that we routinely expect on the playground.*[2]

_Douglas Reeves

Children deserve a fair playing field.

[2]Douglas Reeves in an email correspondence with Harry Wong. Dr. Reeves can be contacted at www.leadandlearn.com.

The First Days of School | 269

## Scoring Guides Everyone Can Use

**S**coring guides are applicable to all grade levels and across all content areas. **Lessons are designed to ensure that students are taught the content; scoring guides are used to confirm that the students have learned what was taught.**

### High School Science Scoring Guide

Karen Rogers, a high school science teacher in Olathe, Kansas, is a National Board Certified Teacher. Although her achievement level in the profession is high, Karen's scoring guides are not sophisticated or complex. She says her students respond better when information is in short and simple doses, thus easy for students to understand and follow.

Karen has some basic scoring guide templates:

- Laboratory Report
- Graphing
- Group Discussion
- Presentations to the Class
- Presentations to the Class (listening)

Karen Rogers

Karen says, "In my science classes, I use scoring guides for writing lab reports and graphing. Writing a lab report can be overwhelming for students. On my lab report scoring guide, I list the criteria for each component (hypothesis, data, analysis, etc.). That way, students can proceed with their experiments and their reports in a simple, step-by-step fashion.

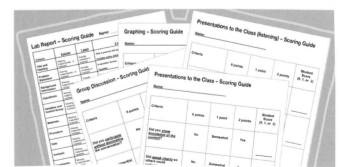

---

### The Talking Dog

A few ladies occasionally ran into each other at the hair salon and Carol would mention that she taught her dog to talk. This went on for years.

One day the ladies asked her to produce this talking dog. So, Carol went outside where the dog was tied. She brought in her dog, and said, "Speak." The dog just panted and wagged his tail.

Carol said, "Speak" and the dog just panted and wagged his tail some more. The other ladies laughed at Carol and told her she didn't have a talking dog.

Carol responded, "I said I taught the dog to talk. I didn't say he learned it."

The scoring guides that Karen Rogers uses can easily be applied to all other subjects where students need to write reports, collect and display data, be involved in group discussions, make presentations to the class, and listen when others are making presentations.

Her students find value in using the scoring guides.

> Bryan Shephard says he likes them because they "tell you what you need to know to do the assignment. You don't have to remember all the directions the teacher said. You know how to get 100 percent."

> Nick Jahner agrees. Nick says, "With the scoring guides, you can control your grade and know what you are going to get in advance."

> Miles Miller likes them because, "they keep the grading standard (uniform) and they give you the basic idea of what needs to be done."

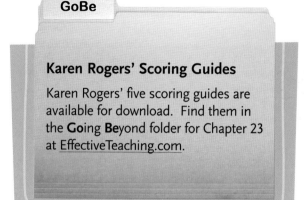

**GoBe**

**Karen Rogers' Scoring Guides**

Karen Rogers' five scoring guides are available for download. Find them in the **Going Beyond** folder for Chapter 23 at EffectiveTeaching.com.

## The Highest Level of Distinction

Just as some people are able to write Ph.D. and M.D. after their names, 55,000 teachers out of the 3.2 million professionals teaching in 2007 can write NBCT after their names. That's almost 2 percent of all teachers. NBCT stands for National Board Certified Teacher and it represents an advanced teaching credential that is the highest level of excellence a classroom teacher can achieve.

To earn this distinction, teachers choose to undertake a rigorous, yearlong, performance-based assessment. Many teachers spend between 200 and 800 hours putting together a portfolio of lessons, samples of students' work, videos, and rigorous analysis of their classroom teaching. They receive written evaluations that probe the depth of their teaching knowledge, and must take a six-hour requisite exam—all at a cost of more than $2,500 out of their own pockets.

Although all states, except for Alaska, reward teachers who attain NBCT status, most teachers who strive for NCBT excellence report that it's not the money that drives them; it is the reward of self-fulfillment and growth.

National Board Certified Teachers distinguish themselves in education by their dedication to the profession and their demonstrated abilities in the classroom. To learn how you can become an NBCT, go to www.nbpts.org.

**The Great Gatsby** Unit Plan Rubric    English 11 Advanced
Teacher: Mr. Dannen

Student:

| CATEGORY | 4 | 3 | 2 | 1 | NS/0 | Total |
|---|---|---|---|---|---|---|
| Content Knowledge 3.1 Reading | The student can easily relate Fitzgerald's idea of "The American Dream" to Jay Gatsby's actions and give three specific written or verbal examples. | The student can relate Fitzgerald's idea of "The American Dream" to Jay Gatsby's actions and give two specific written or verbal examples. | The student can relate Fitzgerald's idea of "The American Dream" to Jay Gatsby's actions, but has trouble giving written or verbal examples. | The student has trouble relating Fitzgerald's idea of "The American Dream" to Jay Gatsby's actions and cannot give any examples. | The student is unable to relate Fitzgerald's idea of "The American Dream" to Jay Gatsby's actions, or give any examples of same. | |
| Compare and Contrast | The student can easily recognize the similarities and differences between *The Great Gatsby* and Fitzgerald's short story, "Winter Dreams, and can give three specific | The student can recognize the similarities and differences between *The Great Gatsby* and Fitzgerald's short story, "Winter Dreams, and can give two specific | The student can recognize the similarities and differences between *The Great Gatsby* and Fitzgerald's short story, "Winter Dreams, but has trouble giving | The student has trouble recognizing similarities and differences between *The Great Gatsby* and Fitzgerald's short story, "Winter Dreams," and | The student is unable to recognize the similarities and differences between The Great Gatsby and Fitzgerald's short story, "Winter Dreams," or give | |

## Scoring Guide for State Standards

New Jersey has core curriculum standards for reading, speaking, writing, and media. This is one of the standards:

> All students will understand and apply the knowledge of sounds, letters, and words in written English to become independent and fluent readers, and will read a variety of materials and texts with fluency and comprehension.

To teach this standard, Norm Dannen of New Jersey created a lesson using the novel, **The Great Gatsby**.

### GoBe

### Norm Dannen's Scoring Guides

Norm Dannen's complete scoring guide with the correlated lesson objectives and the state standards are in the Going Beyond folder for Chapter 23 at EffectiveTeaching.com.

Collette Cornatzer with her teacher, Norm Dannen

### Fair and Easy

Students like the no-mystery approach to learning.

One of Norm Dannen's students, Collette Comatzer, says,

> "I like scoring guides because they make the student aware of exactly how to do the assignment or write the assigned article, and it plots a very fair and easy-to-understand grading system. A scoring guide creates a backbone for your paper."

## The Great Gatsby

**The Great Gatsby** was published in 1925 and is regarded as one of the foremost pieces of American literature. It was written by F. Scott Fitzgerald or Francis Scott Key Fitzgerald—yes, a descendant (second cousin three times removed) of *the* Francis Scott Key who penned "The Star-Spangled Banner."

The setting of the book was a period of great wealth in America called the Roaring 20s. Some of the people and images of this decade include

| | | |
|---|---|---|
| Jazz Age | Louis Armstrong | Al Jolson |
| Charleston dance | Charlie Chaplin | Vaudeville |
| Rudolph Valentino | Prohibition | Gangsters |
| Al Capone | American Dream | Materialism |

The novel centers on a man, Jay Gatsby, the narrator's friend, and Jay's girlfriend, Daisy Buchanan.

Norm took the state standard and created several lesson objectives, one of which was

Draw a parallel between your own life and the life and work of F. Scott Fitzgerald in the context of the Jazz Age (a.k.a., the Lost Generation) and the years leading up to the Great Depression.

Very simply, he asks his students to compare their present lives to the life of Jay Gatsby and the people who lived in the 1920s.

Those teachers who believe standards and objectives can stifle creativity, prevent problem solving, and discourage deeper learning, fail to exercise creativity in their own thinking and lesson planning. For example, the manner in which Norm's students can show comparisons to their lives and the life of Gatsby is limitless. Students can perform a musical recital, write a major essay, submit a portfolio, even create an art exhibit, all to demonstrate higher-order mastery skills and understanding. A student could even take a 1920s jazz song and contrast it to a current pop, hip-hop, or alternative-music song. Just think what a student could do with Prohibition and *gangsta rap*!

Along with the objective, Norm gives his students a scoring guide. He uses this scoring guide as his formative assessment tool to determine how well the students are learning and how well he is teaching the objective linked to the novel, **The Great Gatsby**.

If a student scores 1 or NS/0 in any of the categories, it doesn't mean the student is unintelligent, lazy, or failing. It may simply mean that it's difficult for a young person who is 15 years old and hasn't even figured out life today to relate to a period of time 80 years ago.

This is where the teacher can prescribe a course of action to help the student achieve success. Sit with the student at a computer and go to the Library of Congress website (www.loc.gov) to help a student discover what life was like in America in the 1920s. The teacher can help students who have scored low, according to the scoring guide, see what they can do to earn a higher score—to make **progress toward achieving the objective.**

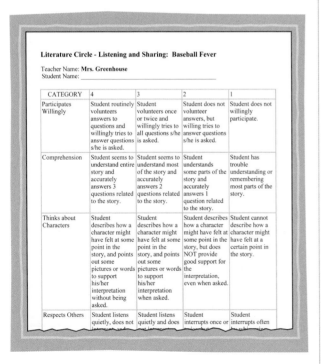

## GoBe

### *Baseball Fever* Scoring Guide

The complete *Baseball Fever* scoring guide is in the **Go**ing **Be**yond folder for Chapter 23 at EffectiveTeaching.com.

**Literature Circle - Listening and Sharing: Baseball Fever**

Teacher Name: **Mrs. Greenhouse**
Student Name: _____

| CATEGORY | 4 | 3 | 2 | 1 |
|---|---|---|---|---|
| Participates Willingly | Student routinely volunteers answers to questions and willingly tries to answer questions s/he is asked. | Student volunteers once or twice and willingly tries to all questions s/he is asked. | Student does not volunteer answers, but willing tries to answer questions s/he is asked. | Student does not willingly participate. |
| Comprehension | Student seems to understand entire story and accurately answers 3 questions related to the story. | Student seems to understand most of the story and accurately answers 2 questions related to the story. | Student understands some parts of the story and accurately answers 1 question related to the story. | Student has trouble understanding or remembering most parts of the story. |
| Thinks about Characters | Student describes how a character might have felt at some point in the story, and points out some pictures or words to support his/her interpretation without being asked. | Student describes how a character might have felt at some point in the story, and points out some pictures or words to support his/her interpretation when asked. | Student describes how a character might have felt some point in the story, but does NOT provide good support for the interpretation, even when asked. | Student cannot describe how a character might have felt at a certain point in the story. |
| Respects Others | Student listens quietly, does not interrupt and | Student listens quietly and does not interrupt | Student interrupts once or | Student interrupts often |

## Scoring Guide for Discussion Groups

Diana Greenhouse, a teacher in Texas, uses a scoring guide for her lesson on the novel, *Baseball Fever* by Johanna Hurwitz. The book is about a boy who wants to play baseball even though his father wants him to play chess. The conflict makes for great class discussions.

**Diana uses the novel to engage the class in what she calls "Inner-Outer Discussion."**

After the class reads a novel, she asks the students to construct five questions for discussion.

In preparation for the discussion, she sets up a double circle of chairs. The inner circle of chairs faces in, and the outer circle of chairs faces out. The chairs are back to back, making an inner and an outer circle of seats. This technique was adapted to her fifth grade class when her daughter came home from high school and reported on the same technique being used by her high school teacher.

Students in the inner circle are the first discussion group. Students forming the outer circle ask questions they've prepared for discussion and they take notes. The questions and notes are all turned in to Diana.

**The students are handed a scoring guide before the activity begins.** It is reviewed and discussed so they are aware of what is expected of them as they prepare for the book discussion.

Diana explains that while the inner circle of students (facing in) is having their discussion, the outer circle (facing out) simply listens. They are not allowed to have verbal input; their role is to be active listeners. When prompted to do so by the facilitator, they ask the discussion questions and take notes. This helps to develop listening skills.

The students in the outer circle are always eager to have their turn at discussion because they have been listening and have a tremendous amount of input bottled up, or written in their notes. Most are very busy writing down important points or scrawling their thoughts.

Everyone has a novel, a notebook with their questions, paper for taking notes, and their scoring guide. Diana randomly selects a discussion group facilitator, and the discussion and learning begin. After 20 minutes, the groups switch roles and a new discussion group begins. Diana says,

> "I look forward to these 'Inner-Outer Discussions,' because I enjoy watching my students take charge of the lesson. They are developing good thinking, listening, and speaking habits. **My students enjoy the discussions and appreciate the use of the scoring guide because they know exactly what I'm looking for and are better able to control their own grades.**

> "There is total engagement," she continues. "They say they feel a sense of power and that thrills me because empowering students is one of my daily goals!

> "This is a wonderful activity to observe. My students amaze me every time!"

### A Multimedia Scoring Guide

Just as Karen Rogers' scoring guides (page 270) can be adapted for use in almost every classroom, on the right is another scoring guide from Norm Dannen that can be changed to suit the objectives being taught. If your students do presentations, you will find this scoring guide in the GoBe folder. It is generic enough to modify and use.

**Multimedia Project Scoring Guide: Travel to Kilimanjaro**

Student Name: _____

| CATEGORY | 4 | 3 | 2 | 1 | SCORE |
|---|---|---|---|---|---|
| Content | Covers topic in-depth with details and examples. Subject knowledge is excellent. | Includes essential knowledge about the topic. Subject knowledge appears to be good. | Includes essential information about the topic but there are 1-2 factual errors. | Content is minimal OR there are several factual errors. | |
| Attractiveness | Makes excellent use of font, color, graphics, effects, etc., to enhance the presentation. | Makes good use of font, color, graphics, effects, etc., to enhance to presentation. | Makes use of font, color, graphics, effects, etc., but occasionally these detract from the presentation content. | Use of font, color, graphics, effects etc., but these often distract from the presentation content. | |
| Originality | Product shows a large amount of original thought. Ideas are creative and inventive. | Product shows some original thought. Work shows new ideas and insights. | Uses other people's ideas (giving them credit), but there is little evidence of original thinking. | Uses other people's ideas, but does not give them credit. | |
| Oral Presentation | Interesting and well-rehearsed, with smooth delivery that holds audience attention. | Relatively interesting and rehearsed, with a fairly smooth delivery that usually holds audience attention. | Delivery not smooth, but able to hold audience attention most of the time. | Delivery not smooth, and audience attention lost. | |
| | Content is well-organized, using headings | Uses headings or bulleted lists to organize, but | Content is logically organized for | There was no clear or logical organizational | |

**GoBe**

### Multimedia Scoring Guide

The complete multimedia scoring guide is found in the **Go**ing **Be**yond folder for Chapter 23 at EffectiveTeaching.com.

## Ready-Made Scoring Guides

**I**t is possible to create your own scoring guides, but many teachers find it simpler to adopt or modify existing guides. We've shared a few scoring guides to get you started. The Internet has many more examples. These range from teachers sharing with teachers on various websites to commercial companies with templates for all grade levels and subject matter. Google the word "Rubrics" and adopt the guides that best suit your needs.

## Assessing Student Progress With a Scoring Guide

> **Unless YOU know where you are going, you will never have students who know where THEY are going.**

**O**ur major role as teachers is to help students make continued progress in what they are to learn. Students want to know the goals of the class. When the students and the teacher are moving toward the same goal, that's when learning happens. The effective teacher does the following to move a student toward learning:

1. Aligns the lesson to district or state standards.
2. Presents the lesson with an objective that focuses the goal of the lesson.
3. Uses appropriate activities that teach the objective.
4. Gauges learning with a scoring guide that is aligned to the lesson objective.
5. Assesses learning based on a test that is aligned to the lesson objectives.

### Assessment Checks Progress

Assessment is not an isolated event. It goes on consistently throughout the lesson, through each day. Assessment takes the form of everything from quizzes, rubrics, questions, and oral presentations to artifacts—**all for the purpose of helping the student make progress.**

As you develop goals for your lessons, always ask WHAT and HOW. But, don't stop there. **The most important part of the entire process is sharing the WHAT and HOW with your students.** Education is not trickery and clever tactics to stump students. Our goal is to open the wonderment of the world and help students discover the joy and fulfillment associated with learning.

Look at the lessons you prepare and ask yourself these three questions:

1. Do your students know **WHAT they are to learn** as a result of experiencing the lesson?

2. Do you know **HOW you are going to help** your students accomplish the goal of the lesson?

3. Do your students know **HOW they—and you—are going to assess their learning** of the lesson?

If you cannot clearly answer these questions, you are not ready to teach your lesson. You will only frustrate the students and yourself trying to figure out what went wrong.

**The purpose of designing a lesson is not simply to ensure that students are taught, but to ensure that they learn.** With a scoring guide, teachers and students have a tool that can easily assess learning.

## The Teacher Is Prepared to Teach

From a student's perspective, it is very important to feel that "the teacher is prepared to teach." **It creates a sense of comfort, security, and confidence to see that the teacher knows what he or she is teaching.** With objectives posted, tests written, and scoring guides created before the lesson begins, the teacher's energy is focused on delivering the content and helping all students achieve the goals of the lesson.

---

**Just Think**

Just think what would happen to student learning if students knew in advance what they would be learning, how they would be tested, and how they would be scored before the lesson even began.

Just think how productive students could be if they knew they could not fail.

Just think what would happen to student learning if the teacher knew this, too!

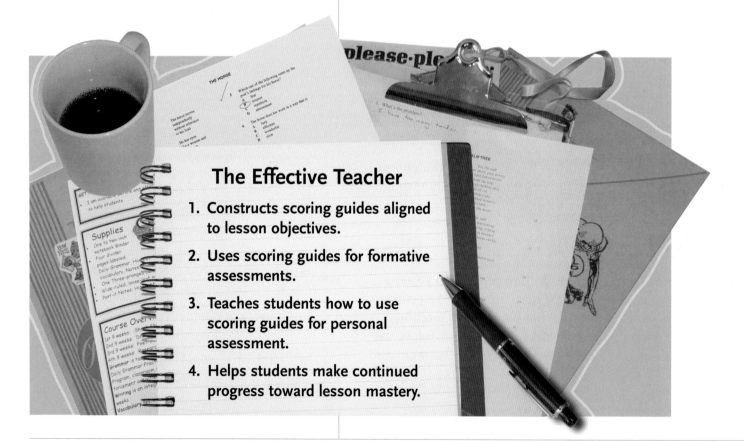

# The Effective Teacher

1. Constructs scoring guides aligned to lesson objectives.

2. Uses scoring guides for formative assessments.

3. Teaches students how to use scoring guides for personal assessment.

4. Helps students make continued progress toward lesson mastery.

## The Tools of an Effective Learning Environment

Teachers that work together to achieve
specific measurable goals
increase the likelihood of improved student learning.

## THE KEY IDEA

**Teachers are more effective when they work together in teams.**

**T**hree teacher characteristics can be found in schools where continuous improvement occurs. These traits serve as the foundation for schools that produce results:[1]

1. Working as a productive team

2. Setting clear and measurable goals

3. Collecting and analyzing ongoing performance data

The Consortium on Chicago School Research found that in schools where teachers worked as teams, students were taught math above their grade levels. In schools where teachers worked alone, instruction lagged behind. In these schools, eighth-grade math teachers typically taught fifth-grade math.[2]

> *A rapidly growing number of schools have made a momentous discovery:* **When teachers regularly and COLLABORATIVELY review assessment data for the purpose of improving practices to reach measurable achievement goals, something magical happens: student achievement.** *How does his come about? Through people working collaboratively as a team in a shared culture.*[3]
>
> _Mike Schmoker

[1] Schmoker, Mike. (1999). *Results: The Key to Continuous School Improvement.* Alexandria, Va.: Association for Supervision and Curriculum Development.

[2] "Rate Your School: Here's How to Do It." (October 2000). *Catalyst.* Available at www.catalyst-chicago.org/10-00/1000rate.htm.

[3] Schmoker, Mike. (2001). *The RESULTS Fieldbook: Practical Strategies from Dramatically Improved Schools.* Alexandria, Va.: Association for Supervision and Curriculum Development.

Even students gather in learning teams to study.

## Effective Schools Have Learning Teams

**M**ost successful companies operate with teams of employees. Notice the bill at a restaurant. You were served by a team. Notice the closed doors at stores: "Team Members Only." A company that wants your business declares, "Our team will take your design and bring it to fruition from beginning to end." The great athletes give credit to the team after a victory.

Effective schools that can demonstrate student learning do it with **teacher learning teams**. These are typically grade-level or subject-matter teams.

Teacher learning teams gather to analyze the progress of students toward curriculum goals.

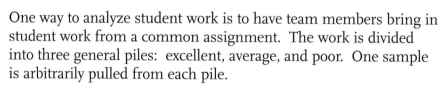

**The core work of a learning team
is to analyze student work
with the purpose of improving student learning.**

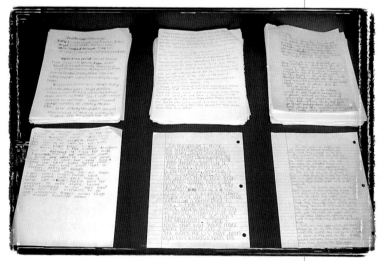

Work is analyzed to help students and improve instruction.

One way to analyze student work is to have team members bring in student work from a common assignment. The work is divided into three general piles: excellent, average, and poor. One sample is arbitrarily pulled from each pile.

The team assesses each of the samples with simple recurring questions: How can we improve or change our instruction to help the student who is doing poor work to at least do average work? How do we help the student who is doing average work to do excellent work? What tools for learning can we prescribe to inspire each student to move up the achievement ladder?

## Schools Where Students Learn Never Give Up

**S** chools are for student learning. In Arizona, where 25 percent of the population is Latino, many schools have low achievement and low graduation rates; yet there are schools performing well enough to beat the national test-score odds.

The Center for the Future of Arizona published a study, *Beat the Odds: Why Some Schools with Latino Children Beat the Odds . . . and Others Don't.*[4] That title says it all.

The report cited several schools, including some along the Arizona-Mexico border, that were doing quite well. The continued success of schools that were considered high-achieving and the newfound success of schools that were labeled underperforming had little to do with funding, class size, reading programs, parent involvement, or tutoring; in fact, these were found in high- and under-achieving schools.

**The schools that beat the odds had these characteristics:**

1. **They assessed and reassessed student work.**

2. **They used the results to teach and reteach.**

3. **They did not stop until they found a way for every student to grasp each lesson.**

One such recognized school that did this was L. C. Kennedy School in the Creighton School District of Phoenix. The first-grade teaching team members Patricia Hicks, Karen Schnee, Julie Kunitada, and Jenny Lopez, call themselves "experts in the trenches." Their attitude reflects their dogged determination not to let anything stand in the way of their students' success—not the parents, the administration, or "the drinking water!"

L. C. Kennedy School's first-grade team, left to right, are Patricia Hicks, Karen Schnee, Julie Kunitada, and Jenny Lopez.

[4] *Beat the Odds: Why Some Schools with Latino Children Beat the Odds . . . and Others Don't.* (2006). The Center for the Future of Arizona. http://www.arizonafuture.org.

The team teaches English language learners and reports that their success **"comes from evaluating test scores regularly, adapting our teaching to each student's needs, and not giving up until they get it right."**

They say, "By meeting weekly, we have created a learning community of teachers that tackle problems and issues. Our team is flexible and pliable, stubborn and persistent. We accept ownership of the children and believe that all children can learn.

"Our goal is to
- create a safe classroom environment.
- give the students something that is meaningful.
- break the skill down into small steps so they can feel successful early.
- build on each preceding skill until they reach the expected goal.
- practice, practice, practice.
- be open to ideas and have conversations.

**"Most importantly, we never give up."**

When she was a new teacher, Julie Kunitada joined the L. C. Kennedy staff, and the other members of the team brought her up to speed quickly by reviewing yearly objectives and discussing how to reach goals. The school did not assign her a mentor. Everyone in the team, available at all times, was more than her mentor. They were her teammates.

Julie Kunitada says, "I was not thrown in, but lovingly accepted into the family."

All the teams at the school meet weekly. They have grade-level learning teams that focus on improving student learning. The teams work together to create a consistent learning environment among the teachers and at grade level.

These grade-level teams do not function in isolation. They communicate with the teams at other grade levels. At L. C. Kennedy School, **the students are assisted by the school and its learning teams—not just one teacher locked in isolation in the classroom**. It's the team approach to learning that helps them beat the odds.

## The Structure of a Learning Team

Pacific Elementary School in Sacramento, California, had an influx of 80 Hmong children in 2003. (The Hmong are Laotians, many of whom were recruited by the U.S. government to fight in the Vietnam War in the 1960s. Because of fear of retaliation, they were offered asylum in the United States, with two of the largest settlements found in St. Paul, Minnesota, and Sacramento, California.)

Today, 40 percent of the student body at Pacific Elementary School is Hmong, yet the teachers and the administration handle the increasing enrollment. How? **The school has a culture that is always focused on student achievement.**

There are learning teams, by grade levels, at Pacific Elementary School. They meet once a week and enjoy the convenience of meeting in one large room where there is interaction during at-grade-level meetings, as well as communication among teachers across various grade levels.

**There is a formal structure or a "procedure" used at the Pacific Elementary School's team meetings.** They use the Schmoker Model[5] the first half of the meeting and the procedure is as follows:

1. **FOCUS** (3–5 minutes)
   - Identify the *specific learning objective* and the assessment that will be used to determine success of the lesson.
   - Write one learning objective/standard that clearly states the purpose of the lesson.
   - Display the objectives/standards for all team members to see.
   - Ensure the team has a common understanding regarding the assessment.

2. **ASSESSMENT**
   - Create the assessment aligned with the standard/learning objective.

The team meetings at Pacific Elementary School are held in a large room to facilitate communication among teachers at various grade levels.

[5] Schmoker, Mike. (1999).

3. **QUIET WRITE** (1 minute)
   - Quietly and privately brainstorm on paper elements, steps, or strategies that might go into an effective lesson (a lesson that would help the greatest number of students succeed on the assessment).

4. **BRAINSTORM** (4–7 minutes)
   - As a team, use good brainstorming protocol (no negative comments, any and all ideas are acceptable, piggyback on others' thoughts) to capture 12–14 ideas for all to see.

5. **SELECTION** (3–6 minutes)
   - As a team, select the best strategies, steps, and elements that combine most effectively to promote student success on the assessment.

6. **OUTLINE LESSON** (4–10 minutes)
   - As a team, use the best ideas selected in the previous step to build an outline of the lesson.
   - Collect related ideas, sequence them, and add or rearrange ideas as necessary.
   - Outline the lesson for all to see.

7. **IMPLEMENTATION** (back in the classroom)
   - Teach the lesson.
   - Assess the results.

8. **NEXT MEETING**
   - Discuss the results of teaching (how many students succeeded), along with the strengths and weaknesses of the lesson or assessment.
   - Discuss adjustments to instruction relative to each area of strength or weakness.

All of the information exchanged at the team meeting is recorded in a "Team Learning Log."

The second half of the meeting time is spent discussing student work. The teachers spread papers, tests, projects, or reports out on a table and analyze the performance of each student. Then they share with each other what they are teaching and how they are teaching it, and how they can help each other to improve the instruction so they can better reach the students.

> **In a learning team,**
> **the teachers have the capacity to work together**
> **to enhance student learning.**

The school is successful despite having a high-minority student body that is rather impoverished. In the 2006-2007 school year, the school only had to hire two teachers. This is a very positive sign because comparable schools have significantly higher teacher turnover rates.

Kieu Nguyen

New teacher Kieu Nguyen says, "I love teaching here because I am not isolated on my own. It's amazing how much I have learned from the experienced teachers. **We, as teachers, are better when we collaborate with each other.**"

### GoBe

### District-Wide Collaboration

Islip Public Schools' new teachers work in collegial teams. Their Regent's diploma rate is at an all-time high of 98.3 percent. Read about the school's process in the **Go**ing **Be**yond folder for Chapter 24 at EffectiveTeaching.com.

### The Honda Story

Honda manufactures cars at its factory in Marysville, Ohio. The company employs more than 13,000 "associates" (not workers).

The associates work in groups. One procedure is for each group to submit complaints and suggestions to management at the end of each shift. In the United States, management generally does not want to hear about problems, and workers do not want to get involved with problems.

The Honda procedure requires answers to three questions:

1. What is the problem?

2. What did you do about the problem?

3. What is your suggestion for a long-term solution of the problem?

Honda works on quality through empowering workers within groups to solve problems and to search for improvement methods so the entire group can achieve excellence.

## Analyze the Instruction, Not the Teacher

In 1993, a group of 23 doctors in Maine and New Hampshire made an agreement to observe each others' operating room procedures and share insights.

In the two years after their nine months of observation and sharing, they reduced the death rate among their patients by an astonishing 25 percent.

For teachers who have traditionally worked as isolated professionals, the analogy holds a powerful message. If their goal is to lower the "failure rate" of students, teachers can succeed with young minds by working together.

Effective learning teams bring to the table their respective students' writing assignments, math problems, science projects, artworks, and whatever else kids are producing every day.

The teachers also bring their own lesson plans to share and try them out on their colleagues. It's scary work, but with ground rules in place (as with brainstorming where everything is acceptable), increasing student learning is the focus of the meetings.

**The focus of team meetings is
the work on the table
and not on the particular student
or teacher who produced it.**

## Assessment in a Learning Team

> Analyze the instruction,
> not the teacher or the student.

**T**he principals and teachers in successful schools embrace regular assessment as a way of identifying problems early and attacking problems immediately. They review the assessment data on a regular basis to identify problems as they arise. Doing "root cause" analysis, they work backward through the data to pinpoint deficiencies and they take steps to immediately correct defects in the instruction.

The deficiency is usually found in the input—the curriculum, the instruction, the amount of time spent on the objective—and not on the output (i.e., the students). The teachers, who are the experts in the business, must be strong and professional enough to analyze their own instruction and have others analyze it. With input, they must be open to making revisions in their instructional delivery in order to reach every single student.

**Teachers who work in groups must recognize that the problem is not a personal attack on the teacher; it's a process of identifying deficient instructional methods of the teacher.**

Early doctors observing while in training.

## Curriculum Maps Inform a Team

**T**he exchange of curriculum lessons in successful schools is done with the use of Curriculum Maps. It is done vertically and horizontally. A curriculum map is a grand spreadsheet that lists what everyone has, is, and will be teaching. The map is dynamic in that it is constantly changing to reflect what needs to be taught to improve student progress toward learning.

Flight controllers at airports can see all the airplanes mapped in their regional sky on their monitors. Train schedules list the arrivals and departures for all the trains on a particular line. In a travel group, everyone is given an itinerary, a listing of their stops.

Likewise, effective schools have something similar to a map, schedule, or itinerary that keeps track of what's being taught and who is teaching it so that no student misses the learning train.

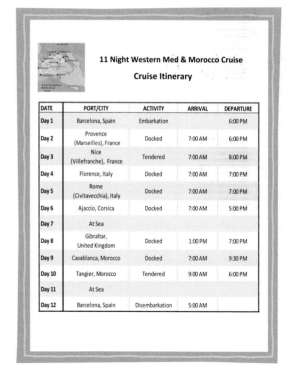

## Curriculum Mapper®

James Westrick served as a Peace Corps Volunteer in a village in Kenya. He was the only science teacher at a tiny secondary school set in the middle of the African bush. He had no laboratory, no textbooks, and no formal curriculum for his biology, chemistry, and physics classes. What he did have in abundance, however, was time.

He began the process of determining what knowledge and skills he wanted his students to acquire at various points of the year. With that in place, he looked at what content knowledge and activities would best be used for his students to acquire the skills. This constituted the crude beginnings of his personal curriculum map.

Upon returning to the United States, Jim became one of seven chemistry teachers at a large public high school outside of Chicago. He had all the resources and textbooks he needed. He even had a laboratory. But, he had no idea what his students knew or had been exposed to in other science classes. He found himself frequently stepping on the toes of other science teachers by duplicating labs or worksheets; consequently, he missed many interdisciplinary opportunities. Although he was surrounded by teachers and resources, he felt more isolated professionally than he did in Kenya.

Early in 1999, Jim attended a workshop on curriculum mapping led by Heidi Hayes Jacobs. **The idea of mapping what actually happens in the classroom to share with other teachers made perfect sense** to Jim because he had used the technique in Kenya to keep track of what his students were learning, even though he was the only one teaching it.

Curriculum Mapper® was born out of Jim's frustration with teaching "in a cave." He wanted to build on what his students already knew—not just re-teach the same content. He wanted to know what other teachers were actually doing in the school so he could support them and make his students' experiences more meaningful. He designed Curriculum Mapper® while he was still teaching. As more schools began using the system, he realized that most schools share common problems, and that getting teachers out of their caves is the first step in building an interconnected curriculum anywhere.

As the demand increased, he devoted more and more time to what began as a personal need to help his students in Kenya. Currently, Curriculum Mapper® is used by schools in 48 states and Canada. Jim is now helping schools and districts implement their mapping initiatives and improve teacher communication and collaboration.

Information on Jim's Curriculum Mapper® can be found at www.clihome.com.

## Tools that Enhance Student Learning

As you meet in learning teams, it is important to focus on and share some basic techniques that students should know to increase their chance for success in the classroom and in life. Some of these techniques include taking diligent notes, reading textbooks for understanding, organizing homework assignments, and keeping track of daily lessons. Some of these concepts may seem like common sense, but the adage, "The problem with common sense is it's not so common," certainly applies.

The skills we are about to share will help students achieve. Teach these skills and review them with your classes throughout the year.

1. **How to Take Notes**

2. **How to Read a Textbook**

3. **Homework as an Extension of Classwork**

Granted, no teacher should lecture too much, but that's not the issue. Effective people have learned the skill of taking notes. That is why they are effective. Note taking is not used only in a classroom. People take notes watching television, during a telephone call, listening to a conference speaker, synthesizing something that is being read, and during an endless array of situations where they want to recall information.

Notes are personal. It's what someone wants for personal edification. Teach a note-taking procedure and you teach a student something useful in life, especially if that individual values collecting ideas to be turned into the next great novel or invention.

> **Note taking is the embodiment of
> one of life's greatest skills: LISTENING.**

## How to Take Notes

The most commonly used note-taking technique is the Cornell Note-Taking Method invented by Walter Pauk while at Cornell University.

Note taking is not complicated. In the simplest of forms, it is a piece of paper divided into three sections. The three sections are called: Record, Reduce, and Review. The Internet even has a site where you can draw your own Cornell page, download it, and duplicate it for your students.

The benefit of the Cornell Note-Taking Method is that the notes do not have to be rewritten. They can be reviewed instantly. The notes are reminders of the details of the lesson and are used for review and studying prior to tests or class discussions.

### The Cornell Note-Taking Method

1. **Record.** Record the notes in this space. Teach the students to use abbreviations and to write in phrases. Leave spaces between thoughts. Neatness is not important; organization is important.

2. **Reduce.** In the left column, write simple phrases, cue words, and key points based on the notes taken. Encourage brevity and simplicity.

3. **Review.** At the bottom, write one sentence or phrase that summarizes the notes on the page. Add any questions that remain, or write ideas for further research.

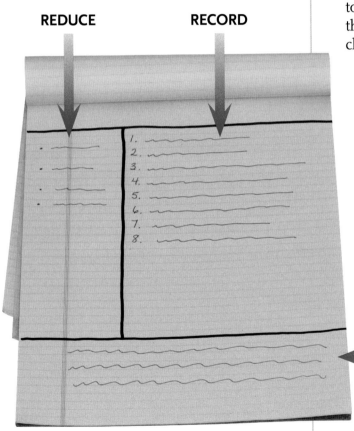

**REDUCE**  **RECORD**

**REVIEW**

### How to Read a Textbook

Effective readers do not necessarily start at the beginning of a book, magazine, or newspaper. Newspaper and magazine publishers know this, which is why parts of the table of contents are put on the cover as teasers to grab your attention.

They know that effective readers skim, scan, and skip from one page to another. This method for reading a textbook is called SQ3R, **S**urvey, **Q**uestion, **R**ead, **R**ecite, and **R**eview. Teach students how to read a textbook.

- **Survey**
  -Read the summary of the chapter first and find out if they all live happily ever after.
  -Read any indication of a key idea or concept.
  -Read all bold-print sentences.
  -Read words or phrases in caps, italicized, highlighted, or in boxes.
  -Look at the pictures and read the captions.
  -Read all the section headings to understand the organization of the material.

- **Question**
  -Ask what this chapter is about.
  -Ask what the subsections are about.

  The better the student has a sense of what questions to ask, the better the student will understand the primary message the chapter or subsection conveys.

- **Read**
  -Read each section with the questions in mind.

- **Recite**
  -Orally, answer the questions asked.

- **Review**
  -Reflect on the questions or the key idea to check for understanding.

Have you ever been in line at a buffet restaurant with no clue as to what is being served? Ask the people in front of you. They have no idea, either. Wouldn't you like to know what's being served so you can ration the space on your plate?

Get out of line and go up to the cashier and ask if you can do an SQ3R of the buffet before you are seated. They gladly allow you to do it.

**Survey** the layout of the buffet. Is there more than one table? Is there a section for hot foods? Is there a carver slicing meats? Where is the dessert table?

**Question** what is under the lids of the chafing dishes. Look at the sauces. Are they cream based? Are there any low-sodium, heart-healthy foods available?

**Read** the labels on all the food items.

**Recite** to yourself all of the wonderful choices you selected as a result of examining the spread.

**Review** the promises you made to yourself about not overeating. Then, get in line, ready to dine responsibly at the all-you-can-eat buffet.

### Homework as an Extension of Classwork

**Homework must fit the lesson objective and the assessment.** If not, it's busy work and has no value as homework.

Any homework given must be part of the lesson objective and it must help when the learning is assessed. Again, if not, it is inappropriate homework.

Understanding this concept, Elmo Sanchez in Miami calls his homework **home learning**. He assigns only what reviews and reinforces concepts the students have learned in class.

Homework is not for new learning; this will frustrate many students and even the parents who are being called upon to teach what has not been taught in the classroom.

---

**GoBe**

**Keeping Track of Assignments**

Carol Brooks of South Carolina has developed a daily method to help students keep track of their assignments. Read about it in the Going Beyond folder for Chapter 24 at EffectiveTeaching.com.

Just as effective teachers use guided practice followed by independent practice, homework or home learning should be additional practice to reinforce what was learned in the classroom.

If a student takes skating or music lessons, the teacher sends the student home to practice the lesson, not to create something new.

The key word is "practice." Ask these questions:

*What have the students learned in the class?*

*What can the students do to practice this new knowledge?*

This becomes the homework for the day. In many primary classes, students get a "take-home" folder with all their work for home learning.

Practice doing homework in the classroom. Spend time during the first two weeks in class teaching the students how to do the homework before sending them home with the assignments. A variation is to have the students start the homework in class and then finish up at home.

## Learning Teams Have a Shared Vision

A successful journey begins with a clear picture of the destination. If you do not know where you are going, then how will you know if you get there?

The journey to improving student achievement is no different. Everyone involved—administrators, teachers, students, and parents—needs to develop a laser focus on improving student learning. They need to create goals and a map that will lead them there together. **This concept is known as a shared vision.**

In a shared vision, the leadership is shared among the teachers; the shared focus is on student learning. There is staff collaboration around learning goals; and this is done with a shared decision-making process.

> In a school with a shared vision,
> the leader works on getting everyone to work together.
> People are connected to, rather than separated from, each other.

To implement this shared vision, every learning team consistently asks these questions of each lesson:

- What are the students to learn? (See Chapter 21.)
- How will we teach what we want students to learn? (See Chapter 21.)
- What will the students need to prepare for learning? (See Chapter 22.)
- What will we assess and adjust for student learning? (See Chapter 23.)

**Teacher learning teams must meet regularly to see evidence of the following:**

1. **Are we teaching to agreed-upon standards?**

2. **Is progress being made toward improvement of achievement goals?**

Ineffective schools have no teacher learning teams and nothing is shared. There is curricular chaos, whereby isolated teachers teach wildly divergent topics in the same grade level at the same school. No one knows and no one cares what else is being "covered." Assessment is for a grade and not for student learning.

**In an effective school, the curriculum is constructed for student learning.** The learning teams consistently assess themselves to see if they maintain and nurture a common, shared focus on student learning.

- They create and use a map to allow the learning teams to coordinate and assess instruction together.

- They consistently ask themselves if students need to be taught or retaught the academic content or procedures needed to succeed.

Common sense says and research supports that **the less time teachers must spend managing classroom conflict, the more time they can spend on instruction.** This improves students' academic outcomes.

The importance of establishing procedures and routines to free up instructional time is paramount to effective teaching.

## The Hallmark of Effective Schools

T hese are the characteristics that are well documented about effective schools, effective teaching, and improved student learning:

- **The era of isolated teaching is over.** Good teaching thrives in a supportive learning environment created by teachers and school leaders working together to improve learning in strong professional learning teams.

- **Teachers thrive when they feel connected to their schools and colleagues.**

- **Teachers need and want to belong.** If they do not belong in a positive way, they will belong in a negative way.

- **The trademark of effective schools is a sense of community, continuity, and coherence.**

- **Effective schools have a high-performance culture,** the hallmark of which is a shared responsibility for learning among all students.

Schools with these characteristics can produce the largest achievement gains in student learning ever reported for educational interventions. This can only happen in schools where teachers work together, assess together, and learn together, all for the goal of improving student achievement.

### When We Wish Upon a School

**The core of student success is having a staff of teachers sharing a vision.** A vision is like a star that gives direction to one's efforts. It aligns everyone toward a common purpose. It forms the basis of a commitment to instructional goals, beliefs, and priorities. Without this shared vision, people have no purpose in teaching.

This may not come as a shock to you, but studies have shown repeatedly that most decisions made in education are not made for the students; they are made for adults and their agendas.

**There is only one vision in education: progress in student learning.** Never lose sight of that fact. Travelers never lose sight of where they are going when they use a map or even a GPS (global positioning system) for navigation. Every decision we consider must be made with the direction pointing toward student learning.

Sometimes we think of schools as being autonomous rooms with a parking lot for faculty and sometimes one for students as well. For student learning to take place consistently, however, each classroom must be connected with hallways, and fully accessible through open doors. When classrooms are intertwined, **everyone has to be following the same shared vision.**

Hold up a compass, a map, a GPS at each team meeting and consistently ask,

**What is our shared vision?**

**Are we following our star?**

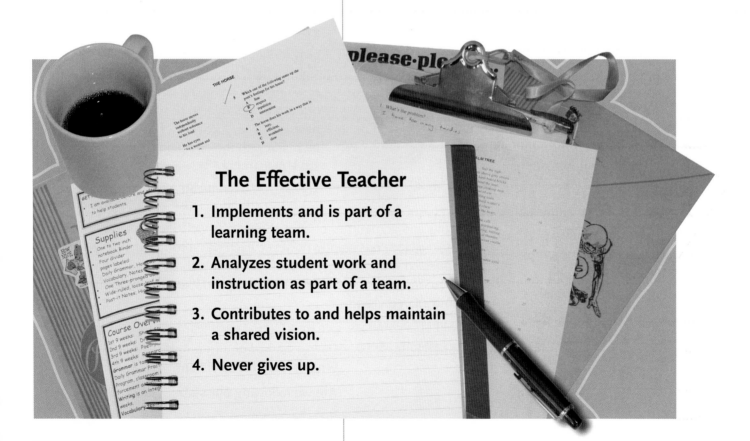

### The Effective Teacher

1. Implements and is part of a learning team.

2. Analyzes student work and instruction as part of a team.

3. Contributes to and helps maintain a shared vision.

4. Never gives up.

# *Future Understandings*

## _The Professional

The teacher who constantly
learns and grows
becomes a professional educator.

# Unit E — Future Understandings _The Professional

The teacher who constantly learns and grows
becomes a professional educator.

## The Professional Educator Is a Teacher-Leader

> You make a statement of dignity to yourself and the teaching profession when you acknowledge and accept that you make a difference.

## THE KEY IDEA

**The more a teacher learns, the more the students will learn.**

**Y**ou have now come to the final unit in the book. The focus of Units A through D has been on student accomplishment. The focus of Unit E is on you, the teacher as a student of learning.

You will soon discover that the more a teacher learns, the more each student will learn; in other words, the more knowledgeable you become in the craft of teaching, **the more you increase the chances that your students will be successful.**

> We teach you to plan so you can plan to teach.

## The Biggest Secret to Teaching Success

**I**f you want to become a professional educator with a successful future, if you want to be happy and recognized as a person who makes a difference in the lives of others, begin by making an impact on your own life. Begin by making a "difference" in your own life. Here's the biggest secret to teaching success:

**Beg, Borrow, and Steal!**

We talked about this earlier in the book on page 14.

**Teaching**

*Teaching is the hardest thing you will ever love.*

Heidi Albin, teacher
Hayward, California

> **" A rock pile ceases to be a rock pile the moment a single man contemplates it, bearing within him the image of a cathedral. "**
>
> _Antoine de Saint-Exupery

The original IBM PC.

Northern California teacher Kris Halverson recently had a change in assignments. She embraced that shuffle with a positive attitude by saying, "I love being on a new learning curve."

Educator Susie Drazen of New York says, "My professors in graduate school suggested that we become eclectic teachers—watching all, and only stealing from the best."

Whenever Rosemary Wong goes to a meeting, no matter how seemingly boring or irrelevant the material is, she starts assessing the potential benefits. **"Before the person is even finished explaining his or her technique, I've already figured out how to do it differently or better in my classroom."**

The human mind is a magnificent personal computer. In fact, it is the original PC! **The effective teacher is always thinking, dreaming, and planning.** Your future happiness and career success depend on your ability to implement techniques and your capacity to grow with new ideas.

If you do not grow, you will have nothing to give; for a teacher cannot give what he or she is not. If you do not take responsibility for yourself, no one else will. It's that simple. **When you acknowledge and accept that you make a difference, only then will the dignity of the profession be elevated.**

## Teachers Who Are Still in Survival Mode

**T**he profession is a mixed bag of personalities, cultures, and ideologies. Nevertheless, they can all be sorted into two categories:

- **There are those who simply want a job to earn money to live on.** They work to live, and survive from day to day.

- **There are those who want to make a difference.** They live to work because the work they do brings accomplishment to themselves and their students.

Unfortunately there are teachers who say, "But I can't use your techniques because I teach high school," "My students are not reading up to grade level," "The buses all arrive at different times so I can't start the lessons on time," or, "You don't understand the culture my students come from."

These teachers survive by making excuses. **The surest path to stagnation is to do nothing or just get by.**

> **When you have a school culture in which many of the teachers do not want to learn, it is obvious the students are not going to learn either.**

On the flip side, there are teachers who have now reached mastery. These are teachers we identify as **professionals** and **teacher-leaders**.

## Reaching Mastery

We expect the plumber, dentist, and lawyer to know what they are doing. We call them professionals. In the same manner, effective teachers are called professional educators.

**A professional is defined not by the business a person is in, but by the way that person conducts his or her business.**

A professional educator is someone who, without prompting, supervision, or regulation, has an ongoing growth plan to achieve competence and strives continuously to raise the level of each new group of students.

**The effective teacher thinks, reflects, and implements.** The effective teacher models what is expected from the students—the ability to think and solve problems on their own. Effective teachers use their cumulative knowledge to solve problems. **The accumulation of knowledge requires perpetual, consistent learning.**

**The professional educator is always learning and growing.** The professional educator is on an endless journey to succeed with students by looking for new and better ideas, new information, and improved skills.

> What counts is not the
> number of hours you put in,
> but how much you put into those hours.
>
> Some people go through life adding
> years to their life.
>
> Others go through life adding
> life to their years.

**GoBe**

**Teacher-Leaders Network**

Become a part of an ever expanding cohort of teacher-leaders. Learn about this professional growth opportunity in the **Go**ing **Be**yond folder for Chapter 25 at EffectiveTeaching.com.

## Teachers Who Become Teacher-Leaders

The effective teacher also has a personal **life plan** to guide that individual's career, with the goal of becoming a teacher-leader. These teachers are easy to identify. Teacher-leaders are optimists. They see daily what they are accomplishing in life, and see clearly the bright future that awaits them.

The term "teacher-leader" is a relatively new concept. For decades, many educators considered themselves "just teachers." They did their jobs, typically in isolation, and if they wanted more money or recognition, they depended on trade unions to get it for them.

As each generation of teachers became more effective, and as they demonstrated greater mastery in improving student learning, it occurred to many of these teachers that they should make a choice to determine or empower their own lives, too.

They chose to step out of the constraints of being "just teachers," and onto the path of becoming **leaders**. These teachers recognized that leaders are not "bosses" who implement rules, regulations, and procedures. Leaders are not merely given the authority to tell others what to do. Real leaders possess certain qualities that are necessary to achieve group successes.

A leader is succinctly defined as someone who motivates, mediates, and mentors.

### 10 Qualities of Effective Leaders

1. A leader has a vision for achievement.
2. A leader sets a good example.
3. A leader has the interpersonal skills necessary to guide a team of colleagues.
4. A leader motivates and inspires others toward mutual goals.
5. A leader remains focused on goals.
6. A leader implements deadlines and achieves milestones.
7. A leader mediates conflicts between individuals and among divided groups.
8. A leader recognizes the importance of proper knowledge and skills, and facilitates training.
9. A leader shares information and mentors younger and less-experienced team members.
10. A leader is well-prepared, passionate, and persevering.

**In the broadest terms,** leadership yields improvement. As it relates to education, teacher improvement leads to student improvement. Without teacher-leaders there can be no student improvement.

**Thus, it is from teacher-leaders that we ultimately get student achievement.**

Think about these two statements.

- **Ineffective teachers are all the same.**
- **Effective teachers are all unique.**

If you have an "aha!" moment after reading these statements, you are well on your way to becoming a teacher-leader. Perhaps you're already there?

If you are scratching your head in wonder, you are still growing and learning. Give yourself time while you continue to study and discover the traits of teacher-leaders.

---

**Teacher-Leaders**

*Teacher-leaders recognize they are forerunners in their profession, working beyond their classrooms by making presentations, writing for journals, supporting new teachers, and sharing with administrators. They elevate the teacher voice, breaking down the walls of isolation that so profoundly limit the work of schools.*

*Simply stated, teacher-leaders take action, accepting responsibility for driving positive change in education.*

William Ferriter
6th grade teacher, North Carolina
Teacher Leaders Network

## All Successful Teachers Are Leaders, Not Workers

ou can predict your life as a teacher 5, 10, 20, even 30 years from now on the basis of these characteristics.

| Teacher-Workers | Teacher-Leaders |
|---|---|
| Manage by crisis. <br> Are full of excuses. | Manage by leadership. <br> Have plans, goals, and vision. |
| Dress like laborers. <br> Sit at the back of the room in meetings. | Dress for success. <br> Sit where they can learn. |
| Complain about professional development. <br> Complain about people, places, and things. <br> Blame other people, places, and things. | Enjoy being part of a meeting. <br> Compliment people, places, and things. <br> Collaborate with people, and improve places, and things. |
| Are frequently late. <br> Run their mouths constantly. <br> Are always asking, "What am I supposed to do?" | Are prompt and have their materials ready. <br> Pay attention. <br> Are able to make decisions and help solve problems. |
| Do not subscribe to or read professional journals. <br> Do not belong to professional organizations. <br> Seldom, if ever, go to conferences, and even complain about district-sponsored meetings. <br> Speak negatively of their obligations, as in, "Do I have to serve?" and, "I'm only doing this because I've got to." <br> Are "I" centered. | Subscribe to and read the professional literature. <br> Belong to professional organizations. <br> Attend conferences and may even contribute professionally at conferences. <br> Speak enthusiastically about their options, as in, "I like being part of the professional learning team" and, "I enjoy working on the district's curriculum committee." |
| Talk about not getting respect. <br> Decide to do what others do. <br> Worry about their jobs and their job conditions. <br> Are victims. <br> Are unwilling to learn or turn elsewhere for help. | Achieve success that earns them respect. <br> Choose to do what they know is best. <br> Have a career and have options from which to choose. <br> Have power and are in control. <br> Are knowledgeable and can turn elsewhere for help. |
| View life as, "Another day, another dollar." <br> Are survivors. | Believe life is, "You strive to be a peak performer and pursue life, love, and happiness." |

Teaching is used by many teachers as a way to earn money to pay the bills and support a family. Their commitment to teaching stops at the dismissal bell, with no time and little desire to partake in growth and learning opportunities.

Like workers, leaders have jobs and put in time to earn money. But leaders are willing to put in additional time to improve themselves, the people they work with, and the environment in which they work. As a result, leaders usually make more money. They make more money not because they put in more time on the job but because they put in more time to improve their skills and enhance their lives. **Life rewards the competent, not the clock watchers.**

> **" Do not follow
> where the path may lead.
> Go instead where
> there is no path and leave a trail. "**
>
> _Robert Frost

> **A job is something a person does to earn a living;
> a career is something a person does as a lifetime pursuit.**

**Teacher-leaders are professionals.** They are not concerned with time and money; they have their minds set on growing and collaborating with others.

## Job Titles Do Not Reflect Worker or Leader Status

A teacher wrote:

*New teachers are not the only beneficiaries of induction programs. The involvement of the education association with the administration has a positive impact on students, colleagues, and administrators. We model teamwork as a way of achieving mutually desired goals.*

Mary Ecker, Executive Board
Port Huron Education Association
Michigan

An executive said:

*The in-service went five minutes over. You owe me five minutes.*

President
Local education association
New Jersey

## Teacher-Leaders Are Proactive

**D**uring the course of this book, we've shared the techniques of effective teachers. We've also written about the successful implementation of *The First Days of School* in our monthly Internet column at teachers.net.

**In all our writings, there are two recurrent themes that exemplify effective teachers:**

**Effective teachers can implement.** Effective teachers have the ability to implement someone else's work, regardless of their grade level, subject matter, or even professional field. They are able to steal the work, change it to fit their own situation, and use it in their classrooms. They observe, reflect, invent, and apply.

**Effective teachers are proactive.** Effective teachers have learned how to prevent problems, rather than reacting to problems. They are proactive and not reactive.

**Ineffective teachers are reactive.** Reactive teachers do not have organized plans for their classrooms, yet they *react* by blaming the school or neighborhood environment for their ineffectiveness.

Reactive teachers have little or no control of their classrooms. Because they are typically disciplinarians, they insist on specific punishments or consequences for certain students.

Very often, however, these students are among the brightest and most apt to become bored in unorganized classrooms. Recognizing—if only intuitively— that they have a reactive teacher, these students learn to manipulate their teachers by engaging them in games that make these students the center of attention. The result is that these students actually control the classroom—not the teacher who is constantly *reacting* to unacceptable behavior by doling out punishments to "disruptive" students.

In short, reactive teachers are not leaders; they are workers, and their students recognize them as such.

**GoBe**

**Are You a Worker or a Leader?**

Workers let other people make their decisions. Leaders make the choices themselves. To understand this concept, go to the **Go**ing **Be**yond folder for Chapter 25 at EffectiveTeaching.com.

Proactive teachers have a classroom management plan that prevents problems from occurring. They have lessons guided by standards and objectives and they have positive expectations for student learning.

## Effective Teachers Have It All Put Together

T eaching is a craft. It requires dedication and commitment. It requires working with others in learning teams. It requires continual self improvement. Although some people possess natural teaching abilities, no one is born with the prerequisite knowledge and expertise of a teacher-leader.

First, you need to understand that your classroom must be managed. Just as running a successful store requires good management skills, teaching a successful class requires thorough preparation. There are no simple, magic bullets for student learning. You have to work at it.

**You have to be willing to learn if you expect your students to listen.**

**The most effective teachers become professional educators. Professional educators become teacher-leaders.**

## The Most Vulnerable Teachers

T he most vulnerable people on the staff are the survivors who cannot make a choice to plan their lives. They know they should be enhancing their own lives and the lives of the students they teach. They know they should work cooperatively with the people on staff who are there to help them.

> " *You must become an advocate of what you believe; Otherwise, you will become a victim of what others want you to believe.* "
>
> —Jesse Jackson

**Think about your favorite store.**
Why is it successful?
It's because of three factors:

1. **The place is well-managed.**
   It's organized and comfortable. You find it a pleasant experience to shop there.

2. **The merchandise is good.**
   There is a good selection of merchandise. It's of good quality and the price entails a good value.

3. **The customers are well-treated.**
   People are polite to you. You are treated with courtesy, respect, and dignity. Salespeople appreciate your business and have built a relationship with you.

You can name these stores. They come in different sizes, sell different merchandise, and can be found in different locations. But they all have the same three characteristics that drive their success. They have all the pieces put together for profitable success.

**Picture the successful classroom.**
It is no different.
It's because of three factors:

1. **The classroom is well-managed.**
   Students find the classroom organized, safe, and pleasant. This is Unit C on Classroom Management.

2. **The lessons are well-delivered.**
   Students learn, have a good experience, and enjoy being part of the classroom. This is Unit D on Lesson Mastery.

3. **The students are well-treated.**
   They are respected. They receive additional help if they need it. They are treated with love and significance. This is Unit B on Positive Expectations.

You've seen or can picture these classrooms. They come in different sizes, have a diversity of students, and can be found in different locations. But they all have the same three characteristics that drive their success. Their students learn because their teachers have it all put together for student accomplishment.

But at the faculty meetings and in the staff room, the toxic people shout about the neighborhood culture, the pay, the conditions, the parents, the administrators, and the students—their very clients. They do not even like what other people say or believe. Remember, toxic people need to blame others to protect themselves.

If you listen to enough people who vilify administrators, parents, and students, you will believe that administrators, parents, and students are the cause of your being a victim.

> **When you see in a given situation what everyone else sees,
> you become so much a part of the situation
> that you become a victim of the situation.**

Successful teachers learn to listen, learn, and lead. **Learn to choose to make a choice!**

## The Surest Path to Success

**T**eacher-leaders practice enhancement behaviors. They spend much of their time participating, learning, and growing to enhance their lives as well as the lives of those with whom they interact. **The surest path to success is with an attitude of enhancement and cooperation.**

They enjoy learning and participating, so they go to conferences, conventions, and meetings. They exemplify the essence of a learning community at a school and can interact with, share with, and listen with other people.

**People who use enhancement behaviors are "we" people.** You keep hearing them use the word *we*, as in, "We need to work in our learning teams to find a solution to reduce the dropout rate," "Do we have some people who can staff the call center for our pledge-night campaign?" or "We can do it—I know we can do it—so let's all work on analyzing the students' work to see how we can improve student learning."

> **"** *If opportunity doesn't knock . . .
> then build a door.* **"**
>
> _Milton Berle

Attending conferences is one of the best ways to grow and learn as a professional.

> **The people who get on in this world are the people who get up and look for circumstances they want, and, if they can't find them, they make them.**
>
> _George Bernard Shaw

When you study a menu, do you choose, or do you decide? Workers let other people make their decisions. Leaders make the choices themselves.

**"We" people have student success foremost on their minds.** They are restless to improve, constantly adding to their knowledge and repertoire of skills. Their attitudes and abilities are their strengths. They do not dwell on problems by whining about people, places, and things, because they have discovered that life is fuller when chasing a future challenge rather than bemoaning the past.

**It takes work and effort to be a professional.** It takes time to go to conferences, read journals, serve on committees, and interact with associates. It requires effort to be part of a learning team, give extra help to students who need it, and take classes to improve personal skills and understanding. But the rewards and the satisfaction go to those professionals who are willing to invest in themselves for the benefit of others. **These are choices they freely make to enhance their own lives.**

## Successful People Choose

Now that you know the difference between a teacher-worker and a teacher-leader, which will you be? **Will you DECIDE to be a WORKER? Or will you CHOOSE to be a LEADER?**

### Decide

Look at the two parts of the word *decide*. The prefix, *de-*, means "off" or "away," as in *defeat*, *destroy*, *denigrate*, and *deemphasize*. It is a negative prefix. The stem, *cide*, means "cut" or "kill," as in *suicide*, *pesticide*, *insecticide*, and *herbicide*. To *decide* is thus to "cut away" or "kill off"—not a very happy activity.

**Many people make decisions by deciding.** Have you ever dined with someone at a restaurant who cannot select what to order from a menu? While everyone at the table waits for this person to place an order, someone impatiently barks out, "How long does it take you to decide? When will you decide? Can't you decide?"

And does the person order? No. Instead the person asks the others at the table what they plan to order and then decides to do the same.

"Oh, you're going to have a turkey sandwich? I'll have the same. No mayonnaise? Oh, OK, make mine the same way. I'll have the same thing."

The meal becomes an act of cloning.

And what happens to people who decide in this way? **Deciders become victims because they allow other people to make decisions for them.**

### Choose

Leaders do not decide. **Leaders CHOOSE!**

**Leaders have control over their own lives.** They know that the good things in life come from what they learn within themselves. They generate their own happiness, and much of that comes from serving and sharing with others. Leaders enjoy tackling problems, obstacles, and challenges.

**Leaders are achievement oriented.** They have a vision that helps them see beyond their task or job. They know what the word *choose* means and how to use it.

- *Choose* means that I am responsible for my choices.
- *Choose* means that I am accountable for my choices.
- *Choose* means that I have control over what I do.
- *Choose* means that I accept the consequences that accompany my choices. If something fails, I deserve the blame. But if it succeeds, I have earned the reward.

Worker-decider teachers do not strive for success, happiness, money, or respect. This is why they do not receive the rewards they long for.

Leader-professional educators are rewarded with whatever they are striving for—be it happiness, success, money, achievement, popularity, or professional respect. **Leaders are people who strive for results and have a passionate pursuit for achievement.**

*Parade of Champions*

*32nd annual*

*Santa Clara County*

*Teacher Recognition Day*

*San Jose Repertory Theatre*

People who are rewarded know the difference between deciding and choosing.

| Workers Decide | Leaders Choose |
|---|---|
| Life's rewards come from what others get for me. | Life's rewards come from what I earn. |
| I expect others to bring me happiness. | I will generate my own happiness. |
| Life will be better when I get a new X or more Y. | Life is better when I share or help others. |
| Life would be easier if I didn't have to do all these things. | Life is fine because I want and choose to do these things. |
| All I want is some peace and quiet. | I enjoy challenges; they are the elixirs of life. |
| I can't do this. I've got to go home and feed the dog. | I'll do this. Then I'll go home and have a wonderful evening with my family. |
| I can't wait for the weekend! | I can't wait for the math conference! |

**Now that you know the difference between deciding and choosing, what will you decide or choose to do?**

## The Choices We Make Determine Our Future

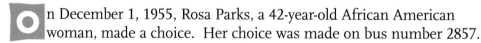n December 1, 1955, Rosa Parks, a 42-year-old African American woman, made a choice. Her choice was made on bus number 2857.

**Today, you can board that bus at the Henry Ford Museum and Greenfield Village in Dearborn, Michigan, and relive history by sitting in the same seat Rosa Parks sat in that fateful day.**

At the time, the Jim Crow law mandated the first 10 rows of a bus were reserved for whites. Rosa Parks sat, correctly, in the eleventh row, the first row behind the white section.

However, on that day, all of the seats in the bus soon filled. When a white man boarded the bus, the driver (following the standard practice of segregation) asked that all four blacks sitting just behind the white section give up their seats so the white man could sit there. Rosa Parks quietly refused to give up her seat.

When the police came on the bus that day, they said to Rosa Parks, "You know if you continue to sit there, we're going to have to throw you in jail." She answered, "You may do that." An enormously polite way of saying, *what could your jail possibly mean compared to the imprisonment I've been subjected to for the past 42 years, an incarceration from which I break out of today?*

**Her action on the bus that day was ultimately her personal choice.**

After her arrest, local civil rights activists initiated a boycott of the Montgomery bus system. Leading the boycott group was a young Baptist minister who was new to Montgomery. His name was Martin Luther King, Jr.

Because African Americans made up about 75 percent of the bus riders in Montgomery, the boycott posed a serious economic threat to the company and the white rule of the community. The boycott lasted 381 days, into December 1956, when the U.S. Supreme Court ruled that the segregation law was unconstitutional and the Montgomery buses were to be integrated.

**It was Rosa Parks' arrest that ultimately gave every American citizen, regardless of color, creed, or national origin, the freedom to sit where one chooses to sit, eat where one chooses to eat, worship where one chooses to worship, and learn where one chooses to learn.**

## You Choose to Learn

**A**lthough we all have the freedom to learn, note where some people sit at team meetings. Some arrive early just to be able to reserve seats in the last row or sit in the most remote corners. Their message is clear, "I do not want to learn, nor do I want to collaborate." They behave like the students they complain about.

Rosa Parks

> **Work your passion.**
> **Listen to the sounds of your heart.**
>
> **Make that your choice.**

If this is your school or the behavior of selected teachers, make a personal choice and stop allowing negative influences and the school climate from being your enemy. If you have children, tell them to do this as well.

**It's a sad reality that you may be one of the finest teachers and have the finest of lessons and programs, but if you work in a negative culture—the culture always wins.**

When Rosa Parks sat down that day, it was partly an acknowledgment that by conspiring with racism, she had helped create racism.

As a teacher, if you conspire to be part of a negative culture, then you help create a culture where the children are the losers.

There was a time when we could discriminate against minorities by restricting them to less appealing places. That way, minorities could not get anything, while the majority got to choose everything—jobs, opportunities, and schooling.

**However, because of activists like Rosa Parks, today the only person who can legally discriminate against you is yourself.**

Thanks to Rosa Parks and her contemporaries, we now have equal access to all the opportunities that are available in a free world. She left behind an inspirational legacy—having **choices in school and learning is one of them.**

**The professional educator chooses to always learn and grow.** The professional educator is on an endless journey; looking for new and better ideas, new information, and improved skills to further student success.

## He Made a Choice to Be an Effective Teacher

Elmo Sanchez teaches in the Miami-Dade County Public Schools and made a choice. His parents made a choice, as well, when they came to the United States from Cuba.

He writes:

*I was hired to teach fifth grade reading, language arts, E.S.E. inclusion, and E.S.O.L.*

*Monday, August 8, was the first day of the academic school year. I struggled through my day's lessons. My students spoke throughout the class period and had no sense of direction. I found myself using my "loud and/or angry" voice. I would go home angry and my family felt the direct effects.*

*At the end of the school year, I reflected on my achievements and failures in the classroom. I labeled myself an "ineffective teacher" because my classroom lacked structure. As a professional, I was disappointed in myself and felt I needed to make changes.*

*Each year the Miami-Dade County Public Schools has a summer professional development meeting. On Friday, June 9, I remember sitting in the Miami Lakes Educational Center Auditorium and I was captivated. Dr. Wong's classroom management strategies, techniques, and explanations made sense. Then, as he says, I had a "light bulb" moment. What would happen if I could take these strategies back with me to improve the way I managed my class?*

*I could visualize the changes in my head that were going to take place in my classroom the next academic school year. By the end of the seminar, changes were occurring in my mind. I could picture ways of changing my failures into successes.*

*After viewing Chelonnda Seroyer's PowerPoint presentation online I began to develop my own PowerPoint presentation. I also read through **The First Days of School** twice and began to formulate a plan that would suit me as a teacher.*

*It took me about a month to develop my classroom management PowerPoint presentation.*

*Picture this: Monday, August 14, the first day of the academic school year. I opened the door at 8:15 A.M. and greeted my students with an extended right arm. Shaking my students' hands, I would say, "Welcome to our class; I'm glad you are here." My students greeted me back with warm smiles.*

*I projected the bellwork assignment as a PowerPoint slide. By the time I closed the door, all of my students were actively working. I could not believe it.*

*After my students completed the bellwork, I began to introduce my students to the PowerPoint presentation I had created.*

*By the end of the day, my students were following the classroom procedures. When the 3:00 P.M. dismissal bell rang, no one got up. They all waited for me to dismiss them. I had control of my class and it was only the first day of school. At the end of the day, peace was with me.*

*I went home happy with an upbeat attitude. For the first time in my professional career I had a feeling that was missing from my life for a very long time. My family noticed the difference in me and liked the "new, happier me." I came to love my profession after the first day of school and my students felt safe in the classroom atmosphere that I created.*

*Last year, I was a stressed-out teacher with a chaotic classroom.*

*Now I feel that I'm an effective teacher with a structured classroom. My students are always happy to come to my class. The parents are always asking, "What do you do that causes my child to become so engaged in your class? My child wants to come to your class even though he is sick."*

*My secret recipe is having a structured classroom with procedures. I'm glad I made a choice to restructure my classroom.*

*I would say that on June 9, my life as a professional teacher was transformed. Thank you for helping me make a choice to be effective!*

## Life Begins When You Make Choices

*Laura was a worker-teacher. She was typical of the countless number of sweet, kind, average people who teach. Laura was a survivor. She did her work. She taught class, gave assignments, wrote tests, showed videos, passed out worksheets, supervised the cafeteria, attended faculty meetings, and baked cookies for the textbook selection committee she was on for the year. She had a family and sang in the church choir.*

*She took early retirement at 53, having "put in" 30 years. During that time, she never read a journal, joined a professional organization, or attended a conference.*

*During her 30 years, Laura never caused any problems, did not abuse her sick leave, and seldom said a word at faculty meetings. She always sat at the back of meetings and knitted. She didn't really harm any children, but then she never really lit fires under any of them, either. She did her job and felt, as workers are prone to tell you angrily, "I did my job, didn't I? What more do you want me to do? I wish they would end this staff meeting. I have to get home."*

*Over a decade later, I saw this familiar face at the mall. I gingerly walked over and said, "Excuse me. Are you Laura? Remember me? We used to teach together." Without much enthusiasm, she said, "Oh, yes."*

*I asked her what she had been doing and she groaned, "Oh, not much. I come to the mall a lot. It's safe here, you know. I see my grandchildren—I have three—and watch television. That's my life. I walk the malls, babysit the grandchildren, and watch television."*

*Then she asked, "And what are you doing?"*

*With a smile, I said, "Oh, I'm so happy I chose teaching as a profession. I've written a book, gave a presentation at the International Reading Association conference, met my wonderful wife at a teacher's conference, and indulge my taste for fine dining. Life has been very good to me."*

*We sat down on a nearby bench, amid passing shoppers and socializing teenagers. She looked at me sadly, with tears welling up in her eyes, and asked, **"When does the good life begin?"***

*I refrained from telling her, **"Laura, the good life begins when you start making choices."***

_Harry K. Wong

**GoBe**

### The Thin Margin for Success

The margin for success is so thin that getting across it is astonishingly simple. To make that step, go to the **Go**ing **Be**yond folder for Chapter 25 at EffectiveTeaching.com.

# The Basics for a Beginning Teacher

**T**he most crucial time in a new teacher's life is during the first three years. Statistics show that some 40 percent of new teachers will opt to leave teaching in their first few years on the "job." Although administrators like to refer to this as *attrition,* in athletics, it's called quitting.

Regardless of the reasons former teachers give for leaving the noble profession, the fact is **successful** teachers DO NOT QUIT.

The professional educator accepts the responsibility of personal growth and invests the necessary time to become an effective and successful teacher.

Don't whine. Don't blame. Instead, make this your mantra in life:

> **What do I need to know in order to do what I need to do?**

> **Repeat:**

> **What do I need to know in order to do what I need to do?**

Of course, you need to know how to manage a classroom and how to teach and assess a lesson for student learning. That is the subject of this book. For additional information go to these websites:

| | |
|---|---|
| teachers.net | k6educators.about.com |
| education-world.com | sitesforteachers.com |

You also need to know what is happening in the profession so that you do not become a victim. These are some websites where you can begin your journey to success. Most are free, but you can also choose to subscribe to their offerings and have information delivered to your email account.

| | |
|---|---|
| ednews.org | tcrecord.org |
| edweek.org | NewTeacher.com |
| gse.harvard.edu/~ngt/ | publiceducation.org/newsblast_current.asp |

Knowledge to help you become a more effective teacher is at your fingertips, waiting to be accessed.

Teachers play a dramatic role in the life of a child.

Our purpose is to help you jump-start the first days of school. Use these same days to jump-start your life, too. Start correctly. Maintain a strong vision of doing those things that will help you become an effective teacher—the subtitle of this book.

**Keep a laser focus on becoming a teacher-leader. It is the teacher-leader who is the most significant factor in improving student achievement.**

Research consistently shows that educational fads and innovations are not the major factors for improving student achievement.

> **The only factor that is able to consistently impact student achievement is the significance of a teacher.**

## The Significance of a Teacher

**S**ociety needs models of leadership. What better models of leaders are there than the teachers of a community?

Teachers can be accurately compared with business executives. Similar to executives, teachers develop, manage, and evaluate the work and productivity of a relatively large number of individuals on a daily basis.

When comparing teachers and doctors, teachers actually make more complex and fewer routine decisions than doctors—and they make them far more frequently.

More teachers go into teaching because of the influence of another teacher. This is not true for other professions. Teachers have influence.

Teaching is the profession that makes all other professions possible. We are the only profession dedicated to making the world a better place for future generations. They are our legacy.

> " *I am quite an ordinary person but I am extraordinary in the sense that every task I undertake, I give it my heart and soul.* "
>
> _Rosemary T. Wong

**Commitment, dedication, and hard work make a person a leader.** Ability and talent are not enough. The world loves talent, but pays off character. Character is the product of ability and talent combined with relentless practice and tempered by years of training. Even then, leaders give more because they dedicate their hearts and souls to helping children achieve.

If you have taught for more than 20 years, then you can recall the significance of that teary-eyed, emotional experience of a student's return visit. Even if you are just starting out, we wish you the same kind of event sometime down the road.

### The Greatest Day of a Teacher's Life

Perhaps the greatest day of a teacher's life is when a former student comes back to visit. There you are, consumed with teaching, when this face suddenly appears in the doorway. It's a former student, but you don't recognize him. Children have a way of changing after 20 years or so.

You suspect he's a parent. So, you directly ask, "Yes?"

"Mrs. Riley?" the person replies.

Agitated at the disturbance, because class is in session and no appointment has been made, you curtly respond, "Yes, I'm Mrs. Riley."

"Remember me? Keith. Keith Marlowe. I was in your class 23 years ago, and I sat right there in that chair. Remember me?"

You don't, but you fake it.

"Oh, yes, Keith. How are you?"

"I'm fine, and how are you, Mrs. Riley?"

"Oh, I'm fine, too."

"I don't live here anymore. I live 2,000 miles away, but I come back to see my parents from time to time. On my way back to the airport, I couldn't help but notice that I had some free time, so I decided to come over here to see you. And, I'm so happy to find you still here.

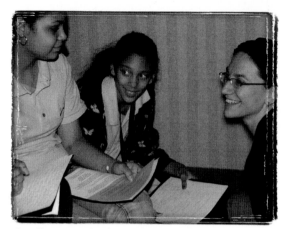

The effective teacher knows that all children are capable of success.

"For you see, Mrs. Riley, I've come here to tell you something.

"I am who I am,
and I am what I am,
and I am where I am in life today,
because of what you represented to me 23 years ago."

Notice that Keith did not say anything about what she taught him. Nor did he say anything about some fun activity he did in class.

Keith described Mrs. Riley as a paragon. She was a role model. She was a significant adult in his life.

He extends his hand to shake Mrs. Riley's hand and says, "I've come today just to say 'thank you.'"

Keith smiles, nods affirmatively, turns, and is about to walk out of her life forever when Mrs. Riley says, "Keith, please don't leave. I have something to say."

With 28 students watching her, and with tears flowing down her cheeks, she says, "Keith, we teachers rarely get any validation for what we do. But what you have done today is all we teachers want—the knowledge that we've made a difference in someone's life."

Her voice choking now, Mrs. Riley says, "Thank you for making my day."

Keith responds, "Thank you, Mrs. Riley. But you made my life."[1]

## You Are the Difference

**Y**ou are the determiner of success in your classroom. You make this possible, not only by what you do, but more importantly through your positive attitude and your strong affirmation of children. It is your leadership ability that can and should make a difference in their lives.

**What you choose to believe is what you choose to become.**

[1]Wong, H. (2007). "The Greatest Day of a Teacher's Life." *So to Teach: Inspiring Stories that Touch the Heart.* Indianapolis, Ind.: Kappa Delta Pi.

### 10 Beliefs of Successful Teachers

1. Believe that every child who enters your classroom wants to grow and learn and be successful and has the capacity to do so.

2. Believe in yourself that you have the skills needed to reach children and move them to new heights.

3. Believe that every day is a new day with the opportunity to start anew.

4. Believe that you are part of a greater community of educators who are proud of their profession and dedicated to their calling.

5. Believe that the smile of welcome you radiate to your students every day will warm the hearts of more bodies than you will ever imagine.

6. Believe in partnerships with colleagues, administrators, and parents that will nurture children.

7. Believe that you are both a teacher and a learner and grow yourself professionally each year.

8. Believe that hard work is required for success.

9. Believe that education is the bedrock of humanity.

10. Believe that we are here to help you and your students achieve success.

What teachers do is nothing short of a miracle that humbles and inspires us all.

**You are the window through which children see the world.**
**You are the sanctuary their heavy hearts come to each day.**

**It only takes one person to make a difference.**
**And we applaud that person who does.**

---

**Know that you don't just make a difference.**
**You ARE the difference.**

---

One hundred years from now it will not matter

What kind of car I drove,
What kind of house I lived in,
How much I had in the bank,
Or what my clothes looked like.

But the world will be a better place because
I was important in the life of a child.

_Forest E. Witcraft

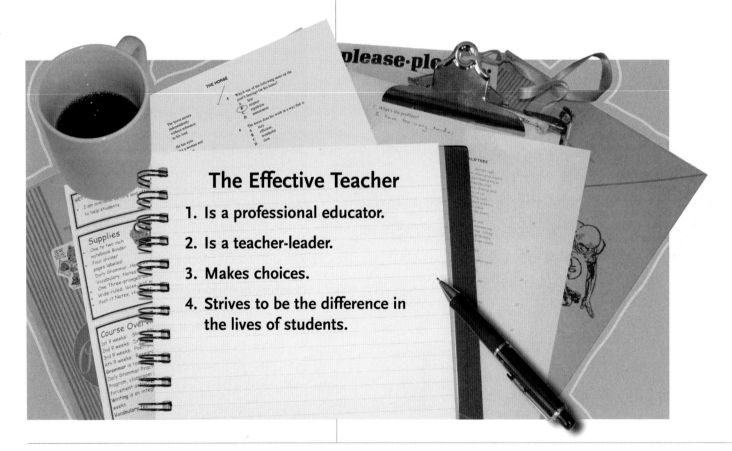

## The Effective Teacher

1. **Is a professional educator.**

2. **Is a teacher-leader.**

3. **Makes choices.**

4. **Strives to be the difference in the lives of students.**

## The Key Is Consistency

The most effective schools have a culture of consistency.

## THE KEY IDEA

The most effective schools have consistency.

**C**onsistency is what you want when you buy a product and use the services of a person or company. That's why you have a favorite hair dresser, cereal, restaurant, and store. Consistent means that you can depend on a product or a service. Consistent denotes meeting an expectation. It means that you know what will happen with a product or service and you can depend on getting a predictable result. Consistent does not mean status quo, never changing.

**An effective classroom is consistent.** Please go back to page 3, the very first page of the book, and reread the concept of consistency in the classroom. In part it says, "Students want a safe, predictable, and nurturing environment—one that is consistent. No one yells at them and learning takes place."

**This book began with the concept of consistency in the classroom and it has taken 25 chapters to explain how to establish that consistency.** You know a classroom has consistency when you see everyone at work in a safe, caring, and focused environment.

    **Safe:** Students are working in a well-managed classroom. (Unit C)
    **Caring:** Teachers have positive expectations for student success. (Unit B)
    **Focused:** Teachers are providing instruction on what needs to be learned. (Unit D)

**And now, this book ends with the concept of consistency in the school.**

### The Future

Epilogues in literary works deal with the future of its characters. This *Epilogue* is no different. It deals with your future in education and what you can do with your years of classroom experience to help those teachers who follow in your footsteps.

The first 25 chapters in this book are directed to teachers. The information in this chapter is for teacher-leaders, coaches, staff developers, mentors, administrators, and most importantly, *you*—the leaders and future leaders of the profession. This *Epilogue* explains how *you* can develop a culture of effective teachers.

## The Last Days of School

I am beginning my third year as principal at a year-around middle school. After I heard you speak, I had an epiphany of how to create an effective school with effective teachers.

Even though the school year was coming to an end, I did not think waiting until next year would be a wise decision. Timing was important and just as important was involving the faculty and staff in this process.

Before the students returned for the fourth nine weeks, we had a teacher workday. I showed DVD 3: "Discipline and Procedures" from **The Effective Teacher** and used that as a springboard for discussion on schoolwide procedures that needed to be established. My approach was simple: **We must create procedures and establish routines as we move into the "Last Days of School."**

Next, I had teachers get into groups and list the top six procedures that we needed to address. Finally, each group presented their list and teachers were given three sticky dots to vote for what they believed were the top procedures:

1. Walk quickly on the right side of the hall with whisper voices and hands to self.
2. Enter each class quietly, sit quickly, and put book bag under your desk.
3. Teachers are the first into the hall after each bell.
4. Quiet signal: hand raised in the air.

Parents were informed and procedure posters of our new schoolwide procedures were displayed around the building and in every class. Teachers spent several days having the students practice the procedures. The students realized the importance of the procedures and liked the structure. Teachers felt less stressed and were able to focus on teaching and learning.

The story does not end here. In July of this school year, when teachers returned for their workdays, we viewed DVD 4: "Procedures and Routines." Once again teachers revisited our procedures and decided to keep the four school procedures and add three additional:

5. All students will sit in their assigned seats.
6. Students will write the lesson objective and homework assignment in their planner.
7. Every class will start with a bell work activity.

We have just finished our last nine weeks. Many teachers have commented on how well-behaved the students are this year compared to prior years. One teacher even stated that this was the best nine weeks of teaching she has ever had. The number of student disciplinary incidents is lower compared to previous years. Teacher moral in general is higher.

Dr. Wong, you are right. The secret is CONSISTENCY with schoolwide procedures to create an effective school with effective teachers.

Thomas Hatch, Principal
Anne Chesnutt Middle School
Fayetteville, North Carolina

## Proficient and Effective

The subtitle of this book is "How to Be an Effective Teacher." **It is our firm belief that everyone can become an effective teacher. Study after** study states that effective teachers produce improved student learning.

> **It is the teachers and their <u>instructional practices</u>, not curriculum programs, changes in school structure, or legislative mandates that improve student learning**

school (skül), A place for teaching and learning; place where children are taught, nurtured, enlightened and loved. *n.*

This sign welcomes children to school in Texas.

Let's look at these two key terms:

**Proficient:** having knowledge and skills
**Effective:** having an effect; producing a result

Teachers who are proficient and effective produce measurable student learning. Programs do not produce achievement; **teachers produce student achievement**.

> **Teachers, not programs, produce student achievement.**

The difference between successful and unsuccessful schools is easy to spot:

- Unsuccessful schools stress programs and make structural changes. They spend millions of dollars adopting programs—fads of the year—in constant pursuit of the quick-and-easy fix.

- Successful schools stress practices. Administrators wisely invest in their teachers—their human capital—and the effectiveness of their teachers. They don't teach programs; they teach basic, traditional academic content. They work at improving the instructional practices of their teachers because they know that **instructional skill is a major factor in improving student achievement.**

**GoBe**

**It's a Happy Place**

Principal Edward Aguiles says, "Teachers and students love to come to this school." Read how he did it in the **Go**ing **Be**yond folder for the *Epilogue* at <u>EffectiveTeaching.com</u>.

## Planning for Learning

To improve student learning, you do not change the structure (i.e., block scheduling, smaller class size, small school size, etc.), you change the instructional practices of the teachers. The schools that seem to do best are those that have a clear idea of what kind of instructional practice they want to produce and then design a structure to go with it.[1]

**Funds are much better spent training and developing teachers than in buying one program after another.** Educational leaders know that what matters is whether schools can offer their neediest students good teachers trained in effective strategies to teach strong academic knowledge and skills.

The ineffective teacher affects little, if any, growth in students. Surrounding these teachers with programs, schedule modifications, school changes, and mandates will never improve student learning.

The effective teacher, even in an ineffective school, produces improved student learning and increased student achievement. (See page 25 for more validation on this topic.)

**That is why effective administrators recruit and then train their teachers to be proficient and effective.**

## The Greatest Asset of a School

**P**eter Drucker, the famed business guru, coined the term "human capital" and considered people "assets." During the industrial revolution, physical capital such as gold, manufactured products, buildings, and money were considered the source of most wealth and virtually all economic growth.

In today's digital age, human capital is what companies invest in to bring wealth and economic growth.

**Human capital refers to what people know (proficient) and can do (effective).** Human capital is not measured by accumulated physical assets, but by knowledge, skills, and attitudes. The very idea of human capital replacing physical capital was so novel it won a Nobel Prize (1992) for its most ardent exponent, University of Chicago economist Gary Becker.

Companies today depend on their people to create the next trends and great ideas. Human capital is the wealth and future of a company. People are its major assets.

[1]Elmore, R. (January/February 2002). "The Limits of 'Change.'" *Harvard Education Letter.*

Peter Drucker says that if you ask any businessperson to name their **greatest asset**, they will tell you it's their **PEOPLE**. An asset is what you invest in to make it grow into greater assets. That's why businesses spend $53 billion dollars each year training their people—their assets—to make them worth more to a company. Thus, they consider their people their **human capital**. The better their people, their assets, the more successful the company.

However, ask a school administrator or policymaker to name their greatest asset and they will often tell you it's money or programs. Rarely do you hear anyone say, their teachers are their most valuable assets—yet the research says it over and over again:

> **Teacher instructional quality is the most critical factor by which to improve student achievement or close the achievement gap.**

**The most effective administrators, coaches, staff developers, and teacher-leaders are instructional leaders.** A study of seven urban districts reported that the only reform effort that clearly resulted in student achievement gains had

- clear instructional expectations,
- supported by extensive professional development,
- over a period of several years.[2]

Ask the baseball manager, construction foreman, or senior partner in a law firm, what they do with new employees. They will tell you that all employees are trained from the day they arrive, and the training continues until the employee leaves.

Now, ask a school administrator what they do with a new teacher. Some do nothing. Most will tell you they assign a mentor to the new teacher and rarely monitor the result of the relationship.

**The only way to close the student achievement gap is to close the teacher instruction gap. Teach the teachers well and they will teach the students well.**

> **Effective schools have a culture where they consistently invest in teacher capital.**

**GoBe**

**Use Coaches, Not Mentors**

Many districts now understand that a critical component of a successful induction program is a coach. Read why in the **Going Beyond** folder for the *Epilogue* at EffectiveTeaching.com.

---

[2]Cross, C. T., and D. W. Rigden. (April 2002). "Improving Teacher Quality." *American School Board Journal*, 189(4), 24–27.

Consistent schoolwide procedures are the foundation for an effective school's culture.

**GoBe**

**A Most Effective School**

Visit a school with a consistent learning environment in the **Go**ing **Be**yond folder for the *Epilogue* at EffectiveTeaching.com. Discover what procedures this school uses.

## Creating an Effective School Culture

**E**ffective schools have a culture, based on their human capital. An effective culture has two characteristics: Beliefs and Practices.

1. **Beliefs:** The vision, goals, and beliefs of a group.

2. **Practices:** What people do and practice to achieve the belief.

> All good schools have a vision or belief and it is always STUDENT SUCCESS.
>
> Schools achieve the belief by what they do— the practices used by the teachers.

Ineffective schools do not have a culture. They do not nurture their teachers as human capital. They have a building with a collection of people isolated in their offices or rooms, doing what they claim are their jobs. The only thing these people have in common is the parking lot.

> The role of an administrator is to establish, nurture, and disseminate a culture.

Lee Douglass is a principal in an urban school district. Her 600 students are mostly minorities with family structures and income levels that are challenging. Yet, the test scores at her school are extraordinary. The kids and teachers love coming to school and the teachers never leave! **Lee Douglass has established a successful learning culture at her school.**

Each school day starts with a teacher beating a drum. When the students hear the drum they gather and stand in a designated line. They know the procedure as they want to be recognized with the "line-of-the-day" award.

Then a group of adults raise their hands. A hush falls over the playground. No voices are used; there are no orders and no yelling.

**The morning routine begins—conducted by a group of students.** Each week a different class leads the routine. A different student from the class steps forward and leads the students in the prescribed order of the day:

- "The Pledge of Allegiance"
- 30 seconds of silent meditation
- The school song (on Tuesday and Friday only)
- The school motto
- The school pledge
- The school slogan

(All of the above are done to cement daily the culture and vision of the school.)

- A teacher reviews the life skill for the week
- Lee Douglass makes a few quick announcements and the line-of-the-day award is given.

The line-of-the-day-class leads the students off the playground and all of the classes follow and fan out to enter various doors of the school building.

As each class walks down the hall, there is no talking, pushing, or shoving. This is because the procedure is "zip and flip," meaning the lips are zipped close and the arms are folded (i.e., flipped) gently across each other.

When the respective classes enter their rooms, *yes*, there is a bellwork assignment awaiting them, and the school day begins.

**Everyone is at work in a safe, caring, and focused environment.**

The kids love the school. The parents love the school. And the teachers love the school.

## How She Created a School Culture

The culture at this school did not just happen. It was guided by Lee Douglass, working with her staff. How did her school achieve this culture?

- She assigned groups of teachers to summarize each chapter in this book, **The First Days of School**.

- Each Friday throughout the school year, a group reported on their assigned chapter and made one or two suggestions for adoption consideration—such as having a bellwork assignment in each class, how to properly walk in the halls, how best to welcome students to class, and so forth.

- The teachers made the suggestions, and procedures were democratically agreed upon. Nothing was mandated from the administration.

- The schoolwide procedures became part of the culture of the school.

With students knowing the structure of the school day, more time was available for instruction. Over time, the students were learning more, and the school's test scores increased.

One day, Lee Douglass reported that she looked up at the group of parents gathered behind the lines of students and there was a 3-year-old child standing at the end of one of the lines. He had learned all the lines and was reciting with the students. He said to her, "I'm ready to go to school!"

**With a schoolwide morning routine the school culture is reinforced every day.**

When Lee Douglass is assigned to start a new school, she takes a critical mass of 8 to 10 teachers—her human capital—with her and they help her instantly implement a positive culture in a new school.

One year, Lee Douglass was asked to consult in a school district where seven schools were on a state probation list. In one year, she turned six of the schools around and they came off the state list. The one school that didn't make it? The principal said, "I lost the notes from the meeting."

## The Importance of Teachers

More than 200 studies have shown that the most significant factor in improving student learning is a knowledgeable and skillful teacher.[3]

**It's the teacher!**

**We've known this for decades, yet we still do not work to implement the obvious.**

As a teacher's effectiveness increases and as the human capital grows, the first group that benefits from this improvement is the lower-achieving students. (See page 23 for further validation of the importance of effective teachers.)

**GoBe**

### It Turned Our School Around

Principal Mike Gee says, "Our scores have hit heights we only dreamed about." Read how he did it in the **Going Beyond** folder for the *Epilogue* at EffectiveTeaching.com.

[3] National Commission on Teaching and America's Future. (November 1997). *Doing What Matters Most: Investing in Quality Teaching*. Washington, D.C.

The achievement gap facing poor and minority students is not due to poverty or to family conditions, but to systematic differences in teacher quality. These differences produce long-term consequences. A student who is taught by an ineffective teacher for two years in a row, for example, can never recover the learning lost during those years.

## The Significance of a Teacher

**A** UCLA study attributed to John Goodlad reviewed 40 years of educational ideas and found that only one factor increased student achievement.

**The one factor that increased student achievement was the significance of a teacher.**

Additionally, a large-scale Harvard-published study found that every extra dollar spent on building human capital and raising **teacher quality** netted greater student achievement gains than did all other uses of school resources.[4]

**It's the teacher and how the teacher is trained that produces student achievement gains.**

## The Importance of Administrators

**E** ffective administrators create a culture where the focus is on how teachers instruct and how students learn, not on programs, structures, fads, or ideologies.

- **Superintendents:** There is a direct link between a superintendent's leadership and student achievement. When superintendents keep their districts focused on teaching and learning (not programs), student achievement improves.[5]

- **Principals:** A study reviewing 30 years of research concluded that principals who are instructional leaders and concentrate on teaching the right *instructional* practices (not programs), can elevate a school scoring in the 50th percentile another 10 to 19 percentage points.[6]

---

**The Three AREs**

*Teachers ARE important.*
*Teachers ARE influential.*
*Teachers ARE able to make a difference.*

_Helen Morsink

---

[4] Ferguson, R. "Paying for Public Education." *Harvard Journal on Legislation.* 1991.

[5] Waters, J. T., and Robert J. Marzano. (2006). *School District Leadership that Works: The Effect of Superintendent Leadership on Student Achievement.* Aurora, Col.: Mid-continent Research for Education and Learning (McREL).

[6] Waters, J. T., R. J. Marzano, and B. A. McNulty. (2003). *Balanced Leadership: What 30 Years of Research Tells Us About the Effect of Leadership on Student Achievement.* Aurora, Col.: Mid-continent Research for Education and Learning (McREL).

**Help at 35,000 Feet**

To not provide comprehensive induction is like asking a pilot to learn how to fly while taking a plane load of passengers up for the first time.

And then if the pilot has a problem, he can call his mentor who is 35,000 feet away— at best.

## The Importance of Professional Development

More than 80 percent of a school district's budget is spent on teachers' salaries, yet many administrators and policymakers turn around and ignore teachers as assets after they are hired.  Teachers are summarily dumped into the classroom to survive with no structured, coherent growth-development program.  As embarrassing as it sounds, some teachers are not even provided with a curriculum.

**The best way to have effective teachers is through a <u>comprehensive</u> induction program that begins before the first day of school.**

You cannot create a good school without good teachers.  It is the administrator who creates a good school.  And it is the teacher who creates a good classroom.

Comprehensive training programs are the norm for most jobs.  Ask the baseball manager, construction foreman, or senior partner in a law firm what they do.  Ask the workforce at leading chains like Domino's Pizza, Starbucks, The Cheesecake Factory, and McDonald's.  Every employee is trained.

**Even the best educated of new employees need on-the-job training.**  Despite completing college and medical school, doctors spend years working as hospital residents before entering private practice.  Newly elected judges, armed with law degrees and years of experience, attend judicial college before assuming the bench.  Pilots receive initial training and recurrent training every time they change positions, such as from co-pilot to pilot, and when they fly a different type of plane, such as from a 737 to a 757.

## Comprehensive Professional Development

In the Hopewell City Schools of Virginia, every new teacher at the school level has access to the following complement of people:

**Buddy:** An assigned teacher to whom the novice teacher can turn for immediate help for answers or quick advice.

**Coach:** A teacher with expertise in classroom management and instructional skills. As the title implies, their role is to develop skills in classroom management and instruction.

**Lead teacher:** A teacher who can help with subject matter questions. There are five on each campus, each specializing in one of five areas—English, math, science, social studies, and technology.

And if you have been hired at Carter G. Woodson School in Hopewell, Virginia, the new teachers are given a "shower." The teachers celebrate your arrival by putting out boxes and baskets where the other teachers can place materials for bulletin boards, sticky-notes, crayons, books, and necessities of the classroom.

**Then, the staff helps you, the new teacher, set up your classroom!**

The Hopewell City Schools is a highly distinguished Title 1 school system and a Standard and Poors Outstanding School Division. Also, all the schools in Hopewell are 100 percent accredited.

New teachers are showered with gifts at Carter G. Woodson School.

**GoBe**

**The Hopewell Model**

Hopewell does not pay big bucks, yet their teachers are happy and their students achieve. Find out how they do it in the **Go**ing **Be**yond folder for the *Epilogue* at EffectiveTeaching.com.

The Gaston County Schools of North Carolina have a building dedicated to professional development. For 20 years they have had a full-time staff devoted to an organized, coherent, and sustained process of producing proficient and effective teachers.

The Gaston County Schools of North Carolina Professional Development Center houses meeting rooms, a media center, and a library all equipped with state-of-the-art presentation equipment. The staff coordinates and conducts training through the year as well as provides space for smaller school team meetings.

Gaston County has had a comprehensive new teacher induction program since 1990. They also have Instructional Coaches at high-needs schools and professional learning communities throughout the district. Gaston County is serious about producing proficient and effective teachers.

## Team-Oriented Results

Most employees of companies work in teams. This is because **teams produce results. People who work in isolation do not produce results.** Most schools are organized so the staff functions in isolation. Collaboration is rare. Worse yet, new teachers seldom see another classroom. Isolation and lack of support further exacerbate the problems of beginning teachers.

Yet, the research is clear—teachers working collaboratively will significantly **raise their productivity** and the quality of their work.[7]

Within high-success schools in low-income areas, teachers and principals have built into their regular schedules time for teachers to intensively share each other's ideas and procedures and work together. The Schmoker Model used by the school on page 283 is an example of a tool schools use to structure their collaboration.

**Professionals do not work alone; they work in teams.** When teachers meet in teams to focus on a problem, they become part of a unit that will work with students who are in need of help.

Professional development is most effective and teachers learn more in sustained teacher networks and study groups than they do with individual mentors.[8] **Collaboration is the most effective way for teachers to learn.**

[7] Guskey, T., and M. Huberman (eds.). (1995). *Professional Development in Education: New Paradigms and Practices.* New York: Teachers College Press.

[8] Garet, M., A. Porter, L. Desmoine, B. Birman, and S. K. Kwang. (2001). "What Makes Professional Development Effective?" *American Educational Research Journal, 38*(4), pp. 915–946.

## Collaboration Helps Keep Teachers

I t's a known fact. Teachers working in isolation make student achievement a next-to-impossible feat.

Susan Moore Johnson of the Project on the Next Generation of Teachers at the Harvard Graduate School of Education says, "Our work suggests that schools would do better to rely less on one-on-one mentoring and, instead, develop schoolwide structures that promote the frequent exchange of information and ideas among novice and veteran teachers."[9]

> **Grade-level teams using carefully developed curriculum consistently get better results than collections of individual teachers using an eclectic collection of curriculum**

The majority of teachers being hired today are part of the Generation Y cohort. The attributes of a Gen Y teacher lend themselves positively toward establishing a collegial learning environment. Gen Ys desire collaboration, assimilate quickly, and have high energy. Schools will see improved student learning if they will harness the collective intelligence, creativity, and genius of this new generation of teachers.

**Just think how much more effective our teachers and schools can be if a new teacher joins an existing team of collaborative learners.**

> *" Teachers should be in teams, working collaboratively around problems identified in their schools and related to students. "*
>
> Kathleen Fulton, director
> Reinventing Schools for
> the 21st Century

**GoBe**

**40 Million Strong**

The Y Generation group has many positive attributes that lend themselves to teaching. These qualities are in the **Go**ing **Be**yond folder for the *Epilogue* at EffectiveTeaching.com.

[9] Johnson, Susan Moore, and Sarah E. Birkeland. "Pursuing a Sense of Success: New Teachers Explain Their Career Decisions." *American Educational Research Journal*, Fall 2003, p. 608.

## It Is Time to Turn the Page!

> Businesses spend $53 billion each year on training.
> Education spends $7.3 billion each year
> to recruit and replace teachers.

**E**ach year school districts spend billions hiring teachers to replace the teachers hired the year before, when a fraction of that money could be applied to a structured, coherent, and sustained professional development program. **Teachers stay when they are successful.**

We know the following:

- The single greatest effect on student achievement is the effectiveness of the teacher.
- New teachers are not as effective as veteran teachers.
- Teachers that work in isolation are not as effective as teachers who work as part of a learning team.
- It is costly and unconscionable to keep hiring new teachers to replace the teachers hired the previous year to fill the same positions.
- New teachers will succeed and stay if they are given training and collegial support.

Therefore, to keep new teachers, to close the teacher instruction gap, and to incrementally improve student achievement, provide every new teacher with the following:

1. A structured and coherent induction program that flows seamlessly into a sustained professional development program.

2. A grade-level or content-level learning team they can become a collegial part of instantly.

---

**GoBe**

**Comprehensive Induction**

Districts that are serious about training and retaining teachers have a comprehensive induction program. Read how to implement one in the **Go**ing **Be**yond folder for the *Epilogue* at EffectiveTeaching.com.

---

It's time for education to have an "aha," a light bulb moment, an epiphany. It is time to turn the page and move forward.

We need a new generation of teacher-leaders and administrators who view themselves as assets, as human capital, as people capable of implementing the already known way to improve teacher instructional skills. We do not need to install another program, structural change, or the same ideology over and over again.

Just as the bottom line in business is profit, the **bottom line in education is academic performance.** The ultimate purpose of professional development must be to improve the academic outcome of every student.

To do this, nurture your human capital from the mix of knowledge, skills, and talents that reside in every person. Developing human capital through sustained professional development is the key to continued student learning and achievement.

Teachers are the only assets that do not show up on the balance sheet, yet they are the most valuable resource of a school. **The teachers we hire today will become the teachers for the next generation. Their success will determine the success of an entire generation of students.**

**The most effective schools invest in their future.**

> **They have a culture of proficient and effective teachers.**
> **They have a culture of predictable results.**
> **They have a culture of consistency.**

With our sincerest thanks for your efforts
and your passion for creating a positive future for kids,

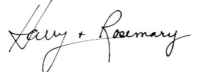

Teachers are our greatest asset.

## Photo Credits

Elizabeth Albers, pp. 26, 260, 269, 321
Mark Tantrum, pp. 62, 85, 90, 119, 212, 243, 254, 280

Doug Hamilton, p. 82
J. F. Walters, p. 217

*Motivos*, pp. 260, 319
A/P World Wide Photos, p. 313

**Grateful acknowledgment is made to the following people and institutions for permission to use their pictures, classrooms, or facilities:**

Chelonnda Seroyer, pp. iii, 24, 47, 117, 166, 179
Douglas Brooks, p. 3
Diana Greenhouse, pp. 5, 117, 274
Kazim Cicek, p. 5
Grand Prairie High School, Texas, pp. 6, 85, 203
Oretha Ferguson, pp. 8, 240
Bill Ferriter, p. 11
Sarah Jondahl, pp. 12, 18, 24, 47, 102, 107, 116, 123, 156, 168, 213
Elmo Sanchez, pp. 15, 315
Beth Sommers, p. 15
Jaime Diaz, p. 16
Lafourche Parish Public Schools, Louisiana, pp. 17, 231
Pacific Elementary School, California, pp. 19, 96, 177, 283
Ersula Bombard, Laura Regan, p. 20
Alex Kajitani, p. 22
Jeff Smith, p. 24
Liz Breaux, p. 24
Steve Geiman, pp. 24, 127
Julie Johnson, pp. 24, 47, 258
Robin Barlak, pp. 24, 118, 202
Norm Dannen, pp. 24, 272
Karen Rogers, pp. 24, 270
Susan Monfet, p. 24
Rita Zimmermann, p. 26
Cheryl Johnson, p. 29
Joe Kitchens, p. 31
Flowing Wells School District, Arizona, pp. 37, 39, 66, 93
Grand Heights Early Childhood Center, New Mexico, pp. 42, 62, 98, 113, 116, 135, 155, 223, 325
Haughton High School, Louisiana, pp. 45, 48
Williston School District 29, South Carolina, p. 46
Julie Wharton, p. 47
Hilton Jay, p. 52

Deborah Haynes, Cherie Lyle, p. 52
Kirk Gordon, p. 52
Angie Cook, p. 52
Steve Seroyer, p. 56
Loretta Keller, p. 56
Christi Shearman, p. 57
Theresa Borges, p. 61
Stacey Allred, pp. 71, 74
Ed Aguiles, p. 81
Judy Jones, p. 81
Melissa Dunbar, p. 81
Bernie Alidor, p. 81
Alice Waters, p. 82
Ed Lucero, p. 85
Art Kavanaugh, p. 87
Camille Snyder, p. 92
Jeffrey Gulle, pp. 97, 216
Jone Couzins, p. 101
Val Abbott, p. 102
Jackie Routhenstein, p. 104
Pam Coombs, p. 104
Chris Bennett, p. 104
Steve Zickafoose, p. 105
Jeanne Bayless, p. 107
Suzanne Laughrea, p. 108
Melissa Boone-Hand, p. 110
Sacha Mike, p. 111
John Schmidt, p. 111
Angie Perry, p. 113
Nile Wilson, p. 117
Sherry Noll, p. 125
Rodney Cullen, Andrew Grove, Kimberly Clayton, p. 127
Debra Lindsey, p. 128

Wanda Bradford, p. 128
Becky Hughes, p. 131
Merle Whaley, p. 143
Jane Slovenske, p. 161
Marv Marshall, p. 162
Terri Schultz, p. 166
Joan Davis, p. 171
Judie Gustafson, p. 172
Sue Moore, p. 177
Holland Meyers, p. 177
Jim Heintz, p. 177
Deborah Chavez, p. 182
Cindy Wong, p. 185
Heidi Garwood, p. 201
Kristen Dardano, p. 217
Kathy Monroe, p. 267
Patricia Hicks, Karen Schnee, Julie Kunitada, Jenny Lopez, p. 281
Kieu Nguyen, p. 285
Jim Westrick, p. 288
Heidi Albin, p. 299
Marty Yoshioka, Terry Ackerly, p. 310
Kim Scroggin, p. 318
Jenee Chizick, p. 319
Tom Hatch, p. 324
Lee Douglass, p. 329
Megan Boyles, Melanie Tocco, p. 333
Gaston County Schools, p. 334
Laurie Jay, p. 337
Angelica Guerra, p. 337
Sam Nix, p. 337
Leland Dishman, Ray Landers, Allen Johnson, Candice Richardson, Rissa Parrish, Pamela Duke, Jenny Franks, Renee Adams, Jeff Sanders, David Lackey, Melissa McRae, p. 337

# Index

# Our Materials for Developing Effective Teachers
## www.EffectiveTeaching.com

Visit our website for a preview of each item, current pricing, and volume discounts.

 Many of our products are available in a Digital format for immediate viewing over the Internet. Look for the Digital icon for instant access.

### *The First Days of School*

This "bible" for new and experienced teachers helps you to know and practice the three characteristics of an effective teacher. Includes a DVD, **"Using THE FIRST DAYS OF SCHOOL"** with Chelonnda Seroyer.

- Authors: Harry K. and Rosemary T. Wong
- 352 page book with Index
- Over 300 photographs, illustrations, and graphics
- Over 1 hour DVD, **"Using THE FIRST DAYS OF SCHOOL"**
- ISBN: 978-0-9764233-1-7, 4th edition

### *Implementation Guide* for *The First Days of School*

This guide was created to help anyone who trains teachers. The consistent format includes key facts, in-depth discussion questions, and activites. Each chapter is treated individually.

- 97 pages
- FREE!
- Download from our website

### *Classroom Management with Harry and Rosemary Wong*

Classroom management comes to life in this eLearning course. Upon completion you will have a binder with your personal Classroom Management Action Plan.

- Featuring: Harry K. and Rosemary T. Wong
- 6 lessons that correlate to the 3rd edition of *The First Days of School*
- 20 hours of course work in eLearning course
- Empty Classroom Management Action Plan Binder
- CEU and College Credit available

### The Effective Teacher

This DVD series showcases best practices used by effective teachers with master motivator, Harry Wong.  Filmed during one of his many legendary presentations.

- Featuring:  Harry K. Wong
- 8 DVDs, 5 hours total time
- Book, *The First Days of School*
- 10 copies, *Successful Teaching* newspaper
- *Facilitator's Handbook* on all DVDs
- ISBN:  978-0-9629360-9-8

### How to Be an Effective and Successful Teacher

Listen as Harry and Rosemary walk you through classrooms that hum with learning.
Their presentation is a detailed account of how any teacher can be effective and successful.

- Featuring:  Harry K. Wong and Rosemary T. Wong
- 2 hours 40 minutes audio CD set

### Never Cease to Learn

This broadcast quality DVD captures Harry Wong's wisdom as he shares from his heart and soul the essence of professionalism—making a difference in the life of a child.

- Featuring:  Harry K. Wong
- Special Introduction:  Rosemary T. Wong
- 38 minute DVD

### That Noble Title Teacher

This motivational essay is presented in a beautifully designed print.  It's a compelling reminder of our responsibility to children and to the profession.

- Written by:  Trish Marcuzzo
- 12" x 18" color poster

### Harry Wong Live! How to Improve Student Achievement

In this 2 audio CD set, Harry Wong invites you to "steal" from him the secrets of effective teaching for all grade levels.

- Featuring: Harry K. Wong
- 2 hours 35 minutes total time

### I choose to CARE

This is a Harry Wong "classic" presentation. This classic recording of Harry captures the exciting performer that he is. You'll laugh, cry, and be motivated to change after watching this presentation. The information is timeless.

- Featuring: Harry K. Wong
- 1 hour total time

### New Teacher Induction

This book offers a comprehensive look at how to structure an induction program to train, support, and retain new teachers and includes contacts for over 30 programs.

- Authors: Annette Breaux and Harry K. Wong
- 240 page book
- Full color photos and illustrations

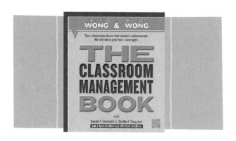

### THE Classroom Management Book – **Our Newest Book!**

This is a solutions book that uses procedures to show how to organize and structure a classroom to create a safe and positive environment for student learning and achievement to take place.

- Authors: Harry K. and Rosemary T. Wong, Sarah F. Jondahl, and Oretha F. Ferguson
- 320 page book
- ISBN: 987-0-9764233-3-1